The Mount Vernon Street Warrens

Also by Martin Green

New York 1913
The Triumph of Pierrot
Children of the Sun
The Von Richthofen Sisters
Tolstoy and Gandhi

The
Mount Vernon Street
Warrens

A BOSTON STORY, 1860-1910

Martin Green

CHARLES SCRIBNER'S SONS · NEW YORK

Charles Scribner's Sons
Macmillan Publishing Company
866 Third Avenue, New York, NY 10022
Collier Macmillan Canada, Inc.

Library of Congress Cataloging-in-Publication Data
Green, Martin Burgess, 1927–
    The Mount Vernon Street Warrens: a Boston story,
1860–1910/
  Martin Green.
        p. cm.
    Includes bibliographical references.
    ISBN 0-684-19109-1
    1. Warren family.   2. Boston (Mass.)—Biography.   I.
Title.
  F73.5.W35G74   1989
  974.4'6104'0922—dc20
  [B]   89-38389
                                                            CIP

Macmillan books are available at special discounts for bulk purchases for sales promotions, premiums, fund-raising, or educational use. For details, contact:

        Special Sales Director
        Macmillan Publishing Company
        866 Third Avenue
        New York, NY 10022

10 9 8 7 6 5 4 3 2 1
Printed in the United States of America

"Now come Mabel Bayard Warren, Samuel Dennis Warren recently called junior, and Louis D. Brandeis, all of Boston in the County of Suffolk aforesaid, and suggest to the court that the respondent in the above-entitled case, Samuel D. Warren, died on February 19, 1910, and. . . . "

—Document "A Suggestion of Death," dated March 11, 1910, in the Warren v. Warren *file, No. 14630, in the Suffolk County Supreme Court records.*

CONTENTS

ACKNOWLEDGMENTS

In the course of writing this book, I have been helped by many people in many ways. I shall simply list names in alphabetical order, even though some people entered into the spirit of my research much more generously than such a listing suggests—the alternatives all seem invidious: Any approach to grading my friends, as one giving more or less help than another, would be grotesque; while any more indirect, humane, and subtle treatment would lengthen the book by yet another chapter.

I therefore simply acknowledge the help of: the Ashmolean Museum Archive; the Berenson Archive at I Tatti; Sylvia Berkman; Michael J. Bohnen; the Bowdoin College Archives; Charles C. Calhoun; Mrs. Rhoda Shaw Clark; the Corpus Christi College Archive; Valentine Cunningham; the Deutsches Archaeologische Institut, Athens; Trevor Fairbrother; the Isabella Stewart Gardner Museum Archive; Andrew Gray; Sandra Grieser; Lin Haire-Sargeant; the Harvard Historical Society; the Harvard University Archives; the Harvard University Law School Library; Erica Hirshler; Rebecca Karo; Ariane Kozloff; Adelbert Mason; Herbert Mason; Marianne May; Maureen Melton; the Museum of Fine Arts, Boston, Archive; David Mitten; Mr. and Mrs. Ed Needham; the Nutter, McLennen and Fish Archive; Patricia Palmieri; Carlos Picon; Charles Rose; the Schlesinger Library Archive; Earl G. Shettleworth, Jr.; Susan Sinclair; Neel Smith; Mr. and Mrs. Snyder; Diana C. Stewart; Evan Turner; Henrietta Tye; Cornelius Vermeule (and the other members of the Classical Antiquities Department of the Museum of Fine Arts, Boston); Mrs. Jessica Warren; Mrs. Margaret Warren; Mortimer Warren; Perry Warren; S.D. Warren and Company; the Warren Memorial Library; Katharine J. Watson; the Wellesley College Archive; John Whitcomb; Diane Wynne; William J. Young.

PREFACE

Who were the Warrens of Mount Vernon Street? This book gives an answer that derives primarily from public records. As a private or intimate record, all that survives is some bundles of family letters, which are both sparse and discreet—often exercises in concealment. We are short of facts. So to begin, let us allow ourselves a moment of fancy, of fabulation.

We stand on Mount Vernon Street in 1870 and look up at the tall brick bow front of number 67, and then at the long street running up Beacon Hill to the State House, and down to Louisburg Square and Charles Street. Transport is horse-drawn, women's skirts almost sweep the ground, street lighting is by gas, and inside each house are two kinds of people, masters and servants.

In the grand but gloomy dining room on the parlor floor of number 67, Mr. and Mrs. Warren and their five children are being served dinner by a manservant and an Irish maid. Mr. Warren is titular head of the household. His real kingdom is his offices on Devonshire Street and the paper mills in Maine. At home he is a tired businessman who offers his family puns, riddles, jokes, and problems in mental arithmetic and general knowledge.

Mrs. Warren is mayor of the palace. Her will maintains the distance of solemnity that surrounds Mr. Warren; he is a great man, even at home, by her decree. She tells them of a lecture she has attended on *The Light of Asia,* Sir Edwin Arnold's verse biography of the Buddha. Its theme, she tells them, is the great renunciation; so like the renunciation of our own Savior. The chandelier's lights glint on the black walnut carvings, the gold plate, and the picture frames.

She speaks slowly, inviting an equally slow and measured response. Her four sons listen, their eyes alert, but they make no response, all resentful, but in different ways.

Mrs. Warren is heavy, imposing rather than beautiful, yet there is something handsome, something bold, in her brows. This is reflected in milder form in her daughter, Cornelia, who is the only one to take up the topic of Eastern religions.

The sons resemble their father. Like him they are short and stocky, strong not elegant. None of them will grow taller than five feet eight. But they have well-marked eyes and brows, and symmetrical features. They are rather handsome, especially Sam, the eldest. In 1870 he is eighteen. He is the most powerfully built, and he has the marks of power—of the anxiety and tension of power—stamped on his brow. He means to be as great a man as his father, to be one of those known as great.

The meal is elaborate and slow, and there are pauses in Mrs. Warren's disquisition. The boys grow restless. Finally, before dessert can be served, Henry, the second son, sixteen, pushes back his chair and says he can sit no longer. He twists on his chair to get off, and we see that he is a hunchback, and when he stands we see that he is very short.

As he reaches the door, Mrs. Warren says, "You may leave, Henry." Those still at the table avoid each other's eyes. But then Ned, the next younger son, ten, says plaintively, "Mamma, *I* don't feel well either." Sam tells him sharply to stop whining. "You aren't a baby. And you aren't a girl."

The boy flushes and lowers his eyes, to conceal tears, but mutters to himself, "I hate you, I hate you." The youngest child, Fiske, hunches over his plate. Mrs. Warren says, "I believe, Sam, that Ned was speaking to me. I am still able to decide such questions for myself."

Silence is reestablished, and the servants, distributing new plates, seem to declare their deafness.

Scenes of that kind, repeated but unrecorded, are what we have to imagine in the background of these lives.

The Warrens' lives and achievements have gone almost unrecorded, and when they do appear, in footnotes to other people's biographies, they are usually misidentified. However, one of them, E. P. "Ned" Warren, did want his life to be remembered, rightly thinking that it was remarkable.

As early as 1897 he asked his sister to send him all the letters he had ever written to members of the family, to help him in an autobiography. He wasn't yet planning publication, but he did want to justify himself to the future. "Sealed letters buried in various libraries to be unearthed later will probably suffice. Someone after our deaths will understand why I did or didn't do what was expected and the knowledge—this is what I hope for—may be such as he wouldn't expect himself" (letter of June 9, 1897, in the Massachusetts Historical Society). This book sets out to fulfill his hope.

After many delays and changes of plan, Ned Warren did write a partial self-description, appointed two literary executors, and left money to pay them for bringing out a book about him. Osbert Burdett and E. H. Goddard were young Englishmen whom Warren befriended in the last third of his life. To them he too was an Englishman, or a cosmopolitan; their book about him largely ignored his American life and his family.

Burdett and Goddard subtitled their book *The Biography of a Connoisseur,* and quite rightly, for it was by being a connoisseur, by helping to invent that concept, that Ned had become a man of importance. (Many people in the field consider him the most important collector of classical antiquities in American history.) They delayed publication, indeed delayed, and never finally performed, all the tasks of turning their manuscript materials into a book. But something finally appeared in 1941, thirteen years after Warren's death, and is referred to in what follows as "Burdett and Goddard." It has been, necessarily, a major source for me.

Unfortunately, it is one of the worst biographies known to man; being written in a fit, or series of fits, of absentmindedness. In the first paragraph, for instance, Goddard tells us that Burdett was supposed to write it, "But his own death in 1936 *and other difficulties* prevented his accomplishing . . ." I need hardly say that the italics are mine.

Nothing but sleepy-headedness can explain this sort of thing, of which there is a great deal throughout the book. Sometimes one cannot even be sure to whom such pronouns as "he" or "they" refer. And when some pressure of impulse or intention can be felt, it is a dull panic lest the reader guess that Warren was homosexual—and so curl the lip at his friends and executors. That panic is understandable, if ignoble, and it clearly would complicate the job of telling Warren's life story, seeing that he was a proselytizing sexual heretic. But they had taken on the job and were getting well paid for it.

In addition, their panic or paralysis of discretion cannot justify, or even explain, how Burdett and Goddard obscure every issue, deaden every theme, and even leave half the interesting moments of their subject's life undescribed. Their book really constitutes an act of betrayal of their friend and patron (he was very generous to them, as to dozens of other people), and it is an act one is bound to resent on his behalf. Thus I thought this note necessary: to explain what "Burdett and Goddard" means in my book, and why my tone of voice in referring to it is so often acerbic.

Dramatis Personae

The main characters in this story are the five children of Samuel Dennis Warren (1817–88) and Susan Cornelia Clarke Warren (1825–1901). These were Samuel Dennis "Sam" Warren II, the lawyer and businessman (1852–1910); Henry Clarke Warren, the scholar of Sanskrit and Pali (1854–99); Cornelia Lyman Warren, the philanthropist (1857–1921); Edward Perry "Ned" Warren, the collector of classical antiquities (1860–1928); and Frederick Fiske Warren, the political radical or utopist (1862–1938).

The parents are referred to herein as Mr. and Mrs. Warren. The younger generation are referred to by their first names when involved in dealings with each other or their parents. But when they are linked to a partner or rival in some public enterprise, as Ned is linked to John Marshall, or Sam is linked to Louis Brandeis, they may be called Warren.

We also meet, listed here in alphabetical order:

J. D. Beazley, professor of classical archaeology at Oxford

Bernard Berenson, connoisseur

Mary Bliss, cousin of the Warrens and wife of John Marshall

Louis Brandeis, lawyer and public servant

Erskine Childers, British soldier and Irish patriot

Molly Osgood Childers, wife of Erskine Childers and sister of Gretchen Osgood Warren

John Fothergill, protégé of Ned Warren and innkeeper

Alice Freeman, president of Wellesley College

Isabella Stewart Gardner, art collector

Charles Lanman, professor of Sanskrit at Harvard

Maurice Magnus, author of *Memoirs of the Foreign Legion*

John Marshall, collector of classical antiquities

John Mason, Irish husband of Sarah Mason

Mortimer Mason, son of John Mason and partner in S.D. Warren and Company

Mortimer Phillips Mason, son of Mortimer Mason and professor of philosophy at Bowdoin College

Sarah Warren Mason, sister of Samuel Dennis Warren and wife of John Mason

George Herbert Palmer, professor of philosophy at Harvard

Matthew Prichard, protégé of first Ned and then Sam
   Warren, and officer of the Boston Museum

Edward Robinson, curator of classical antiquities at the
   Boston Museum

Denman Ross, benefactor and trustee of the Boston
   Museum

Robert "Robbie" Ross, friend of Oscar Wilde

George Santayana, philosopher

Vida Dutton Scudder, professor of English at Wellesley and
   worker at Denison House

Harry Asa Thomas, protégé of Ned Warren

Daniel Berkeley Updike, printer

Mabel Bayard Warren, wife of Samuel Dennis Warren II

Gretchen Osgood Warren, wife of Fiske Warren

Charles Murray West, secretary to Ned Warren

The Mount Vernon Street Warrens

Introduction

O n the night of February 18, 1910, in his country home at Dedham, Massachusetts, Samuel Dennis Warren II took a gun and killed himself. The son of a self-made hero of industry, the elder and leader of five gifted siblings, a husband and father of six himself, he was also a prominent figure in Boston Yankee society. He had been or was: founder of the Dedham Polo Club, law partner of Louis Brandeis, head of the family paper firm, trustee of Massachusetts General Hospital, and president of the Museum of Fine Arts.

What was in his mind when he decided to kill himself we do not know. He left no message, to his family or to the world. But he was enmeshed in a painful and shaming suit brought against him by one of his brothers, which he was probably losing. The conflict between the two men had been lifelong and now exceeded the limits of divergent interests and ambitions. Each cherished and embodied an idea of manhood that was deadly to the other. Each *despised* the other. When the elder Warren shot himself, he shot his own idea of manhood, the father-husband-master idea, the sportsman-trustee-president idea, which he had gleamingly manifested to the world of Boston. He lent his gun to a man who had failed to meet that idea all his life, had suffered from it bitterly, and vowed to destroy it.

In September 1909, E. P. Warren, called Ned, was summoned to Boston from his home in England for conferences on the family quarrel about the trust fund they shared. He wrote his friend Bernard Berenson on September 22 that this was "the time of crisis in Boston." Berenson, and Warren's other aesthete and connoisseur friends, knew that the quarrel had been going on for several years, and that a great deal depended on it, for Warren and—in a sense—for art.

Ned Warren was then fifty years old and a well-known figure in the world of art collecting, especially of classical antiquities. Ninety percent of the classical holdings of the Boston Museum of Fine Arts came from or through him, while his former partner and lover, John Marshall, was doing the same work for the Metropolitan Museum in New York. Ned was also known in other circles and for other things, and most of all for Lewes House, near Brighton, where he lived with homosexual or bisexual male friends and protégés. His word for people like himself was "Uranians."

Since Oscar Wilde's death in 1900, Lewes House had sheltered former members of his circle. It was a college for the study of classical art, a museum for art of all kinds—Rodin sculpted the best-known version of *Le Baiser* for Warren—and a center of one kind of erotic liberation. Warren was at work, intermittently, for most of his life, on a three-volume *Defence of Uranian Love.*

The Warrens in Boston lived in a very different style or styles. (Ned openly hated all that "Boston" stood for and intended his nude Greek sculptures to lead to the subversion of Boston values.) His parents, and his brother Henry, were dead by 1910, but two other brothers and a sister survived. The oldest, Sam, was a leading figure in Boston society and a trustee of great Boston institutions, dining out with Cabots and Lowells and the dignitaries of Harvard. He lived on Marlborough Street in the Back Bay, with his Southern belle wife and six children. The youngest brother, Fiske, lived on the single tax enclave and commune he had founded in Harvard, to the west of Boston. His was a name quite often in the headlines for his life-style (reform clothing, vegetarianism, nudism) or for his anti-imperialist activities in the Philippines. Cornelia lived on their mother's estate in Waltham, where she ran a model farm and was busy with a variety of philanthropies—notably the College Settlement House in Boston's South End, which built social bridges between Yankee society and its immigrant neighbors.

All four siblings were serious people, but they did not find it easy to take each other seriously. This was particularly true of Sam and Ned. The latter had always been the aesthete and poet, impractical and unmanly, first a sissy and then a fairy. Sam was a lawyer and businessman, sailor and sportsman, a proper Bostonian in his work and his play.

During the first decade of the twentieth century, Ned had begun to change the scenario one expects for these roles. In 1903 he hired an attorney to check the accounts of the S.D. Warren Company and to investigate the family trust. After receiving the attorney's report in 1906, he began to ask for hundreds of thousands of dollars, for changes in the trustees and the trust, and most recently, for changes in the running of the paper mills themselves. The aesthete was challenging the businessman on his own ground.

The Mills Trust, as it was usually known, had been set up in 1889 by the law firm of Warren and Brandeis, and was mostly the work of Louis Brandeis. It was he who was expected to defend it and Sam against Ned's attorneys. Brandeis was as much Sam's friend as Berenson was Ned's; the two brilliant Jews had been introduced into Boston society by the Warren brothers. But just as the Warren quarrel reached its crisis, Brandeis was asked to take part in the Ballinger-Pinchot case in Washington, the case that made him a national figure as defender of citizens' rights against the money trusts. His absence from the Boston courtroom was to be a dramatic feature of the *Warren* v. *Warren* suit and to have an effect on his own later career.

Cornelia had grown alarmed as early as 1902 at the bitterness between her brothers. In a letter to her of July 28, 1902, Sam referred to Ned's hate for him as "the author of all his ills"; "I would like to step out [and] let another take my place who can keep the family together. I have very likely deemed myself over necessary to the business. My dear good father would have done better. I have tried to do my duty but it may have been with too proud a heart and too arrogant a point of view."[1]

This note of pathos sounds recurrently through Sam's letters, but we should take into account also the way he had, for instance, squeezed Fiske out of his partnership. The latter was originally assigned 16⅔ percent of the firm's profits, to Sam's 33⅓ percent (the other 50 percent going to a more experienced partner, Mortimer Mason). But in 1896 that distribution was altered to Fiske 10 percent, Sam 40 percent; in 1902, Fiske got 5 percent, Sam 45 percent; and in 1903 it became 2½ percent and 47½ percent, respectively. This obviously left sore feelings in Fiske, for he too hired an attorney to investigate the trust. Sam was often accused of arrogance, outside the family as well as in.

Nevertheless he was forced to yield. In a letter to Cornelia dated July 25, 1907, he says that when the company's six-month report is ready, she and Ned's attorney, a Mr. Youngman, should come for an oral report from him and do so every quarter.

Ned grew bolder in his complaints. In an October 1908 letter to his sister he asked why he, the yielder so often before, should yield yet again to Sam, on pain of being blamed as a troublemaker. Why shouldn't those in possession yield for once? An established government has only to ordain, it need never be "obstreperous"; but he and Fiske will not get their rights unless they make trouble. Were he Sam, he would have come to terms long ago. It is she and Fiske who have, unwittingly, been in the wrong for many years, by not standing firm against Sam.

The family legal conferences went on until December 1909 and ended in an ultimatum from Ned: Sam must either agree to change the workings of the trust and the company or he would sue. Sam evidently refused, for on December 13, 1909, Ned wrote Sam that he had filed a bill in equity; adding, "First. I hope that you will make me contented to withdraw it; and Second. The phrases are such as in a legal document I have felt obliged to sign, but are very far from representing my feelings towards you aside from the business or my desire for unanimous fraternal procedure. Let us try to agree; it would be much pleasanter. Your affectionate brother, E. P. Warren."[2]

Daily hearings began in January 1910. In a letter from Ned's attorney, Youngman, to Sam's attorney, Gorham, it appears that the latter pleaded estoppage, arguing that Ned had accepted the trust by not protesting it. Youngman countered that Sam Warren and Mortimer Mason, his partner in the mills, had asked Ned to leave everything to them: Youngman quoted a letter of Sam's, dated May 31, 1889, that accompanied documents for Ned to sign. "All the others have been carefully into the matter, and approve of the present arrangement; and I shall have to ask you to take my word for it, as far as you do not understand it."[3]

Ned was not told how much capital his father had left or what his own income would amount to. He was given no inventory of the estate, nor any explanation of how the trust would work. Thus he had been in effect "an heir induced by executors to act in almost absolute ignorance of the facts. . . . In such a case it is unnecessary to show action or intentional concealment [on their part]." But though he waived the question of intention, Youngman continued, it was hard to believe that the information was *accidentally* withheld. Someone was to blame, but it was not the person one might think. "Of course, as you know, I do not suggest a purpose in Mr. Samuel Warren, in withholding information, to defraud his brother. It was a brain other than Mr. Samuel Warren's that conceived the scheme and the method of accounting and invented the arguments to defend the same."[4] This is a thrust at Brandeis, whom many Boston lawyers hated.

Sam seemed to have realized before his death, says Youngman, that his and Brandeis's arguments were fallacious, that in setting up the trust he had indeed "meant to assume the position of a quasi-guardian." Ned didn't learn the basic facts of the matter until 1906, when he got Youngman's report, and the full facts only in 1910, when Sam was questioned in court. For instance, the administrative charges of the company, Youngman claims, should not have exceeded $40,000 a year, but much more had been reserved by the partners in payment to themselves. He also claimed that the partners owed the heirs $1.5 million, plus interest.

In the *Pleadings in Warren* v. *Warren,* Youngman argued that at the time the Mills Trust was set up, Mrs. Warren was entirely inexperienced in business matters, and so were the children, except for Sam (and Fiske, who had occupied a subordinate position). They had no suspicion that Sam would in any way violate the trust and confidence reposed in him.[5] His duty was to act with utmost fairness and scrupulous regard for the interests of the other beneficiaries. He knew that his mother was unlikely to take any active part, and Mortimer Mason was so situated that he could not oppose anything desired by the defendant. Fiske, Youngman said, "held a small interest and had but little voice in directing the affairs of the business."[6]

The case thus had a moral as well as a legal character. Sam "undertook the solemn duty of resisting all temptation to sacrifice in any way the interest of the other beneficiaries under said trust for his own personal gain. . . ." On January 4, 1890, he obtained power of attorney from Ned, which continued until 1903 when Ned had it revoked "being no longer satisfied with the doings of said Samuel."[7]

The defendant, Youngman said, was subjected to a temptation no trustee should meet, and he failed to withstand it. The partners had taken $2 million in profit—twice as much as they should.[8]

If this was a moral indictment, it still had to be settled legally. Sam, being in 1909 the only trustee, was claiming the right to terminate the trust; Youngman strongly felt that he must be restrained by the court.[9] Sam was no longer suitable to be a trustee, nor should he be allowed to appoint new trustees. He should be removed, and the court should appoint three new trustees.[10]

On December 13, 1909, the court issued a Writ of Injunction temporarily forbidding Sam to appoint a new trustee. On the seventeenth, Cornelia and Fiske sent a joint note to the court, saying that they disapproved the attack on their brother and were satisfied with his management of the trust. On the twenty-second they were appointed co-trustees.

Cornelia was largely on Sam's side; Fiske yielded to pressure from his sister at times, but from Ned at other times. Ned was scornful of them both, and resentful of Cornelia. In a letter to his cousin, Lois Shaw, written after Sam's suicide, he said, "The New England woman is accepted in New England. I apply my standard and find her cold, hard, inhuman, so that even honesty will not save her. . . . Witness the amazement of the dame who pitied Cornelia for having such a brother, when you pitied me for having such a sister. Now Cornelia isn't cold, and hard, and inhuman, but she isn't warm, and soft, and human, like the red rose of England, and she has a monstrous confidence in her own judgment. Indeed, she is always spying about, whatever is discussed, for a judgment seat that she may sit on the question. Unfortunately I am often the question. Fiske does the opposite. He believes in a count of heads, and, when he ought to act, he tries to find a majority to outvote him. When he has found it, or as the Romans said, has invented it, he desires it to suppress him, what time he clamours lustily against the injustice of the majority, though by a fine distinction, not against the injustice of the suppression . . . the conclusion of the whole unnecessary fight is that business men and the woman [have the] right to keep the control of those anomalous beings who are not business men nor women."[11]

On February 15, 1910, just three days before Sam's death, Ned wrote to Cornelia about his plans to intervene in the running of the mills. He had been talking to disaffected workers there. His thoughts had long been with the mill people, he said—he saw himself as the defender of the proletariat—but his art collecting had been a big work, and there had been no chance as long as their mother filled the third trustee slot. He had planned to abate the collecting long ago, once the museum had built up its collection, but that hope passed when the museum trustees voted to build. (Another quarrel between the brothers was that Sam spent the museum's money on erecting its new building—the present one, on Huntington Avenue—while Ned wanted to spend it on the purchase of art.)

Ned also had hoped to live at Longley House, in Westbrook, just across from the mills, and to take an active role in their operation. Sam objected to that, so instead he was living at Fewacres, a house a few miles from Westbrook, which was as close as he could get, and talking to the workers.

At the same time as he was taking all this punishment, Sam had had to accept a restructuring of the mill's partnership, with four new members besides himself and the rebellious Fiske. One of these new partners was Herbert Mason, the son of Mortimer Mason, who had died in February 1909. (The other three were Charles W. Ward, Roger D. Smith, and Walter B. Nye.) The profits or losses were to be shared, 45 percent going to Sam, 7 percent to Fiske, and 12 percent each to the other four.

Moreover, after his partner's death, Sam had induced Mason's two sons to accept a settlement of the company's debt to Mason's estate that was considerably less than was provided for in the articles of partnership. However, in this same month, February 1910, the Mason brothers went back to Sam and said they were dissatisfied with the settlement. (We know this because of a legal document filed after Sam's death in which his executors agree to pay the Masons another $32,000, in accordance with Sam's wishes.) He may well have felt like an aging lion, a king of the jungle whose jackals turn against him.

So much had already gone wrong, and the suit seemed likely to go in Ned's favor, in circumstances of great potential publicity. It is easy to imagine the shame that must have been felt by Sam and his wife, Mabel, given their high position in society, and given a feud they already maintained with the popular press. What strains it fostered between the two of them we don't know, but in mid-

February Sam went, apparently alone, to their Dedham house, Karl-stein, to spend a few days, and left no note of explanation when, on the night of February 18—the day on which the new partnership came into effect—he took a shotgun and killed himself.

His eldest son discovered the body and had to tell his mother. The family immediately wired, or went, to Brandeis in Washington to ask him to come to their aid despite the very cool relations between Mabel Warren and Brandeis. (It is not surprising that they did not ask Ned or Fiske to act for them, but Mabel Warren had several brothers—and her oldest son was twenty-five.) In any case, it was given out that Sam had died of apoplexy, brought on by the strains of the suit, though many people must have guessed the truth. On February 21, under the headline FIGHT FOR MILLIONS SUDDENLY ENDED BY DEATH OF S.D. WARREN, the *Boston Evening American* reported that mystery surrounded the death.

The report bristled with suspicions. The death had been officially ascribed to physical exhaustion, "augmented by the fact that his brother, E.P. Warren, had brought a suit to have Samuel ousted as trustee of the big Warren estate." But, the reporter said, he was not too exhausted to walk the two miles from the station to Karlstein or to spend the afternoon chopping wood. The suit was summed up as Ned's attempt to prevent Sam's appointing trustees he could control. The Warrens' social position was gloated over; Sam's estate was reported as between $4 and $5 million, and his son's marriage the previous year was described as an event of the social season.

Sam's death was announced as occurring on the night of the nineteenth-twentieth. In fact, it was twenty-four hours earlier, though the reporter does not seem to guess that. Dr. Andrew D. Hodgdon, the medical examiner for the district, had been called to Karlstein, but Sam was already dead. When interviewed, Hodgdon said, "I do not care to say anything about the case. You better see the Warrens [*sic*]. They will tell you anything about it." An under-taker named Higgins, of Flynn and Higgins, had been called and had embalmed Sam the same night. No death certificate had been issued. (As preserved in the Dedham Town Offices, the certificate gives the cause of death as "Cerebral Hemorrhage"; the certificate at Mount Auburn Cemetery leaves cause of death blank.)

Louis Brandeis had hurried home from Washington to take charge of things at the Warren home, where he stood as a guard between the family and news reporters. It is believed in the family that Sam's eldest son went to Washington to fetch Brandeis, who reportedly told the press, Sam "came here to rest for a few days last week. He had been in poor health for some time. . . . [Without transition or explanation] I should not think that he left much to the Boston Art Museum (he was president) because he gave liberally to it during his life. . . . Hodgdon was the family physician." The reference to the museum, obviously in response to a question, reflects an earlier scandal of Warren's forced resignation from that institution and implies, however vaguely, that this may have played a part in the tragedy.

When the reporter went back to Hodgdon, the latter denied being the family doctor. "I was simply called in this time and I may have been called in once or twice before in my life." Warren's real consulting physician was Dr. Arthur G. Cabot of Boston.

E. P. Warren, the newspaper said, had issued a statement through his lawyers: "While litigation concerning the management of the Warren paper mills interests the Warren family, there has been no personal feeling over the matter. The question turns over the interpretation of certain legal documents." Nobody is likely to have believed that. (Ned was probably in Boston at this time; his letter to Cornelia of three days prior had been mailed from the Hotel Bellevue on Beacon Hill. They were all attending hearings five days a week, so he was probably in Boston even on weekends. On the other hand, if Sam had gone to Dedham for a few days' rest, perhaps the hearings were in recess. Ned may have gone to Fewacres, where they would have had to wire him the news.)

Thus the readers of the Boston paper were given a dozen reasons to disbelieve the family's account of the death, and those who knew that it had occurred twenty-four hours earlier than announced could easily imagine how that time had been spent, in Dedham, Boston, Waltham, Washington, and perhaps Maine—how many people, in the family and outside it, had to be reached and talked to, how many plans had to be proposed and amended, how much grief and anger, charge and countercharge, against the living and the dead, had to be dealt with. On top of everything else, for some days after that report, the family no doubt felt grave anxiety about whether the paper would follow up those clues.

In fact, the death had profound repercussions in Boston and beyond. As the newspaper reporter's questions suggest, many people thought Sam had been driven to his death by the trustees of the Museum of Fine Arts, who had forced him to resign his office of president there not long before. This forced resignation had been a scandal in the art world, in which Ned had played a part. Isabella Stewart Gardner's friends in the Boston art world, who loved and admired Sam, never forgave those trustees for that. Many of Sam's law and business friends, on the other hand, thought Louis Brandeis was to blame; either for having failed to come to Sam's defense or for having long before set up a flawed trust. They never forgave Brandeis. And in the family, of course, Ned was bitterly blamed. He was in effect excommunicated, so far as Sam's branch went. The *family,* which Mr. and Mrs. Warren had built up to be a powerful social and financial and even intellectual unit within Boston culture, was broken beyond repair.

1

The Parents

*He had been so constant to his lights, so constant to
charity, and to his love for his neighbour. Perhaps he
had loved his neighbour even better than himself—which
is going one better than the commandment.
Always, this flame had burned in his heart, sustaining
him through everything, the welfare of the people. He
was a large employer of labour, he was a great
mine-owner. And he had never lost this from his heart,
that in Christ he was one with his workmen. . . . For
Gerald [his son] was in reaction against Charity. . . .*

—D. H. Lawrence,
Women in Love

Samuel Dennis Warren, who was born in 1817 and died in 1888,
had two homes. He piled up a fortune making paper in his Cumberland Mills in Westbrook, Maine, and he had six children, of whom
five grew to maturity, on Beacon Hill in Boston. This story is about
those children and their pursuit of art, learning, philanthropy, and
political reform—various forms of idealistic work. It is in some
sense a Beacon Hill story. But the fortune, and the factory in Westbrook, are forces within it.

The children imbibed their father's idealism, both directly (from
his conversation) and indirectly (through the education he lavishly
funded for them at Harvard and elsewhere). He himself had been
denied a college education as a young man, and thereafter esteemed

its advantages to the point of exaggeration. For him, as of course for many others, book learning was almost synonymous with "idealism," with higher moral values. Later his children modified that moral enthusiasm, choosing different ideals from his in accordance with the thinking of their own generation. Above all, they had to choose between his puritanism and the more aesthetic modern values. But they did not cease to be idealistic.

In their hands, Mr. Warren's money (and zeal) took forms still visible today as one goes about Boston and its environs. It became, through Samuel Dennis Warren II, the Museum of Fine Arts on Huntington Avenue; through Cornelia Warren, Denison House, now on Leyland Street, Roxbury, the College Settlement House for social work; through Henry Warren, the slice of Harvard Yard lying across Quincy Street; through Fiske Warren, the restored Shakerton and his own Tahanto, a twentieth-century "commune" at Harvard. But buildings were only one of the forms their achievements took: Through Henry the Warren money became the Harvard Oriental Series of books, and through Ned it became the classical antiquities collection of the Museum of Fine Arts. One could prolong the list.

Mr. Warren could be proud of his children; all five became noteworthy citizens of Boston, divergent though their lines of activity were; better citizens and more creative minds than the average. But this story has other and opposite themes—money, suicide, and sex. Its main action could be called a tragedy of sexual politics. For a fortune the size of Mr. Warren's, in nineteenth-century idealistic Boston as in other times and places, bred passions of jealousy, ambition, resentment, repression, and hatred.

It was not just as a pile of dollars, a purchasing power, that the Warren fortune stirred up such strong excitement, but as an achievement, as a manifestation of the father's energy, imagination, self-application, and virtue. S. D. Warren's life was an American success story and a moral exemplum. He had started with nothing and ended up with a fortune, and it seemed that he had made it without cheating, indeed by being good, on the way up. He was seen as a hero of the business ethic, a man who showed that Christianity was good for business. (Later generations, including his children, were more skeptical about the business ethic in general, but none of the children seem to have doubted their father's virtue.) Thus a large audience surrounded and applauded his later years, and to the front row of that audience, his gifted children (perhaps we should say they sat on the platform with him), his wealth was a constant incitement to achieve something notable themselves. Contemplating his life at the time of his death, his loyal employees said, "One fact comes to mind—the opportunity that this country affords to the ambitious young man to achieve success."[1]

Mr. Warren, called Dennis by his parents, was born in Grafton, Massachusetts, the eleventh child of fourteen. There had been Warrens in Massachusetts since 1630, but they had been inconspicuous—except for one witch, arrested in 1674. Dennis Warren's father, John, fifty years old when his son was born, was a peddler, traveling regularly from Massachusetts to North Carolina, and sometimes to the West Indies, carrying to the backward South shoes made in semi-industrialized New England. He drove a team of horses that pulled a cart full of shoes. This was a line of enterprise he had invented; he had persuaded three Grafton shoemakers to entrust him with trunkfuls of their work (mostly coarse cowhide shoes, suitable for Negroes, Cornelia Warren tells us), and each spring he returned from the South with a sufficient profit.

Meanwhile the family lived and ran a store in Grafton, from where the children launched themselves into the outer world, one by one. Dennis's mother, born Susannah Grout, was a second wife and a strong personality, who reinforced her son's conscience and will to succeed. The oldest Warren son, John, was wild and was sent out to Texas, never to be heard from again. Two other brothers went West and settled in Wisconsin. But the five Warren children we are concerned with still had lots of uncles and aunts in New England, and lots of cousins who went to work in the Cumberland Mills. Elevated above the common herd as Warrens, though not of the royal blood themselves, these cousins surrounded our five Warren children like courtiers.

After four years of secondary schooling, Dennis Warren went to work for Grant and Daniell, a Boston paper firm (sellers, not makers) in 1832. This was four years before the battle of the Alamo and one year after Nat Turner's slave revolt. Racism and imperialism were already forces to be reckoned with in America, and during the decades to come the Warren children, some of them, would do battle against those forces. But their consciousness was not primarily political. This is a story in which we can say that cultural issues, rather than political ones, dominate; as long as we let "culture" cover the whole range from social work to art and scholarship, but exclude the major dramas of political history. For instance, Mr.

Warren's life seems to have been little affected by the Civil War. His energies were all absorbed by his job and his family and his charities.

Mr. Warren was a very hard worker for Grant and Daniell, was made a junior partner in 1838, and by denying himself minimal comforts, provided money to send his younger sisters to school. His affections were strong and his sympathies imaginative. In 1841 he became engaged to a girl named Ellen Fiske, whose brother was his best friend. She was a religious, sickly, and high-strung girl, who at one point registered herself as a patient at a Waltham asylum for the insane; she died young. In 1847, on his thirtieth birthday, he married a girl of very different character, and thereafter his world revolved around her and their children. Susan Clarke was the daughter of a Massachusetts Congregationalist minister.

The Reverend Dorus Clarke (1797–1884) was a man of letters— he had studied at Williams and Andover—as well as a minister. Some twenty items are ascribed to him in the National Union Catalog, including a memorial volume and one devoted to his life and work, published during his lifetime. But it seems likely that his audience was narrowly sectarian. From 1842 he edited a journal called *The New England Puritan,* and later others called *Mothers' Magazine, Christian Alliance and Family Visitor,* and *Christian Times*. His best-known book was *Orthodox Congregationalism and the Sects*.

In 1878 he published an essay, "Saying the Catechism," describing his home town of Westhampton, Massachusetts, as he remembered it from his childhood: Here, everyone observed Saturday evening as a part of the Sabbath; and three Sundays of the year were devoted to testing (or displaying) the children's knowledge of the catechism—which was taught in the family, the church, and the school—and everyone took pride in their familiarity with it. It was part of the secular culture of that time and place. Mr. Clarke yearned back to that culture, but it was already, in 1878, a part of the past, the possession of his memory, a subject for him to write about, not a part of contemporary America.

The Warrens and the Clarkes were similar families. There is some evidence that Mr. Warren (his wife could not bring herself to call him Dennis) felt inferior to his wife in terms of genteel culture, but the difference was not categorical enough to be called a difference in social class. Girls from both families attended Miss Hubbard's School, where they became friends, and it was thus that Susan Clarke met Mr. Warren. They were both serious people, and in the same style. At the time of their engagement her aunt described him as "a sober staid man, no dandy, no fop." That was the language both families used.

The Warrens at least lived in genteel poverty; genteel in the sense that although neither well-to-do nor with any tradition of wealth, they clearly belonged to the responsible class in society and allied themselves to the privileged in the way they saw things. A striking feature of the story to be told here is how quickly they adapted themselves to the wealth Mr. Warren made; they did not need to acquire new tastes or interests or manners. Cornelia Warren's *Memorial* mentions pieces of furniture that had long been handed down and appreciated in both families. This shows a vein of feeling that linked the older generations with this century's otherwise heretical Ned Warren, the homosexual aesthete. Also, both families believed that their sons should go to college, even in generations when the family could not afford to send them. Further, Dorus Clarke was an officer of the New England Historic-Genealogical Society. And perhaps the most telling point in establishing the connection is that Mr. Clarke was a Congregationalist minister and Mr. Warren once thought of becoming one.

Certainly there was no gulf between the families morally or religiously. "Puritan" was a word invoked to explain and praise Mr. Warren as well as Mr. Clarke. The former was a reader of the latter's journal, *The New England Puritan*. He was a devout young man, one of a group at the Bowdoin Street Church who got together in 1842 to found the Mount Vernon Church, dedicated in 1844.

At the same time, Mr. Warren was known for his jocularity, although such of his jokes as have come down to us have the quality (very evocative of the times) of a faintly grim teasing, especially about money matters. For instance, in a letter of 1884 to Mrs. Houghton, the wife of Henry Oscar Houghton of Houghton Mifflin Publishers, we find what is presumably a reply to a request for a donation to some charity. "I do not know how much 'a few dollars' is. I was taught that one is some, two a few, three a good many, four a crowd, and five a room, and I think about fifty right for you."[2] Such was the pecuniary humor of even pious Yankees.

Mr. Warren made a profession of faith in 1836, after some agonizing of spirit. In those days he went to five church services on a Sunday and had thoughts of becoming a missionary. In 1846 he renewed his 1836 "Agreement with Myself" to live to Christ's glory and to forward His kingdom.[3] It was, rather strikingly, Mrs. Warren whose sense of religion was the more liberal, and she transferred the weight of her spiritual enthusiasm away from church work and into the world of art. At least in Cornelia Warren's novel, *Miss Wilton,* the Mrs. Warren character does not always go to church, distrusts foreign missions, and criticizes her husband's religious friends from a hedonist or vitalist point of view. "Jim" has, she tells him, one very important quality that they lack; he is not too afraid of the universe to have a good time in it. "They'd be mortally alarmed if they enjoyed themselves."[4]

Our major source of knowledge about the couple is the two books their daughter wrote, *A Memorial of My Mother* (1908) and a novel, *Miss Wilton* (1892). The first is an exercise in the too-pious, too-reticent tradition of Boston memoirs, but it does make clear that the writer saw her parents in the same terms as she saw two characters in the much more revealing novel. In the latter she tells of the courtship and early married life of Jim Willcox and Bessie Folsom, a businessman in the iron trade and a music teacher. He is middle-aged, with sandy whiskers and merry eyes; she is significantly younger but the dominant figure in the relationship. He makes mistakes in dress and manners, being a simple and ardent soul, but worships her. She is dainty and decided, in the *Jane Eyre* tradition of fictional heroines. "Dainty" here means scrupulously fresh, plain, and neat of dress, not frilled or flounced or jeweled; and "decided" means something equivalent in manner—a demureness that is full of principle. (In the detail of physique and temperament, Bessie Folsom is not much like Mrs. Warren; she resembles another powerful woman of Cornelia's acquaintance, Alice Freeman, who struck many of her contemporaries as a novel heroine.)

Bessie is the one in charge in all her relationships, in the name of taste, and in the name of womanhood. "It is, I think, the right perception of feminine sentiments that constitutes the gentleman," she says.[5] Jim acknowledges that he has everything to learn from her, and she gradually "softens in the face of his utter humility."[6]

This is after he has told her, "You can never be sorry for having been so wonderfully good to me today. I am not the man to be blind to the difference between us."[7] She was superior. Her taste was very definite, and his was uncertain. (We gather from more than one source that this was true of Mr. and Mrs. Warren; he was rarely allowed to buy her any kind of ornament or such a thing as a tea service. Ned Warren says his father's taste was "inconspicuous.") Later, Jim felt "an inward shudder that he was of a coarser mold.

He loathed himself, his unmanageable clothes, his uneducated manners."[8] Cornelia's language tends to hyperbole, and the reader
should not think that Jim is being presented as Dostoevski's Underground Man. But the idea that men do offend women by their
"coarseness," that women are, by nature, more refined and cultured,
was an important idea among the Warrens (and other people in their
world) and one that Ned Warren was to react against.

It is also worth noting that Bessie is in one way quite hearty; she
is very fond of horses and riding. So was Mrs. Warren, and most
of her children—Ned and Sam, so different from each other in other
ways, and Cornelia. We don't hear this about Mr. Warren, which
perhaps fits with the general symbolic map of the family; riding
does seem to figure in all their lives as an elegant upper-class activity. Sam founded a polo club; Ned had Arabian stallions in his
stables in England. Perhaps this was one of the inherited tastes that
made it easier for the children to rise socially.

Miss Wilton, the other and opposite heroine of Cornelia's novel,
a proud beauty who sins and repents, gets into financial difficulties
and appeals to Jim—and would get his chivalrous help except that
Bessie, recently married, puts her foot down. " 'I do not see, I cannot
see,' exclaimed Bessie wildly, 'why we are to suffer in health or
comfort to meet Miss Wilton's bills.' "[9] She speaks in the name of
principle, but also in the name of family egotism; and when she has
won her point, and Miss Wilton is sent away, Bessie dances win-
somely round the room—now they can have the cellar and the
dining room put to rights. Cornelia Warren had clearly read a lot of
George Eliot, and Bessie is conceived as rather like Mary Garth in
Middlemarch, Lilla Wilton as rather like Gwendolen Harleth in *Daniel
Deronda.* But for our purposes the important thing is that Cornelia
saw the moral and emotional transactions between Mr. and Mrs.
Warren in similar terms.

We must of course be tentative in drawing these connections.
Bessie Folsom is more modern than Mrs. Warren; she is doubtful
about the value of foreign missions. Mrs. Warren continued to press
the claims of all sorts of missions on her children to the end of her
life, and in 1895 she wrote to Henry that she had the best children
in the world—if they would just take their stand as Christian men.
But in recommending missions, her stress fell on the secular educational work done by the churches, and above all her own work was
done in the field of art.

In terms of family ego, at least, the novel character seems to

represent the novelist's mother. More than most people, the Warrens—because of Mrs. Warren's decisiveness—lived at the center of
a series of concentric circles, with a sense of responsibility that
increased palpably with every inward move toward the nuclear
family. Cornelia, at least as a novelist, but probably as a daughter
too, feels uneasy about this; the novel's other story, about Miss
Wilton, embodies a more radically Christian sensibility, but the
issue is treated in some sense dialectically in the novel.

The *Memorial* also gives us the feeling that Cornelia was fonder
and more admiring of her father. She tells us that his life was sweet
and wholesome, and his words merry, and that happy echoes of his
life were still coming to her twenty years after his death.[10] Her
words of praise for her mother are slightly more judicious and less
spontaneous sounding. Mrs. Warren was "firm," and "just," and
"capable." She ruled, or over-ruled, and Mr. Warren was one of her
subjects. During her widowhood she apparently spoke of her fears
that she might be "left behind" by her husband's soul because of
the spiritual life and development he might be experiencing beyond
the grave. This is all funerary sculpture, of course, very vague as
well as very proper; but there are suggestions that she and her
children felt he was a saint and she had given him a hard time. He,
not she, was the fragile figure who might get hurt if they collided,
though there is no evidence that they often did so. They seem to
have worked well together.

It is worth noting that after their marriage, Dennis Warren and
Susan Clarke took with them on their wedding journey both one of
his sisters and one of hers. The two families resembled each other
in the strong sense of responsibility the older siblings felt for the
younger, the stronger for the weaker. (In Cornelia's novel, Jim and
Bessie first get together over the latter's anxieties about one of her
brothers.)

The families also intermarried. Susan's sister Ellen, who looked
after the Warren children when their parents traveled, married Dennis's cousin, George Warren Hammond (who worked at the Cumberland Mills). On at least one of Mr. Warren's long trips to Europe,
Ellen accompanied him, while Mrs. Warren stayed at home. A Mr.
Bliss who was a cousin of Susan married two of Mr. Warren's sisters
in succession; and his daughter Mary Bliss married John Marshall,
who was Ned Warren's great love. By the time Mr. Warren died,
four of his nephews were in key positions in the business—one was
a partner in the firm, three others headed three of the individual

mills. The company in a sense belonged to the entire family; the elegant Warren House in Westbrook, the company town, belonged not to Mr. Warren or any of his children, but to a nephew, John E. Warren.

These facts are suggestive in various ways, but most importantly, for this story, they suggest the privilege the five siblings must have at least sometimes felt. Mr. and Mrs. Warren were clearly the royal family of this far-spreading cousinage in which their five children were central and prominent, like young princes. And while the cousins managed the mills, below them stood the workers of Westbrook, who attended a Warren School and a Warren Church, and so on. Even today the profile of the S.D. Warren mills, a cluster of giant smokestacks rearing above the town as if an ocean liner had stranded there, dominates the area. There was and is a Warren Block in Westbrook, where the Oddfellows met; a Warren Memorial Library; a Warren Swimming Pool; Warren Baseball Park; and so on. The company town was something like a little kingdom, dynastic and feudal. (The "book" about Mr. Warren, compiled when he died, was subtitled *A Tribute from the People of Cumberland Mills*.)

This did not pass unnoticed or unprotested. Charles Fairchild, Mr. Warren's partner in the 1870s, was appalled by what he called the company's "rank nepotism."[11] In that decade George Warren Hammond was agent of the mills; his brother Billie looked after the shipping; his sister Mary's husband, William Longley, was superintendent; Bert Warren (son of Mr. Warren's brother Jonathan) was in charge of the shops; John E. Warren (son of Joseph) was all-around man and later agent; Henry Merriam (son of Mary Warren) ran the Copsecook Mill; Kit Blasland (grandson of Anna Warren Hammond) ran transportation. At the end of the next decade, Mortimer Mason, son of Sarah Warren and John Mason, became a partner. According to the company's official history, it prospered because of some of these men but despite others. (There is a tradition that the Warrens were a family of bookmen rather than businessmen.) As far as the five Warren children go, these facts remained a distant background most of the time, most felt in that sense of a private kingdom up in Maine, where they were royal; but at the tragic end of our story, the accusation of nepotism—as a sin against good business practice—was one of the charges that Ned Warren (the aesthete) brought against his brother Sam (the businessman) in the quarrel that ended the latter's life.

During these siblings' later lives, their link to the mills, and therefore to the cousinage, grew more remote, but it is still notable how many bequests to cousins there were in Cornelia's and Ned's wills; and the two men who most assisted Fiske in his utopian schemes were Mortimer Phillips Mason, a cousin, and Charles White Huntington, the husband of a cousin. How large a proportion of the family helped and were helped by the successful branch is hard to calculate, for I am using the word "cousin" wherever the family used it—to cover every variety of second and third and once- or twice-removed cousin. And though in the family documents cousins figure as loyal recipients of patronage, or as grateful recipients of charity, had we heard the voices of the disaffected or proudly independent, or the less favored, we might have been given a different picture of Mr. Warren and his children.

The nearest we get to that picture is in the story of the Masons. (This is oral anecdote, handed down by Adelbert and Herbert Mason.) Mr. Warren's sister Sarah married a John Mason who came over from Ireland shortly before 1848 and set up as a ship-carver in Boston and Salem. (Some of his work can be seen in the Peabody Museum in Salem.) He was also something of a poet. Unfortunately, in him artistic skill was linked to moral weakness, as it was in so many artist-types in Victorian novels; he had abandoned a wife and children when he left Ireland, and sometime in the late 1850s he forged Mr. Warren's signature to a check and had to flee New England. Mr. Warren told him he would have him prosecuted unless he left town, for Canada or the West. Mr. Warren then also gave his sister a choice: She could either go out West with her husband and children or stay in New England with *him,* where he would provide them with the necessities of life, but she must then promise never to see her husband again. She chose New England, for the children's sake, and they moved to Gorham, near to the mills. However, she was often red-eyed with weeping and the children were often without boots in cold weather. One hears also that the house Mr. Warren found for them was quite handsome, and that he sent them a wagonload of food on occasion; but it seems agreed that the family had a hard time.

So far the story is largely pathetic, but its second part is more variously suggestive. The oldest child, Mortimer Mason, at the age of fifteen went to the mills and asked Mr. Warren for a job. He was told he could "make himself useful"—without pay. This was in 1870—at least that is when he joined the firm. (There are discrepancies among different sources. In 1870, Mason would have been twenty, not fifteen; perhaps in that year he came back after a time away from the firm.) He was an industrious apprentice and rose up through the ranks of employees, accepting a tough commercial discipline. By 1880 (according to another source, 1883) he was a partner, and when Mr. Warren died and the Warren trustees handed the business over to three men to run for the benefit of the heirs, the three were Sam, Fiske, and Mason. And, as the most experienced, he was the principal partner, with a 50 percent share of the profits. When he died in 1909, Mason left a fortune of $1,316,000.[12] Thus his too was a success story and a moral exemplum. Nor do we hear that he or his sons ever reproached Mr. Warren for his severity. On the other hand, however, the legend of Mrs. Mason's red eyes and her children's bare feet was handed down.

There is a disconcerting grimness also in another family anecdote about Mr. Warren: After he had begun to rise at Grant and Daniell, his elder brother asked him to find a place for him in the firm. Mr. Warren responded that he could only give him his own position, and he himself would start again from scratch. The brother got the point and set out for the West. The modern reader is likely to interpret this offer as artificial and entirely to Mr. Warren's discredit, as moral bullying; and one must indeed suppose that he did not expect it to be taken up; but one should also suppose that if his brother had accepted, Mr. Warren would have fulfilled his bargain. His kind of sacrificial ethics would not have been grim if it had not been sincere.

The crucial step in founding the fortune was taken in 1854 when Mr. Warren bought the Androscoggin Paper Mill at Westbrook, on the Presumpscott River, an area where the Penobscot Indians used to live. The site was well adapted to Warren's purposes. The river runs twenty-two miles from Sebago Lake to tidewater, with a drop of 270 feet: The average volume of water discharged annually is 20.4 billion cubic feet, which means a flow rate of 39,000 cubic feet per minute, of which 37,000 feet was, in 1952, used by S.D. Warren and Company.[13]

The site was one mile downstream from the Saccarappa Falls and four miles upstream from tidewater. The first large industry there was the Westbrook Manufacturing Company, an outgrowth of the Portland Manufacturing Company, founded in 1829, which used the waterpower to make duck canvas for sails and tents. There were also sawmills in the area, and because of them the river water was not pure enough to use in papermaking, and Mr. Warren had to seek out spring water. But the twenty-foot head of river water at the Coggin Falls was invaluable in driving the mill machinery. Questions of landslides, alterations of the river's course, new land purchases, negotiations with the town over waterpower, and so on, continue to occupy management throughout our story.

Mr. Warren clearly perceived, in 1854, that his opportunity lay in making, as distinct from selling, paper. The year before he had leased a mill at Pepperell that produced 2 tons a day. The Androscoggin Mill, which he bought from the firm Day and Lyon, made 3,000 pounds of paper a day, using two Fourdrinier machines, of 62 and 68 inches, plus a 36-inch single-cylinder machine. In 1863 he added a third 68-inch machine, which brought production up to 7 tons a day. (By the time of Ned Warren's death in 1928, the firm made 250 tons a day; the plant covered 410 acres, 190 of them in the mill yard proper, and there were 36 acres of floor space and 2,000 employees.) He originally made brown paper and manila from old bags and jute butts for the Portland market, and newsprint for Boston from bleached cotton and linen bags.

Mr. Warren's partners in 1854 distrusted the venture, so he went ahead on his own. He borrowed money from two friends, Dr. Crehore and William H. Hill of the First National Bank, and bought the mill for $28,000. He changed the mill's title to Cumberland (the name of the county) and began to build a working community around it. The work was arduous and disagreeable; workers were hard to find and harder to keep; and, no doubt for that reason, it was a common theory that you could not build a respectable town around a paper mill. Mr. Warren used to tell his daughter of that prejudice, enlisting her interest in what had been achieved at Westbrook.

The company paid fair wages: seventy-five cents a day in 1854 and $1 a day during the Civil War. It was very much a company town; though there were other firms there, Mr. Warren paid 30 percent of the total taxes. There was never a union at the mill in Mr. Warren's time, despite the efforts of outside agitators, we are told. Workers were forced to live in company housing (at first, boardinghouses) unless they lived at home, and they could be dismissed if they failed to abide by the boardinghouse rules. They did, however, get running water and electricity there. An eight-hour workday was introduced in 1901, earlier than in other firms. And later, under Fiske Warren, a loan fund was set up that enabled many workers to become shareholders.

Moreover, a prominent feature of Mr. Warren's achievement was the family housing he provided for his workers. In the first year he either built or brought in thirty homes for them. Later he grew ambitious in matters of design; in the 1870s he had eight homes built that were direct adaptations of "Design A—A Working Man's Cottage," to be found in Andrew Jackson Downing's *The Architecture of Country Houses,* published in 1850. These were wooden structures, a story and a half tall, with a central gable on the facade. The architectural trim is a horizontal molding over each window, supported by brackets, and a series of simple brackets on the roof. Then, in 1881, he had a series of Queen Anne cottages erected from designs by John Calvin Stevens. (Stevens, born in 1855, was Maine's leading architect, most famous for his work in the shingle style.) These were followed in 1882 by three of Maine's most elaborate Queen Anne structures, the Warren Block, a community hall; the Longley House (now "The Elms"), a residence for the family when it visited; and the Warren House.

In 1883, Stevens began to experiment with the new shingle style, begun by H. H. Richardson and W. R. Emerson, and in 1886 Warren commissioned the same architect to build Cottage Place, a series of gambrel- and gable-roofed cottages with lots of space between—it is a very attractive street even today.

By 1883, the company owned 150 houses, with rents running from $75 to $200 a year. Electricity was provided in some at $35 a year, and water at $10 a year. In 1889 a sewerage system was begun, a public hall was erected in the town, and the company loaned employees money for the purchase of homes, the payment of bills, and the education of children. In 1891 it began a profit-sharing plan that was designed to increase wages and decrease the employees' fear of new machinery. Newspapers, we are told, often held the company up to others as an example, during the troubled time of strikes, in the 1870s and 1880s.

Stevens and his partner, W. W. Cobb, published *Examples of American Domestic Architecture* in 1889, which illustrated Cottage Place, and praised the company—the largest paper mill in the world—tracing its success to its treatment of its operatives. "They are glad while they are doing their work. Under the beneficent management of the mill proprietors, homelike cottages have been built. . . . Here is an example suggesting the solution of certain social problems. In all the history of Cumberland Mills there is no record of a strike."[14] By the time of Mr. Warren's death there were four hundred houses around the mills and two thousand people living in them.

Clearly the company was paternalistic and tried to make the social atmosphere of the town very respectable. At first, the people who came to work at the mill neither attended church nor sent their children to school, both institutions being a mile away. "A large percentage of the children were growing up without the restraining influence of the sanctuary, and the Sabbath was held in light esteem."[15] Mr. Warren set out to change all that and succeeded; church and school became his allies in building a socially solid community in Westbrook. (Solidity and stability were concepts or slogans he and his allies often employed.)

It was his belief that people should not have things done for them, but should be helped to do things for themselves. They too might then succeed, just like him. When the people of Westbrook felt they needed a new church, he promised to give them $5,000 once they had raised the same sum themselves; and he made a similar offer for the church furnishings. The Warren Church (Congregationalist) was organized in 1869; Mr. Warren gave the lot and a rose window that he bought in Italy. In 1880 he gave the church its parsonage.

Some people were disappointed that he would not simply give to the poor and needy, but that "He helped those who recognized the identity of their own highest interest with faithfulness towards him and his interest."[16] He declared that he did everything from business motives; but, said a speaker at the memorial service for him, "It requires a large faith in men to use such methods."[17]

It is said that Mr. Warren was sociable and jocular with both other businessmen and his workers. But, says his nephew John E. Warren, "What might to a stranger seem like thoughtless banter was to him a screen from which he looked out to take the measure of the man before him, and in this estimate he was rarely mistaken."[18] At the same time, when a competitor had to sell his machinery at a loss, Mr. Warren put himself out to get him the best price. And when, in 1858, he bought a spring a mile or more from the mills, although his prime object was to supply his customers with "uniform clean white paper at all seasons of the year," he also wanted his employees to have pure drinking water.[19] He managed to make the two motives coincide.

His son Fiske, though in some ways a political radical, in 1917 wrote a letter to his children and their cousins about their grandfather, describing him as a man whose religion it was to benefit his fellowmen, a purpose to which he subordinated his church creed, his business interests, and even his work hours.

He had been, as we know, a young man of marked religious piety. He was still one of a group of eighteen people who supported the Anglo-American revision of the Bible, finished in 1881 (this was a project Dorus Clarke was concerned with too). But in later years his charitable giving seems to have gone mainly to educational causes. According to Fiske, he believed in the church as an educator, and that education would solve all sorts of social problems at their roots. This was not a novel interpretation of religion, of course: It was certainly not new to Dennis Warren. As a young man he had passed a whole winter without a fire in his room or even stockings to wear so that his sisters might go to school.

Fiske described his father as the chief papermaker of his day. But he was also a dealer in rags, a pioneer in their large-scale importation; in the 1850s and 1860s his company made more money out of buying and selling rags to others than out of making paper.[20] By 1870 the company's turnover was evaluated at a million dollars a year. But Mr. Warren also early recognized the possibilities of wood pulp, made with soda. He bought the Forest Fibre Company at Yarmouthport and began to produce three tons of the pulp a day for the use of the Cumberland Mills. Poplar wood was suitable for this purpose, and great numbers of such trees were floated down the Presumpscott River to Westbrook.

After the Civil War it became possible to make newsprint from "mechanical fibre," which was made by disintegrating spruce wood on a grindstone. This became its preferred source. S.D. Warren and Company, however, had no access to spruce forests, so it turned its attention away from newsprint and concentrated on the superior quality paper used in books and magazines. In 1881 it started making coated paper, with a layer of pigment; this paper made possible the printing of glossy magazines because it took half-tone illustrations. The half-tone printing plate, made from a photographic negative, replaced the woodcut. One of the first of these publications was *Century Magazine,* which published, for instance, Theodore Roosevelt's *Ranch-Life and the Hunting Trail,* with the illustrations of Frederic Remington. The spread of such magazines even affected the history of literature, because they created a broader public for quality short stories and essays. By 1889 the output of the Cumberland Mills was forty tons a day, by 1895 fifty tons, and by 1900 sixty-one tons.

Mr. Warren also appears on the edge of literary history by the way he intervened in the development of Houghton Mifflin, the

Boston publishers. He was the friend and ally of its founder, Mr. Houghton. In Ellen Ballou's excellent history of that firm, the hero is Henry Oscar Houghton, who is contrasted with both his partners (Melancthon Hurd and later G. H. Mifflin) and his rivals (James T. Fields and later James R. Osgood). The partners were well born and bred, the rivals were genial, Anglophile, name-droppers and party-goers; while Houghton was "taut, unpressed, guarded, impervious, forthright, implacable."[21] Through the crowded realistic detail of the history, the scenario emerges of this contrast between the Lincolnesque hero and these comparative lightweights. It is to some degree a contrast between slick Bostonians and a stiff-necked back-country puritan.

The interest of this for us is the likeness between Houghton and Warren. (Lincoln was the hero invoked, again and again, in the obituary tributes to Warren.) Houghton was the son of a Vermont tanner. Six years younger than Dennis Warren, he began work at thirteen, and set up as partner in a Boston printing firm in 1849 and as a publisher in 1864—all in step with Warren. Ballou suggests that when Houghton got the contract to print the Merriam-Webster dictionary, a big step in his career, it was perhaps Warren who brought the two firms together. Certainly Warren supported Houghton through the crucial decade of the 1870s, when he was expanding and taking over from his rival, Osgood. Warren supplied $20,000 to buy the *Atlantic Monthly* in 1873, and attended the *Atlantic* dinners, a feature of Boston social and intellectual life, when Houghton revived them; and supplied most of the money to buy Osgood out in 1880.

The families knew each other socially, and Houghton and Warren were both, even in their heyday, old-fashioned figures, with the stamp of the old puritan, reformist, and egalitarian New England upon them. In 1852, Houghton helped found the Printers' Literary Union, which declared its belief in the religion of brotherhood and saw knowledge as a golden key to admit men into the Temple of Equality. He was suspicious of England and of Boston Anglophilia, especially after the Civil War, when so many Englishmen favored the Confederate side. (He wanted to publish children's books written by Americans, for instance, objecting to the class-ridden character of English children's books.) The triumph of the North in that war, and the martyrdom of Lincoln, set the seal upon the revival of "puritanism" as an American ideology. Houghton began a profit-sharing scheme in 1872 and believed in education as much as Warren; he started an educational magazine and an editorial department at the *Atlantic* for education. He tried—again with Warren's support—to start an educational magazine for working men.

Ellen Ballou makes a good case that W. D. Howells was thinking of Houghton when he wrote *The Rise of Silas Lapham,* the classic novel about new business money and old Boston culture. Silas Lapham makes a fortune, without the benefit of education, but in the eyes of old Boston families makes mistakes in spending it. Ballou can point to things in Houghton's Riverside Press that Howells describes in the novel, but other things remind us more of the Warrens. It was they who had shot up the Boston social ladder so strikingly.

But to return to the history of the papermaking, the rags themselves are of interest. Mr. Warren bought them from many sources overseas, including Japan, Belgium, and Sweden, but most notably from Italy and Egypt, and in the last case actual mummy wrappings were imported. Old cultures that were subsiding into piles of dirty rags were to be redeemed by America. It was his father's pride, said Fiske, "to convert dirty useless rags [from the Old World] into clean useful paper."[22] That very American symbolism must have struck many imaginations.

At the same time, an unpleasant wet-paper smell emanated from the Westbrook mills. Charles C. Calhoun, in his recent essay on E. P. Warren, says the company still gives its whole neighborhood the smell of a damp paper bag.[23] In the nineteenth century the rags apparently crossed the Atlantic to Portland, Maine, and were then taken by wagon to Westbrook, where they were first sorted and shredded and then subjected to a fermentation process that broke the fibers down. This smell, being associated with rags from Egypt, in times of pestilence brought suspicion on the importers, and even the Warrens of Beacon Hill grew embarrassed and uneasy. (We hear of Sam Warren, the son, eagerly arguing to friends that the rags could not be the source of infection.) Thus there were Promethean aspects even to this most virtuous kind of capitalist industry; S.D. Warren and Company were seen as heroes of the business ethic much of the time, but also, on occasion, as spoilers of nature (air and water) and poisoners of their fellowmen.

I have assigned the year 1860 as the beginning of this story because it was the date of birth of E. P. "Ned" Warren. He is in some sense the central figure in the drama, especially in its tragic denouement in 1910. But I am concerned with the whole family, and as a year in which to date this prologue to the story, out of several possibilities, 1854 seems the best because that is when Mr. Warren purchased the mill.

However, in that generation, besides Mr. Warren, there is his wife to give some account of. The stuff of the tragedy was the children's feelings about each other, which seem to have been tense and angry from early on, and to have grown worse as time went by. And judged by ordinary standards, Mrs. Warren impinged more than her husband on those feelings—on what the children felt about each other and about themselves, in their formative years.

Indeed, judged by any criteria, she was clearly remarkable and forceful. Her own mother seems to have been a mild and gentle personality who made no demands on, and exerted no control over, her husband and family. Perhaps by reaction, Mrs. Warren was the opposite. Cornelia, in her *Memoir*, says that even as a girl, her mother was a better housekeeper than her grandmother, and that she kept every member of her own household, servants and children, under rigid control. "Wishing," she used to say, "is the worst of employments."[24] She was calm, confident, and systematic: If she took on a task, everyone knew it would be done; if she searched a closet for something, there was no point in anyone else searching it again. She herself said she dealt better with things than with people, and she was naturally silent and not social.[25]

Susan Clarke was born in 1825, eight years after her husband, in Blandford, Massachusetts, where her father was then minister. The family moved to Chicopee Falls in 1835, and from there to Boston in 1841. The Reverend Clarke seems to have identified himself with the New England puritan: the journal, the historical idea, and its modern equivalent. He was, for instance, a vehement enemy of alcohol and, according to his grandson, Ned, preached an evangelical Christianity of anxiety and fear.

"My grandfather, an old-fashioned Calvinist Congregationalist, used to pray on Sunday mornings at Mount Vernon Street for outpourings of the Holy Spirit, for awakenings. . . ."[26] (Ned's tone here is satirical.) Mr. Clarke understood conversion as a spiritual crisis, and one of the motives of that crisis could properly be fear. Ned, and probably the other Warren children, disapproved of anything emotionally grim or melodramatic that called itself religion. He was taken to hear evangelists Moody and Sankey as a child, but as an adult turned his back on all that. He tells us in disgust how in his mother's home he once saw an old woman "distressing herself with self-questioning: 'Do I love Christ? I think that I do.' In this atmosphere [Ned observes] not only concerts but nearly all our doings were logically impossible."[27] It is to be presumed that "logically impossible" implies morally reprehensible, and that "our" doings included those arranged by the children's mother.

According to the same source, Mr. Clarke's grandchildren thought him an egotist and were glad when their father declined to finance the publication of his works in a uniform edition. (Ned speaks of his grandfather snuffing up incense from no matter what source and supplying his own when no other was available.)

Dorus Clarke published *Lectures to Young People in Manufacturing Villages* in 1836, *Fugitives from the Escritoire of a Retired Editor* in 1864, *Orthodox Congregationalism and the Sects* in 1871, and a volume commemorating his Golden Wedding in 1874. The last is presumably an example of the self-congratulation his grandchildren complained of, and there are others. A "book" about him and his writings was published in 1876, and a memorial volume after his death.

Growing up, Susan had looked after siblings, notably her younger sisters, Ellen and Mary, in her commanding and unquestionable way. Mary was mentally handicapped after a childhood accident. After the marriage, Susan also cared for some of Mr. Warren's relatives. But soon, we gather, she employed others in such tasks, devoting most of her own energies to the collection of art and fine furnishings. Thanks to her, the Warrens were notable for the speed with which the money they made in the smelly paper mills of Maine was converted into fragrant tapestries, bronzes, china, and paintings on Beacon Hill; the speed with which the tenets of puritanism were turned into the habits of the connoisseur, without any period of shamefaced self-doubt. While the story of the Warrens is very like *The Rise of Silas Lapham* in some ways, a striking difference is that it took Mrs. Warren only a decade, from the purchase of the first mill, to install herself on Beacon Hill and in the position of connoisseur.

With her children, she insisted on truth; the implication being that other values, like affection, counted for less, and that her moral style had force. Cornelia says Mrs. Warren let her children cry themselves to sleep and speaks of a "certain hardness of moral tissue."[28] In their childhoods they all probably suffered at her hands. More than one of her sons spoke of her grandeur, referring both to her behavior and to her taste in furniture.

On the other hand, Cornelia says that her mother had a very just mind and was always calm, though we shall see exceptions to that rule and stormy depths beneath that calm. It is above all interesting, in a moralist of force, that her favorite son, Ned, was the most evasive and plaintive of them all, the least truthful and manly. But in her daily behavior, she was apparently irreproachable as well as formidable. As compared with her husband, for instance, she was less accessible to appeals for charity or sympathy, but on the other hand, she noted and remembered all sorts of details about such applicants, while he forgot them. In other words, she was a serene and rhadamanthine judge.

In the early years of her marriage, Mrs. Warren bore six children and began her collections. Her first child, Josiah Fiske Warren, born in 1850, died in 1853. Before he was a year old, Mr. and Mrs. Warren traveled to Europe, leaving the baby in the care of another couple. Mr. Warren had business to attend to—perhaps he was already finding sources of rags—and also needed the trip for his health. Mrs. Warren spent the trip buying bronzes and porcelain, and probably looking at pictures too.

In 1852 and 1854 two more boys were born, Samuel Dennis II (known as Sam) and Henry Clarke, to be the lawyer-businessman and the scholar of Pali, respectively. Next came their only daughter, Cornelia, born in 1857, who became one of the best-known philanthropists in the state. And finally Edward Perry Warren, called Ned, and Frederick Fiske Warren, called Fiske, the collector of classical antiquities and the leader of anti-imperialist protest, respectively.

What little we know about the relations between husband and wife comes to us from Cornelia and celebrates their mutual love and happiness. The subsequent history of the family, however, suggests that there came to be tensions between them. In later life Mr. Warren seems to have been—at least when they were abroad together—reduced to inertia and impotence in family matters, while his wife remained a remorseless surge of shopping energy.

Earlier, Mr. Warren seems to have been, in certain ways, emotionally exuberant; for instance, in his gratitude to his wife for giving him a marriage and a family and a home. For example, when their first child was born, he was so happy that he dragged an old man in off the street to look at the child.[29] Mrs. Warren is said to have been amused by his passion of paternalism, and he to have been shocked that she thought the baby looked like a little old man. This may, of course, be nothing more than the role-swapping of mutually happy parents, but it stuck in the family memory the way items

of hidden significance sometimes do. Mrs. Warren was said to have
been usually impassive, and we shall see that she was also secretive.
Mr. Warren's naive exuberance may have irritated such a temperament.

Two weeks after the baby was born, Mr. Warren wrote home
from New York, "I have thought of you and the dear little one God
has given us a great deal today and wished a thousand times over
that I could be with you. . . . Though I am not with you, dear Susan,
I often imagine myself to be so, and have little Josiah in my arms
half the time." And the next day, "You cannot tell what sensation
passes through my mind every time I think of that little boy, especially every time I speak of him to others. I hesitate, and think, Is
it possible I am a Father and have a nice little black-headed boy?
Is it not all a dream? It takes some time to convince myself that I
am in my right mind, but it is true. I am not only a happy husband
but a happy Father. I have something to live for, I feel that my life
and health are of some importance to my wife and boy, if no
other."[30]

One seems to hear there the release after long tension of a man
who had denied himself so much for fifteen years before marriage,
and a personality perhaps permanently strained and full of self-
doubt who needed a strong calm tenderness from his wife. Strength
and calm Mrs. Warren seems to have been able to give at any time,
but in the matter of tenderness, it may be that the demands of her
own psychic economy made her inept in reassuring such an emotional man. There was a period during their engagement when he
had "misgivings," and she felt she had to offer him his freedom.

Mr. Warren was subject to headaches that sometimes lasted as
long as three days. Cornelia has said that a doctor once con-
gratulated him on them, saying that they guaranteed he would
never go mad, since nature was finding its outlet in this minor
way.[31] Mr. Warren traveled a great deal for his health. And though
he was obviously a successful businessman, that career too must
have been strainful; for he was in debt, as Sam said, all through his
career, up to his last years.

As for Mrs. Warren's calm, it is striking to reflect, as one reads
Mr. Warren's letters after Josiah's birth, that the mother left that
baby, not a year old, when the parents made a long trip to Europe.
From that journey Susan Warren wrote home to friends and relatives with advice on their problems—according to Cornelia, typical
was advice on how to put the best face on unpleasant situations.

Meanwhile, the family's prosperity steadily increased. In 1855, Mr. Warren bought out his old partner, Daniell, so that the firm became Grant, Warren and Co., until 1867, when they split, and the mills belonged to Warren alone. Then, in 1871, when Charles Fairchild became a partner, it became S.D. Warren and Company, the name it kept thereafter. Fairchild chose the opposite side in the Houghton Mifflin struggle—backing Osgood in his struggle with Houghton; he withdrew from S.D. Warren in 1880, and Mortimer Mason replaced him.

Of course, commercial prosperity varied with the times. The Civil War stimulated the paper trade considerably, giving a decisive advantage to large mills, and saw the end of the old system of individuals or small groups making paper by hand. But in the financial crisis of 1874 the workers knew that Warren kept the firm going as an act of faith and without profit to himself.

When the Senate Labor Committee consulted Mr. Warren in 1883 about the secrets of his success, he spoke for two hours. When he finished they said that it had been a red-letter day for them. He was a hero of commerce and industry. The image we get of him and his family is thus bound to remind us of novels of the time; one of them being, as already stated, W. D. Howells's *The Rise of Silas Lapham.* In the shape of their early careers, in the matter of their class and birthplace and early setting, Lapham and Warren are very similar. Moreover, as we shall see, Warren's oldest son made a socially brilliant marriage, rather like the one in question for Lapham's daughter. Sam Warren married a Southern belle, the daughter of a senator from Delaware. Indeed, since his marriage occurred in 1883, and the novel began to appear in 1885, the coincidence is very striking. There seems no reason to believe that the novelist was secretly referring to the Warrens—though it is quite possible that he *was*—but one can confidently say that the sort of people who read novels at that time would be as interested in Mr. and Mrs. Warren as they were in Mr. and Mrs. Lapham; everyone was thinking about new money and its relations with old manners. The Warrens were a representative couple.

All this is merely prologue to the main action, which concerns the five children of Mr. and Mrs. Warren. Coming of age on Beacon Hill, and making their first flights from that high nest, all of them had a sense of privilege and an attendant sense of duty that derived from their heritage, material and moral. Having different talents and ideas—and not being much at ease with one another—each worked toward a destiny, an intervention in history, that separated him or her from the others. But they were tied together all their lives—materially and morally—by a family trust that linked their personal fortunes. Thrusting away from each other, but returning upon each other, they entangled themselves in tragedy.

2

Cedar Hill Childhoods

1860–70

. . . that secret hostility natural between brothers, the roots of which—little nursery rivalries—sometimes toughen and deepen as life goes on, and, all hidden, support a plant capable of producing in season the bitterest fruits.

—John Galsworthy,
The Forsyte Saga

*I*n 1854, Mr. Warren, in Maine, wrote to Mrs. Warren, in Massachusetts, that she was just as busy with building Cedar Hill, the family home in Waltham (a few miles west of Boston), as he was with building the mills in Westbrook. They were putting up an eighteen-room mansion in Waltham on a hilltop overlooking the home of Mrs. Warren's parents, who had moved to that town in 1849.

Perhaps we should not say *they,* for it seems to have been very much Mrs. Warren who was putting up this mansion. "I like Mill-building better than house-building," Mr. Warren wrote; adding, with Yankee wit, "Probably I should not, if I did not suppose it would pay better pecuniarily." He implies both it is natural that she should be absorbed in the work at Cedar Hill, which is not "pecuniary," and that she is not much interested in the mill, which is.[1]

The act of building, especially a family home, is always an important symbol, and for *nouveau riche* families like the Warrens it was a very self-conscious one. In *The Rise of Silas Lapham* the new house the Laphams build on Beacon Street, where the old Boston families live, is full of meaning to themselves, to their acquaintances, and—with a slightly different meaning—to the reader. The five Warren children were also to be builders in their turn, or renovators and adapters, and had notable houses all over Beacon Hill and the Back Bay, but also in Mattapoisett, Dedham, and Harvard. Later we shall see how important Lewes House was for Ned and Beck House was for Henry, and how the construction of the Museum of Fine Arts was one of the major episodes of Sam's life. Cornelia was content to live in her mother's mansion house at Waltham, simply developing the estate, but her life was defined by that property to an unusual degree. The only real exception was Fiske, who designed himself a house at Harvard, of a typically odd originality, but who defined himself by the somewhat opposite symbolism of constant travel.

Mrs. Warren devised the plan of Cedar Hill, and the only thing she later regretted was that it was only forty-four feet square: She could have wished it to be forty-six feet square.[2] Her taste tended toward size and grandeur, and the house was described as "a Victorian mansion" in style, solid but not beautiful (it was demolished in 1950). A hall ran through the house, from front to back; there were eighteen rooms and sixteen fireplaces; and massive mahogany doors with silver hinges. She supervised the whole construction, snatching hours of sleep in her carriage as she was driven to and from Boston. She later attributed the delicate health of her son Henry, born that year, to the stress which that work caused her.

From the broad porches of Cedar Hill you looked out over Watertown, Waltham, Waverley. The Warren estate spread over 148 acres on one side of Beaver Street, with acres of corn and rye fields on the other side of the road. The house cellar had to be blasted out of solid rock, and the project became more expensive than had been foreseen. The idea had originally been to build a house for Mr. Warren's sister Sarah—formerly married to John Mason—but Mrs. Warren, seeing how worried he was about the cost, with a house needed for themselves also, suggested that he fuse the two plans and reassign this one to them. Cornelia, who tells us this, does not say what Sarah thought of this neat way of solving the family problem. But it seems likely that there were several such incidents in which Mrs. Warren rode roughshod over the hopes of the less important, or the remoter, relations. Henry once told Ned that it was useless to protest against or try to modify what upset them both in their mother's behavior: They must think of it as a storm that would have to blow itself out.[3] She was, in their eyes, a domestic juggernaut.

The children were troubled also by the splendor of Mrs. Warren's furnishings, paintings, upholstery, bronzes, china, and so on. Cornelia, writing in 1908, said she had been influenced in her youth by "social theories"—theories of and enthusiasms for social justice—and so was very critical when her mother bought a vase or a picture for a high price. Ned, on the other hand—though he had his social theories too—was probably more troubled by the suggestion of ostentation or commonplaceness in what was bought. His own taste was severer, purer, plainer than his mother's. There were too many rooms in their house on Mount Vernon Street, he said, and too much gilt and inlaid ivory decorating them.

She made her first purchases in china, glass, textiles, furniture, and so on; what Erica Hirshler of the Boston Museum of Fine Arts calls "an eclectic and encyclopedic collection, favoring the 18th century."[4] Her later collecting, of paintings, was more original.

The fifty years following the Civil War was the period when taste-conscious people were especially interested in new-money vulgarity: They read about it in novels by James and Howells, by Mann and Proust. This suspicion was installed in the consciousness of the new-money families themselves (perhaps that was its main locus and field of influence) and all the Warren children were, in various ways, afraid of incurring that kind of odium. All but Sam turned decisively away from "high society" in their youth; he secured his position by marrying into an old Southern family. The others did not simply spend or enjoy, much less display, their money; they set it to work, for one ideal or another. Fiske came to live in some ways like a poor man. (However, none of them renounced his or her money; they all lived and died rich.)

Mrs. Warren did not make mistakes of the grosser kind in the art she bought—granted that her taste was of her time and class. She was clever in such matters, and she had, from quite early on, clever advice from Ned. Her bolder ventures in purchasing pictures came later, and we will associate them with her Boston house, but while they were living at Cedar Hill she appreciated French painters of the nineteenth-century Barbizon school (country scenes). Her collection later included works by E. T. P. Rousseau (1812–67), C-F. Daubigny (1817–79), N-V. Diaz de la Peña (1807–76), and Constant Troyon (1810–65)—the last famous for his sheep and cows. She also had works of some nineteenth-century Spanish painters—Eduardo Zamacois (1842–71), known for depicting monks and friars, and Mariano Fortuny y Carbo (1838–74), often compared with Meissonier, the highly esteemed painter of battle scenes—and seventeenth-century Dutch masters, such as Pieter de Hoogh and Bartolomaeo Van der Helst.

She was a pioneer among Americans as a collector. Beacon Hill houses in her day and later displayed, admittedly, copies of European paintings, but Mrs. Warren collected old master originals—or what claimed to be original; just as Ned was to be a pioneer in collecting Greek sculptures instead of plaster casts. Mrs. Warren was, in a less important way than Ned, a priest of the cult of authenticity, cherishing the pristine source, scorning educative facsimiles.

As for the interrelations of these people, the prime document for this period is a letter from Mrs. Warren to Ned. It was written as late as 1897, when he was thirty-six years old, but it describes the months before he was born.[5] It is addressed, "Strictly private and personal to you, my son." Mrs. Warren tells Ned that the reason he is more "nervous" than her other children is that she bore him alone—unhusbanded. That is, the winter she was carrying him his father had been in Rome because of a bad throat, and in the company of his sister-in-law. (This was Ellen Clarke, seven years younger than Mrs. Warren; another Clarke relative was in the party, but Mrs. Warren does not mention her in this letter.) Mrs. Warren had not told her husband that she was pregnant (perhaps she did not herself know when he left) because she did not wish him to be "anxious." She had written him "cheerful" letters about other matters (and presumably had warned his other correspondents against mentioning the pregnancy) because the doctor had said he should stay abroad until the weather grew warm in Boston. She had also been busy again with Cedar Hill ("getting it in running order") and was looking after one of their relatives as well as her own three children.

Nevertheless, as the moment of her husband's return approached, she grew nervous about how to tell him. She was almost at the point of giving birth. Mr. Warren arrived home on May 20, and the baby was born on June 8. She was also troubled by other perplexities, or rather fears. "I met him dissolved in tears with a fancy he might possibly think it was not his child. Oh how many times I prayed you might be made in his very image, for now, I saw, I ought to have prepared him. . . ."[6] Ned, in any important sense, was *not* made in his father's image; of all the children, he was the changeling, and of the parents, it was his father who must have found it hardest to acknowledge him. Ned later admitted that he had grieved Mr. Warren by his obstinate resistance to all his father wanted him to do and be, by his "whims and apparent perverseness" as his biographers put it.[7]

Mrs. Warren continued: "I have always meant to tell you what to me was the terrible strain of that winter. It made you very dear to me, but it was not good for you." She went on to sketch a theory of how her other pregnancies had affected the characters of *those* children: Before Sam was born, the Warrens traveled in Europe—"a time of some agitation"; Henry was born unhealthy because of her work on Cedar Hill; Fiske was a seven-month baby and therefore delicate; only Cornelia (a good daughter) was born after "a peaceful quiet time."

There are several provocative points about this letter. First, of course, we note the mother's symbolic parthenogenesis, and the consequent guilt she later felt before both her husband and son. She had kept her son to herself, away from her husband. (When Ned later commented on the story of Medea, who murdered her children, he explained that her crime, for the Greeks, was partly that she deprived her husband of his heirs, of his succession; by then Ned saw his mother as a tragedy queen.) Then comes her idea of how pregnancy determines the child-to-be's character, an idea that extends the claims of the biological mother to create her children. And then we must be struck by the pattern this letter reveals of a family life in which a businessman spends eight months in Rome for a bad throat, and in the company of a woman seven years younger than his wife. Ellen Clarke was, we are told by Ned, very pretty and a great favorite of Mr. Warren's. Whether *she* knew of Mrs. Warren's pregnancy, we cannot say. There seems no reason to suggest infidelity in Mr. Warren (he is described as very devoted to both wife and family), but there is some reason to suspect jealousy on Mrs. Warren part—though it was jealousy of her sister's freedom and opportunities in Rome rather than of anything sexual. One way to read her behavior is that she was saying, You have Rome; I have the baby.

Ned was indeed "nervous." He grew up evasive, devious, unreliable, a hypochondriac but with plenty of energy and pertinacity. Perhaps his most striking feature was his failure or refusal to be boyish—and later, manly. When his brothers played Indians, he ran around by himself in a toga. In kindergarten he refused to learn to tell the time, priding himself, he says, on being dreamy. He hated both mathematics and adventure stories like *Robinson Crusoe* and *Swiss Family Robinson*. Instead, he loved sculpture and music.[8] At his grammar school he was nicknamed "Tassels"; he carried around in his pocket three photographs of Venus statues (a Canova, a Thorvaldsen, and the Venus de Medici), plus a small silver Venus de Milo statuette. Long after he left that school, he tells us, he would hear the cry of "Tassels" coming from the alleys as he walked the streets by the Massachusetts General Hospital; and he sometimes got knocked down and roughly handled.

Ned early felt himself an exile in Boston, out of place in America as a whole; the family trips to Europe gave him his only sense of real life. "I was a boy cloistered from the American world in a domestic museum on the top of Beacon Hill, yearning for" what only Europe and art could give him.[9] On the mornings that their trips abroad began, he was out on the sidewalk early, waiting.

He was not in every way a rebel, of course. He was pious as a child, and dreamt, like other pious boys, of becoming a missionary to the Indians, but he decided later that that dream had come because the braves wore no clothes. In the great European museums he asked to be left alone in the sculpture gallery, but his excitement, he later said, was partly sexual and provoked by the naked bodies. At this point—in 1868—his aesthetic interest seems to have been strongest in music. He was a pianist, a lover of music, and even a composer. It is understandable that he was thought to be a remarkable child. He identified with all composers but especially with Beethoven, because of the latter's stormy temperament and painful experiences. He himself meant to lead a "grand but blighted life."[10]

Ned makes it clear that as a boy he had bitter experiences as a sissy, and because of it he hated Boston for the rest of his life. He suffered the derision of other boys, both for his failure in manly sports and tastes, and for his sexual "abnormality." He in some sense hated his family, above all Sam, but it is not clear what his parents and siblings felt about his homosexuality—or what he felt they felt. His brothers at least must have known, but it seems possible that they never named it to each other. They must have made allusions, to him, but they may have been very indirect.

Ned was not ever a screaming queer, and it seems unlikely that he ever patronized male brothels, but he was a nervous eccentric, openly afraid of women—not all women, but all queenly ones. There was something of the spoiled child about him; he referred to himself, even in writing, as "Ned." He involuntarily drew attention to himself as queer, and in the locker rooms of his brothers' schools and clubs there must surely have been coarse jokes about the likes of Ned Warren. His brothers were men of refined and puritan imagination, and younger generations of the family, even those brought up to hate his name, did not know that Ned was homosexual. It is likely that Sam, who had a strong sense of responsibility, and a tactless way about him, tried to make Ned more of a man; and if he did, it is also likely that he used expressions and methods that left a bitter memory behind.

The sort of thing we learn from Ned is, for instance, about a conflict between them over (Johannes) Ernst Perabo (1845–1920), a German pianist and composer who gave Ned piano lessons, and whom the boy loved. Perabo was a prominent figure on the Boston music scene in the second half of the nineteenth century. Born in Germany, he had been an infant prodigy, trained at Leipzig Conservatory, 1862–65, even though his parents had emigrated to the United States in 1852. He played with the Harvard Music Association in 1866 and soon gathered a number of Boston pupils and admirers around him. He is said to have taught piano to over a thousand Bostonians altogether, and gave concerts—Schubert was a composer he especially favored—and transcribed orchestral music for the piano.

Perabo had apparently had an unhappy childhood himself, being driven by his father to be a prodigy, and he told Ned anecdotes of those times and wept as he did so. He had "an extreme and almost morbid tenderness."[11] When Sam told Ned that composers usually had poor characters, Ned said that Mr. Perabo was an argument to the contrary. "But you wouldn't be like him," Sam said. To which Ned replied, "Indeed, I would."[12] The anecdote is rather flavorless as Ned tells it, but it obviously stands for a series of disputes between the brothers over the dignity of the artist (when Ned got excited about Shelley later, Sam took the same tone about *him*), and those disputes were of great importance, at least to the younger brother.

What, if anything, they said to each other about sex is a matter for speculation; perhaps it was never the subject of overt conflict, but we can say quite confidently that there was a lifelong and bitter conflict between the manliness incarnate in Sam—the kind that displayed the social prescriptions of that time and place—and the manifold unmanliness of Ned. (Here I am using the word as Sam did: Ned gave a lot of thought to what he called virility, and by his definition, *Sam* was unmanly.)

Ned obviously betrayed his gender in all kinds of ways, some of them remote from sex itself; for instance, in his recoil from adventure, sports, and even mathematics. The Warrens, like other New Englanders, made something of a cult of mathematics: of calculation, of statistics, of balanced accounts, sheerly of numbers—they had what might be termed a quantifying or Robinson Crusoe imagination. The other four children were often the treasurers of the societies to which they belonged. (Fiske was treasurer of the Cumberland Manufacturing Company in 1888, Henry was treasurer of the American Oriental Society, Cornelia and Sam were treasurers of various charitable committees.) In Fiske's genealogical history of the family, the relationships are expressed in fractions and decimals; in Cornelia's novel, the heroine's debts and the rates of interest she pays on them are expressed in numbers.

This sort of mental activity seemed to the Anglo-Saxons of that generation to mark them off from other human types, and especially from "natives," or premodern peoples (see Mark Twain's *Connecticut Yankee in King Arthur's Court* and Richard Henry Dana's *Two Years Before the Mast*). They also thought they were more masculine than other races (see Francis Parkman and other nineteenth-century American historians). So, to refuse to learn to tell the time, to dislike mathematics and *Robinson Crusoe,* to prefer music and sculptured nudes to games and sports, all this was more directly an offense to masculine and racial pride than we may at first think.

But Ned knew, he more than once said, that he was his mother's favorite child. Quite apart from the history of his birth, he was like her in his passion for beautiful objects. (It may also be that she recognized in his secretiveness something of her own temperament.) He loved the beautiful china she collected and took pieces of it up to his room at night. The next day pieces would be found hidden under his bed. She bought him china of his own, and he spent hours arranging it in his bedroom when he was supposed to be sleeping. He also spent time as a child arranging the fall of their damask curtains, for Mrs. Warren and her sister Ellen to appreciate. When he dressed up as a priest (in a nightgown and blue Japanese sash) and conducted a religious service, it was his mother who played the congregation. Presumably, in those early years, he loved her as his protectress against the rest of the world. The real world, he says, was identified for him with working in his father's business, and it was something he was determined to stay out of. What he felt later about his mother, however, was a bitter resentment and even (to judge by pieces of symbolic and imaginative expression) a wish to have killed her. For he came to blame her for losing him that virility that became his deepest desire.

In the 1860s, however, they were allies. Mrs. Warren's relations with Sam were apparently always difficult. She complained of his being hard to handle as an infant: "his future well-being depends almost entirely upon his training . . . he requires a pretty steady hand. I wish you were here sometimes to advise me. He yields, however, well at last, but I sometimes fear I shall yield first."[13] And he was sent to a series of schools, some of them as a boarder, which did not happen to the other children. (The other boys went to Hopkinson's School in Boylston Place, in Boston.) A letter of Sam's has been preserved, written when he was eight, in a handwriting that suggests dyslexia—his adult hand is often almost unreadable—and there is a family tradition that he suffered from that disorder, which is to be found among his descendants. In 1868, when he was, though young, ready to enter Harvard, he went, instead, abroad for a year and then spent another two years working with the firm. He finally began college in 1871, but since he was then only nineteen, he was not much out of line with the other freshmen.

We seem to see a precocious boy, difficult for his family to handle; easier for them to be proud of than to live with. Much later, Ned, who had most reason to disparage him, said Sam had a profound head though not a clever hand.[14] In his eulogy in 1910, his friend Arthur Cabot said Sam had been a hard man to work with or for because of his high standards, his "idealism."

As for family relations per se, Cornelia, in her account of their joint childhood, says Sam was away so much that he scarcely counted as one of the children.[15] Mrs. Warren told Ned, at the time of the latter's confirmation, that while all her other children were "right" in their hearts, Sam was "against God." He was a known doubter or disbeliever.[16] When Ned defended Sam, and blamed her for blaming him, she wept and sent Ned to talk to his father. (This is Ned's story.)

However, if Sam got on badly with his mother (and we hear nothing of his relations with his father) he seems to have remained a dutiful son and sentimentally attached to his family. He took the position of *head* of the clan very seriously. He certainly never rebelled against the family, which Ned did. Sam perhaps tried to compensate and conciliate the rest of them, for the various ways in which he irritated or offended, by so conscientiously representing them in public matters, by excelling in public performances, and by being a success at Harvard, in his many clubs, in his law firm, and as trustee of Boston institutions. He even gave up the practice of law, which he loved, to head the family firm, at his father's request.

He had a reputation at Harvard for being stiff, haughty, and conceited, but it seems likely that this was partly the result of shyness—though partly of ambition. His brothers seem to have condemned an ambitious worldliness in him and resented the authority he tried to wield over them (though we get a lot of this information from Ned, who is a suspect source), but other men often both admired and pitied him as a victim of the disciplines of manliness. Like his father, he lived under strain—a strain that in Sam's case came to a tragic end. He was not at ease with his parents or siblings, nor perhaps (to judge by the circumstances of his death) with his own wife and children. It was only, one of his friends tells us, when he was playing games, like polo, that he could relax and lose the stiffness that otherwise held him remote from people.

As to the other siblings, Henry Warren's fate was largely dominated by his health. He was delicate from birth and suffered from bad digestion and bad circulation, and had boils on his feet and ears. He was also deaf, according to Ned as a result of scarlet fever. But the most serious problem happened at the age of three when he fell out of the buggy his mother was driving and landed on his head. He cried only a little at the time, but two weeks later complained of pains in the groin. It became clear that the accident was having grave consequences. Though he had before this begun to talk, he had to learn to do so all over again. The doctors prescribed a supporter for him to wear and long periods of rest in certain postures; everyone (rightly) began to fear a spinal "affection." In 1859, Mr. Warren consulted Professor Symes of Edinburgh University, who recommended bathing and rubbing, and quick alternations of rest and activity. The professor was displeased to hear that the boy could not be kept entirely quiet during his periods of rest.[17]

Some of the anecdotes Cornelia tells about Henry suggest a clever and willful boy, perhaps rather like his older brother, his will always engaged. He spent his rest periods (from eleven to one and from five to six) doing mental arithmetic: He would ask visitors for their date and hour of birth, and then, lying in bed, calculate how many hours, minutes, and seconds they had so far lived. When he was asked what he supposed he himself would be doing fifty years hence, he got out his watch to calculate, but finally said, "I shall be taking my long rest."

Like his father, Henry liked to tell funny stories—though today they sound rather mechanical. Acknowledging a gift of brandied peaches, he praised the spirit in which they were given. He was supposed to resemble his father in certain physical ways, though a more important filial resemblance (but this he shared with all his brothers) was his cleverness and determination to succeed. But his fate was decided by his illness. He grew to be only five feet tall and grotesquely hunchbacked, and he withdrew from most forms of ordinary life. There are family photographs, of Mr. and Mrs. Warren and their *four* children and dog.

Like Sam, if for more obvious and excusable reasons, Henry was of a "difficult" temperament. According to Fiske's sister-in-law, Molly Osgood, Henry repelled the sympathetic interest of visitors. Ned said, "His mental isolation was so complete that he could not enter into the purposes of others; he could show himself parsimonious."[18] Though not emotional, Ned continued, Henry must have always felt he was battling the odds. He showed no signs of loneliness and appeared to be very self-sufficient, but he once asked Ned to choose a soap dish for him, which Ned interpreted as a hidden appeal for affection.

Cornelia did not allow herself so much temperament, it seems, at least not until later in life. She was a good daughter and sister, and even the anxieties she may have early given her mother may be explained as the result of loyalty to her father. She seems to have been devoted to him and admiring of his care for the workers at the mills. She interested herself in those workers, often accompanying her father on visits there. This concern eventually expanded to include the disadvantaged of Boston as a whole and involved her with people and projects that deserve to be called socially radical.

In most likelihood, this probably was not exactly what her mother had envisioned, if she was as ambitious for the family as was thought (though we should remember that she was not primarily a social being). Anyway, with time, Cornelia changed and yielded without any sense of grievance that we find expressed, without complaining of any pressure. (She praised her mother for not expressing anxiety about her children, and it may be that Mrs. Warren's invulnerable calm had this advantage for them.) In the matter of the art collection, for instance, Cornelia later declared that she had learned, as a result of guiding groups of visitors around these high-priced paintings, how much pleasure they gave to even the poorest viewers. It was not a mean envy but a broader vision of life that these works of art aroused. (The language of the *Memorial* does not show Cornelia at her best.) Ostensibly, then, Mrs. Warren, and everybody else, was lovely. When Cornelia was severe with a family member (which never happened in print or in public, of course) it was with Ned, and the severity was in some sense on the family's behalf, when they were hurt by his wayward behavior.

We know less of Fiske's childhood, but he was of delicate health then. He was a stutterer, apparently until he was at Harvard. As a cure for this, he learned a lot of poetry by heart, and it was claimed that he could recite seventeen thousand lines, most of them by Sir Walter Scott. (He also collected Scott autographs, letters, and rare editions.)[19] That dogged obsessiveness—and that quaintly old-fashioned taste—are clues to his personality. There was always something comical about Fiske, as there was about Ned too, but it was a different kind of comedy. Though none of the Warrens were big, Fiske was the one often referred to as little. At Harvard he had a reputation as a grind. He grew up, of course, in the shadow of four siblings who were all, in their different ways, strikingly clever; he also grew up in an environment of family stress, and it may be that, so far as he could, he turned his back on not only those relationships but all intimate relationships. Emerson's essay "Self-Reliance" was Fiske's Bible. He grew up to be a crank, a man of ideas and causes, who made other people feel that he wasn't sufficiently aware of them, or sufficiently respectful of the common wisdom on any topic.

What Cornelia tells of their joint childhood makes it sound full of fun. The Warrens kept lots of pets, and there were farm animals at Cedar Hill, and wide-spreading grounds, with foreign trees brought home by Mr. Warren, and gardens and borders planted by Mrs. Warren. The summerhouse had windows with red-, yellow-, green-, and blue-stained glass, like the one Vladimir Nabokov describes on his parents' estate. There was a marble fountain and several draped female figures (the drapery was specified when they were ordered) and a pony that pulled a yellow cart named "Queen Victoria" because it was bought in England.

The children played imaginative games, some purely childish, some parentally inspired. When they made a trip to Mount Auburn Cemetery to their dead brother's grave, they would lie on the grass to measure themselves against it, to see if they could fit in. They also

constituted themselves a Benevolent Society and held formal meet-
ings (with Cornelia keeping the minutes) to decide which charity to
support. Mr. Warren started their fund with the gift of a dollar, and
they each made a contribution, from his or her allowance, of as
many cents as each had years. They sent $25 to help rebuild a
burned church in Chicago and $65 (Mr. Warren adding $60) for a
font for a church in Waltham. In 1874, with their parents away,
they compiled a mock newspaper, the "Cedar Hill Transcript,"
for ten weeks.[20] Clearly, they were training themselves to join
the responsible ruling class of which their parents were leading
examples.

Cornelia's account of their childhood, that it was "memorably
happy,"[21] must of course command our attention, but it may be
doubted if that takes account of everything. The family was, to
judge by the Warrens' later lives, composed of barely compatible
individualists—not easily compatible with other, milder people, let
alone with each other. Of course, Mrs. Warren's powerful will was
set to make everyone *think* they were happy, and Cornelia carried
out her mother's wishes. But even in those days, if Sam was too old
to play childish games, Henry was often too sick, and Ned too
nervous, so who was left but Cornelia and the baby? (Fiske was ten
years younger than Sam.) Happy families have been composed of
even more disparate material, but among the Warrens it seems that
the will to group happiness got lost or twisted. Of them all, it was
only Cornelia who, in later years, extended herself in family hospi-
tality. She made Cedar Hill, when it became hers, a friendly home
for her nephews and nieces, and I think we must take her *Memorial
of My Mother* to be a literary or fictional equivalent, a garden of
guaranteed happy memories. It is a risky move, in the teeth of her
assertions, but I think we must see those mahogany doors and solid
silver handles as shutting in a lot of mutual anger and muffling a lot
of bitter grief.

Religion played an important role in the life of the family while
the children were young. On Sundays there were morning prayers
and then a church service (two of the children walked to church, the
others rode; on the way back they reversed those assignments).
After lunch three of them attended another service, and in the
evening they sang hymns. This was of course Protestant Christianity, with evangelical and missionary projects. Cornelia tells of how
the children went as a group to convert Bridget, their grandmother's
servant. Ned tells how, while staying in a hotel in Philadelphia in

1876, shrinkingly he felt that he ought to be asking the worldly people around him if they were saved.

Congregationalism was their original faith, but later the family also attended an Episcopal church when Phillips Brooks preached the social gospel there. (Ned, however, found him too emotional, insufficiently sacramental, and doctrinal.) It seems clear that, as time passed, the difference between the ecclesiastical forms became less important, and that Christianity in any organized form seemed a fading story to them (as to most other people). We hear of no dramatic change of faith, except in Ned, and in their wills, Mr. and Mrs. Warren and Cornelia left money to church organizations. Cornelia indeed was seen by everyone as "Christian," which meant that she had a predilection for good works and self-sacrifice. Only Ned can be said to have preached *against* Christianity. But clearly a large change came over the family during the fifty years of our story, though it was one that only kept them in step with the world around them—a change from a Christian to a post-Christian religion.

Ned had a strong ecclesiastical interest as a boy, but it led him toward the Episcopal church, specifically toward its ritualist wing. This set him at odds with the family, especially with Cornelia. She said his religious interest was retrograde, and he was retreating into the tortoiseshell of dogma and ritual; he thought her kind of dogma and ritual too elastic.[22] She thought his religion "aesthetic," that he was drawn to the Episcopal church for aesthetic rather than Christian reasons.[23] He said that in fact his aestheticism led him out of Episcopalianism; what attracted him was that church's image of a "continuity of sober, quiet, and godly self-discipline."[24] It was the opposite of the "conversion" Christianity he was brought up in, which he decided was a religion of *beginnings* only.

However, he also replied that Cornelia had no aesthetic sense and extended the accusation to cover everyone in the family except his mother. The 1870s and 1880s were a time when "aestheticism" was an issue for everyone, and one that affected more than one's experience of art and beauty. Ned was a figure in the aesthetic movement, indeed deserves to be considered one of its key examples. His career illustrates a philistine cliché of the times, that Catholicism, aestheticism, paganism, and homosexuality were interdependent. As Irish priests declared, with some heat, there was no necessary sequence from one to another of these ideas, which contradicted each other in important ways. But in fact they were often to be found in the same people; they did go together, for instance, in Ned Warren. And a fifth congeniality that his career also illustrates was classical scholarship. The historian of the Boston Museum of Fine Arts, W. M. Whitehill, says that Ned "agonized his way from the Calvinistic Congregationalism of his grandfather through the Episcopal church to a state of active disbelief in everything except classical Greece."[25]

In many ways Ned's experiences were typical of a group of people (from the intellectual point of view, a generation) who grew up in Boston then and were affected by the aesthetic movement. One of those was George Santayana. He was so gifted a social commentator, and so temperamentally similar to Ned, that we can invoke his help in describing the world of the Warrens. There were points of connection between them; Santayana's grandfather Sturges lived on Mount Vernon Street, like the Warrens, and his cousin Russell Sturges distributed evangelical tracts, like grandfather Clarke. In other ways, his family situation was very different (he and his mother were both wholly Spanish by blood), but his account of his Boston home is very like Ned's account of *his.*

Santayana tells us, for instance, that a schoolmate who visited his home said that it was like a boardinghouse, everyone was so separate.[26] No one could love Santayana's mother, a powerful and dominant personality like Mrs. Warren, and so there was sullen disunion and hostility in the house.[27] At the same time, he understood his mother and felt himself to be like her: "Perhaps she resented the tendency, meant for kindness, to assimilate and absorb her, and she emphasized her separateness in self-defense, as I had to do afterwards in personal and intellectual matters." While at school and college, he, like Ned, always felt like a stranger.[28] "America in those days made an exile and a foreigner of every native who had a temperament at all like mine."[29] One of those was Ned Warren.

He and Ned both grew up in, and resented, the businessman's America that had displaced the culture of an older Boston. Santayana spoke nostalgically of the Boston of the 1850s, which he only heard about. Both he and Warren saw the new America as practically dominated by businessmen and culturally or at least morally dominated by women. In his famous lecture-essay "The Genteel Tradition," Santayana says, "The American Will inhabits the sky-scraper; the American intellect inhabits the colonial mansion. The one is the sphere of the American man; the other, at least predominantly, of the American woman. The one is all aggressive enterprise; the other is all genteel tradition."[30] These concepts all

apply well to the Warrens, and their case was not unique in showing
that the will of the American woman in her mansion could impinge
on her sensitive children with considerably more power than that
of the American man in his office.

Like Ned when young, Santayana loved religion, though he re-
acted against his father's liberalism: "Hatred of religion had acquired all the dogmatism and intolerance of religion . . . I belong to
the next turn of the tide . . ."[31] He loved religion in the same
aesthetic way Ned did, a way that we should not think is limited
to a fondness for rites and ceremonies. When he said that "Religions
are the great fairy tales of the conscience,"[32] he was paying them
a large tribute, even though his terms were "aesthetic."

He was, however, puzzled by the Protestant combination of ear-
nestness with waywardness, and he found that Unitarian sermons
flattered their congregations.[33] It was Roman Catholicism that attracted him most. The reason takes us to the heart of aestheticism
as it affected him and Ned: "Liberalism, Protestantism, Judaism,
positivism all have the same ultimate aim and standard. It is prosperity, or as Lutheran theologians put it, union with God at our
level, not at God's level."[34] In other words, it is the dominance of
the businessman, and the material prosperity he brings, that ruins
modern culture; and religion can be a major ally in defeating that
dominance.

The last important figure to note in the Warren children's family
experience was "Aunty," Mrs. Warren's sister Ellen, the most intimately known representative of that league of dependent relatives.
She looked after them when their mother was away on trips, and
her rule was lighter. She was imaginative, quick-minded, and
quick-moving. (Physically, she may have been another of the models for "Bessie Folsom" in Cornelia's novel.) They could persuade
her, against her better judgment, by joining hands with her and
dancing her round the breakfast table.

Cornelia says that she finally decided that she preferred her
mother's severer, juster rule. This was clearly an important step in
her moral education, and it makes us see the effect Mrs. Warren's
"harder moral tissue" had on her children. "I came to have a secret
contempt for mothers who for no consideration could see their
children suffer."[35]

Aunty's moral style was quite different. She first brought the love
of pictures (of "pretty things") into the Warren house, and (perhaps
because of Ned's influence) underwent a parallel change of religious

sentiment. Ned tells us that though she continued to disapprove of Catholicism, she bought a beautifully printed and bound book by Dr. Pusey, the notorious leader of the ritualist Oxford Movement, and some pictures of the Catholic saints; she also hung on the wall of her room a painting by the British aesthete painter Simeon Solomon that depicted a priest dispensing the sacrament.

It was Ned who gave her the painting, and we can see in the incident a miniature example of not only the changes coming over the Warren household but the role Ned played in them. Solomon (1840–1905) was a convert to Catholicism and also a member of that branch of the aesthetic movement that we associate with Aubrey Beardsley and Oscar Wilde, which is often called the Decadence. He had a brilliant career up to 1872, the year he painted Walter Pater's portrait at Oxford (Pater was a kind of pope to the English aesthetes), but after that year Solomon went into a spectacular cycle of disgrace, involving alcoholic and homosexual scandals. He had been a friend of Pater's, and his tragic history is thought to be one reason Pater so secluded and protected himself in his later years. How much of all this Aunty knew cannot now be ascertained, but it may be significant that she hung this painting in her bedroom rather than downstairs. Ned of course knew all of it, and so knew what kind of symbol he was introducing into the family home.

3

Beacon Hill Connoisseurs

1870–80

The old charm of Mount Vernon Street, for instance,
wandering up the hill, almost from the waterside, to the
rear of the State House . . . Oh, the wide benignity of
brick, the goodly, friendly, ruddy fronts, the felicity of
scale, the solid seat *of everything . . .*

—Henry James,
The American Scene

*F*rom 1870 on the Warrens were a wealthy Boston family. Their houses were luxuriously appointed, Cornelia and Mrs. Warren ordered their gowns from Worth in Paris, and they traveled in style throughout Europe and North Africa, and later in Asia. Henry and his father were in Egypt in 1873, and Mrs. Warren bought some famous scarabs there in 1874. On another Egyptian trip, twenty years later, Cornelia described her mother as riding high like a sacred boat on the shoulders of her four bearers and the army of servants and hangers-on who accompanied them everywhere.[1] They were demi-gods, if we set them on the world-historical stage. Mrs. Warren wrote home to Henry that year that the captain of their Nile boat wanted them to take his ten-year-old son home to America with them, and she wondered if he or Ned might not find a use for him.

They were a Beacon Hill rather than a Waltham family by then. They continued to summer at Cedar Hill, but in 1863 they had bought 67 Mount Vernon Street, and later the house behind that one, which fronted on Pinckney Street. By building an extension, they converted the two houses into one. Since they kept their horses on Joy Street, and before the Mount Vernon Street house had owned 11 Bulfinch Street, there were traces of them all over the hill.

Number 67 was designed by George Minot Dexter in 1847 for the Amory family, who sold it to the Warrens for $45,000. (Dexter was one of those who designed the Boston Athenaeum.) The Warrens bought some of the Amory furniture, and the personality of the original house seems to have survived; even today the main rooms on the parlor floor are much as they were. There were five floors: a cellar and then a basement, which we today would call the ground floor; the parlor floor, which has ceilings perhaps twenty feet high, massive fireplaces and cabinets, chandeliers and marquetry parquet floors; and then a chamber and an upper-chamber floor—the last presumably inhabited only by servants. In the census report of 1870 seven servants were listed, one of them a man; five of the seven were Irish, one Nova Scotian, and one—perhaps a lady's maid—French. In 1880 eight servants were listed.

It is worth noting that the Warrens did not buy on the newly filled Back Bay. Eighteen sixty-three was the date Howells assigns to a general perception in Boston that the Back Bay was where one should live. Silas Lapham buys a house in the South End that year cheap, because its owner suddenly realized that everyone was moving to the new area. The Warrens' choice is perhaps a sign that they were sure of their own, old-fashioned taste. However ambitious Mrs. Warren may have been, she was not fashionable in the crude sense.

A sketch of number 67 will help us understand the family in this decade. There were a great many rooms, quite haphazardly arranged—partly because of the amalgam of two houses—with a rather haphazard jumble of decorating styles.

Ned describes an octagonal room on the ground floor, used for breakfasts and decorated in a Pompeiian style. Behind this, moving inward, were a china closet, a kitchen, the servants' dining room, a laundry, and a man's bedroom. On the parlor floor was a little parlor right over the front door, which contained pictures, plate, and Venetian furniture, ebony with an ivory inlay. Its large French windows were often kept ajar because the whole house was overheated by furnace and registers. (It was in this parlor that Ned played priest to his mother, reading out Morning Prayers and the Litany.)

Next came the front library, in which Mrs. Warren had left the decorations as the former owner had had them, as she did the next apartments, the drawing room and the "grand big hall." In the library the cornice and frame of the mantel-mirror were painted to look like old oak. The wallpaper was dark, and the "Walter Scott" furniture was covered with dark velvet. (This style reflected an earlier phase of aesthetic taste in well-to-do Boston.)

The drawing room was paneled, with oval portrait insertions of Louis XV court beauties. Over the doors, and also inserted into the panels, were bucolic courtship scenes in the style of Watteau. Here Mrs. Warren had also introduced portraits of herself and her husband by the fashionable painter Alexandre Cabanel, and there were also Oriental embroideries and vases on the French furniture: all rather a jumble, as Ned points out; a variety not composed into a harmony as it was at Mrs. Gardner's Fenway Court. (Boston's most famous collector in the next generation, Isabella Stewart Gardner, built an "Italian villa" on the Fenway, to house her works of art.)

Next came an anteroom with a grand piano and another Venetian cabinet filled with china. This led into the grand big hall, which had been designed for dancing but was made into a black-walnut dining room "in some French style," Ned says, with a built-in sideboard sustained by griffins. This can be seen today, still sumptuous and severe. There were also then two gas globules of ground glass, borne aloft by half–life-size figures representing a Roman and a Gaul, guarding a great mirror. (Here we must imagine a strong note of scorn in Ned's voice.)

There were no doors between this and the anteroom, so a huge tapestry depicting Elijah with the Woman of Sarepta hung along the wall and was let down when either room felt drafty. The Warren meals were slow and dull, says Ned, and he was "not allowed to leave till they were over, and was full of nervous impatience."[2] He was always eager, as a child, to get down from the table. (Henry, it seems, began to stay away from family meals while still young.) Behind this dining room, moving north, toward Pinckney Street, was Mr. Warren's "retreat"; one does not know how much to read into that word.

This description refers to the house before it was extended backward. When Ned came home from Oxford he wrote to his friend John Marshall an acid description of the splendors that had been added. The room just mentioned as Mr. Warren's retreat had become a picture gallery (built-in cabinets to contain drawings still survive) and behind it there were now two new rooms; one was to be Mr. Warren's new "retreat," the other had no function. People had to go through Mr. Warren's room to get to the second one and to a stairway that led to another two rooms above and one below. Ned deplored the expenditure and flamboyance—the ceiling of the dining room had been painted to look like lacquer inlaid with mother-of-pearl—and thought the new rooms (all but two of them were sunless) unnecessary.

As a child, of course, "I did not know that it [his mother's house] was not in pure taste."[3] During his Harvard years, he tells us, he taught himself taste by walking the streets, peering in the lighted windows of rooms decorated in ways he saw immediately were better than the Warrens'. He once remarked at home, obviously with some reference to taste, that none of the Warrens were "born to the purple." His mother, he tells us, reproved him for saying so.

On the floor above were the bedrooms, only a few of them sunny but one with a view of the Milton hills. Fiske had a suite, opening on Pickney Street. Henry had a tiny southern, or Mount Vernon Street, room, which he kept so hot that Ned called it Tophet (Hell). Henry needed to keep his room warm because he could not bear heavy bedclothes on his sensitive back.

Henry's life ran along eccentric lines in matters of schedule and much else, and he must have been a difficult person to live with. Not eating with the family, he had cold chops, and so on, left outside his door at night, which he emerged to consume as and when he needed nourishment. Ned describes once finding his brother lying in *his* bed, because it was too much trouble to get into his own. At night, Henry had to get himself into a bag, and then had to be lifted on to the bridgelike top of his desk; a blanket hung down in front of the latter, and once he was in position, the blanket was drawn up over him, and the desk was pushed against the wall, to trap the blanket into position. Normally, one presumes, a servant did all this for him, and perhaps on this occasion for some reason he didn't want to call for help.

We do not know just when, but while still young he hired a black servant who, because of Henry's disabilities, necessarily played an intimate and important role in his life. Mrs. Warren does not appear in anecdotes about the adolescent or the full-grown Henry. She perhaps gave up the attempt—perhaps she had been rebuffed too often—to solve his problems or to figure in his life. According to Ned, Henry was sympathetic to him but made critical judgments on other family members, saying that Aunty's was a wasted life, their mother was a juggernaut, and Sam wanted only to live as stylishly as possible.

Of course these things were not said in public. The family kept up the forms of mutual fondness. On a much later birthday Henry sent his mother a letter in which he described her as an ideal American lady.[4] She wrote to him quite often, at least when she was abroad; recommended doctors to him, recommended massage as a treatment, solicited his contribution to charities, bought Buddha statues for him. And Cornelia asked him to oversee some work she wanted done at Cedar Hill while she was away.[5] But it seems clear that the family did most of the work of maintaining the relationship: They had to invite him several times to get him to come once.

By Ned's account, which no one has denied, he was the family member closest to Henry, and in fact the latter left him a legacy of $25,000, singling him out from the others. Ned was also closer to Fiske than the other members of the family. The fondness Ned attracted is surprising considering how very idiosyncratic his interests were, how eccentric his temperament and behavior, and how much trouble he caused other people. But he spoke the language of the heart more freely and more convincingly than the rest of them, and in that sense, he was the least nervous of all. This was not just—perhaps it was not primarily—a matter of talk, of professions of affection. He took note of other people's comfort, health, feelings; he watched over them—especially over the men he loved; he fussed attentively. He invited others to smile at him, in affection or in amusement. One of his Harvard Class Reports, written by a fellow classman, says he was "deemed eccentric, but he made friends easily." The same may have been true of his family relations. And then, all three younger brothers seem to have been somewhat allied together against Sam.

As for the paintings at 67 Mount Vernon Street, our only comprehensive record of them dates from after 1901, when Mrs. Warren died; an exhibition of them was held in Boston in 1902, and then a two-day auction of them was held in New York in early 1903. The catalogue of the collection had an introduction by the art critic Charles H. Caffin. Concerned primarily with certain valuable paintings purchased after 1870, the introduction did praise Mrs. Warren's choice of the lesser artists, saying she displayed a feel for color and for "painter-like painting," further explicated as "art in the artist, rather than in the subject."[6] Mrs. Warren was credited with an individual, and cultivated, taste. Pieter de Hoogh—"a painter not everyone likes"—exemplified the qualities Mrs. Warren preferred.

Another kind of logic to her taste seems to have been the preference for women as picture-subjects. The Goya was of young girls, the Jan Bruegel (another painter "not everyone likes") is of *Circe Calling Ulysses;* there is a quadroon by George Fuller, a *Bürgermeister's Wife* by the Dutch Van der Helst (one of Rembrandt's contemporaries), and others painted by Reynolds, Gainsborough, and Lawrence. In the Reynolds *Lady Hervey of Bristol,* "the fragrant personality of a true woman peers through the affectation of her pose."

There was nothing idiosyncratic about this preference for women as subjects, even in puritan Boston—where Charles Eliot Norton, the doyen of art historians, was particularly fond of Madonna paintings. But Ned, who was consulted so often about his mother's purchases, and who helped arrange the sale, may have felt oppressed by their predominance. He wanted to install men in the place of women, Greek athletes instead of medieval Madonnas, Donatello and Michelangelo in place of Millet and Ingres. (And though Warren's homosexual creed explains something here, quite different people, for instance Henry James and William Dean Howells, also saw American culture as dominated by women.)

Erica Hirshler tells us that Mrs. Warren bought over a hundred paintings; including at least six Corots, four Daubignys, three Rousseaus, and five Millets, including *The Young Shepherdess,* "one of Millet's most monumental and heroic figurative works."[7] (Mrs. Warren spent $20,000 at the Vose Galleries in a single year.) Her collection also included several American paintings "in the Barbizon style," by John La Farge, William Morris Hunt, J. Foxcroft Cole, George Fuller, and George Inness. But there was also a group of old masters.

Mrs. Warren's Temple of Art

This was the period of the aesthetic movement, a broad and powerful tendency in the world of ideas and institutions. Through their service to the museum, all members of the Warren family, at one time or another, took some part in the Boston branch of this movement. Ned often complained that he was the only one of them who had any feeling for art, but that was partly because he (like other aesthetes) had such high standards in these matters.

In Galsworthy's *Man of Property,* it will be remembered, Soames Forsyte, though condemned as the archetypal philistine, is himself a connoisseur: His feeling for art is *wrong* (a matter of property), but it is, by any ordinary standards, very strong. Ned's feeling about Sam was like Galsworthy's about Soames. It is worth noting that Ned and the novelist attended the same Oxford college in roughly the same years; obviously aesthetic ideas were in circulation there.

The aesthetic movement corresponded, in the world of ideas, to a new importance attributed to art by even the philistine ruling-class mind. The white nations', perhaps especially America's, consciousness of new wealth expressed itself partly by treasuring art objects as the most refined kind of valuables. In the Warren family, for instance, not only Ned, but all the members of the family, became connoisseurs.

The movement was made up of complex and shifting ideas and can be defined in various ways, but whichever formula we use, there was a new devotion to art, especially the visual arts, in the last quarter of the nineteenth century, to which both Ned and Mrs. Warren bear witness. This was shown partly in collecting, partly in new public institutions. Eighteen seventy was the year that both the Museum of Fine Arts in Boston and the Metropolitan Museum in New York were incorporated. According to Francis H. Taylor, the museum director, it was only after the Civil War that America saw her manifest destiny and demanded a share of the art treasures of history.[8] And since 1870 (he was writing in 1945) two thousand museums of art, science, and history had been established, representing an investment in land, buildings, endowments, and collections of $3 to $4 billion.[9] That is the aesthetic movement seen in its institutional form.

On the whole, however, the Warren children when young found the art they knew in their own home, and we may in this chapter properly look at the psychological aspects of life in the Warren museum or treasure house. In the autobiographical chapters printed in Burdett and Goddard, Ned speaks of his mother's maintaining "a grand considerate placitude."[10] This typical neologism is probably meant to evoke the image of a great idol at the center of her temple, for that is how, in the autobiographical part of his *Defence of Uranian Love,* Ned depicts 67 Mount Vernon Street. The house was her achievement, her palace, where everything spoke of her. He blamed the luxurious furnishings and artwork for the effeminate sensuality it developed in him. "Not in vain was the shape of an ornamental vase voluptuous, a house proud, a room worldly, the heavy fall of velvet drapery luxurious, a metallic or flamboyant color infernal. He was solicited by the over-rich in poetry, his blood was aroused by the rebellions of music. But most of all did he know temptation in a deep-set brow and a full, disdainful lip."[11] The last sentence would seem to refer to sculptures and paintings of young men, but perhaps also to their living counterparts. This may seem an oddly puritanical attitude to art for an aesthete, calling attention to its moral dangers, but the sense of sin was one of the essential flavors of Paterian aestheticism. In Ned, that attitude also led to the austerer taste that he practiced in preference to his mother's, and to the cult of classical Greece. This was closely connected to his sexual theories and his own sad fate as a man.

In his story "Alcmaeon" (published in 1919), under cover of retelling a Greek legend of the Theban war featuring a wicked mother, Ned seems to accuse his own mother of emasculating her husband and seizing power and wealth at the expense of the family, even at the expense of the son for whom she did it. Alcmaeon's father was only a shadow to the boy because his wife despised him. He was too gentle. "He had never been the hot, ambitious youth which he had seemed. Kingship was nothing to him; and he would have resigned it but for the needs of the people."[12] As time went by, Alcmaeon's father devoted himself more and more to priestly functions.[13] (In *Women in Love*, D. H. Lawrence depicts a *good* industrial magnate whose Christian humility literally maddens his queenly and pagan wife: Their children inherit suicidal conflicts.) His wife's decisions prevailed over his own, and she domineered, though she would have yielded to "a rougher hand and a frank mastery." Thus, when Polynices "Bent over her with gallant deference and soft impenetrant eyes, she was released from the long strain of alternate discouragement and determination." And when he left, "she sobbed in thankfulness for that there was such a man and that he was gone, since she would have forgotten her queenliness for him."[14]

When Alcmaeon looked at the poor people of his kingdom (as Ned looked at the workers of Westbrook) he realized that his mother's gold vessels and soft raiment were bought with their poverty. The symbols of what she wants are "the necklace of glory and the robe of dominion."[15] (Mrs. Warren had bought some twenty scarabs in Egypt, some of which turned out to be 3,500 years old. She had them set in gold and made into a necklace by a Parisian jeweler.) In the final scene of the story, more modern than Greek, Alcmaeon is sent by his father's ghost to avenge him; he awaits his mother in her room and examines her beautiful robes and jewels, and then executes her.

Ned and Sam

In the first part of this period, which ended when he was nineteen, Ned was still religious. He was sixteen, in 1876, when he feared it might be his duty, at the Centennial Exhibition in Philadelphia, to go around the hotel spreading the gospel. The evangelical side of religion was never as congenial to him as the ritualist side. He shared with a schoolfriend a fascination with candlesticks and the colored ribbons to go with the candles, and with the sacrament of confirmation. He bought missals and breviaries.

His parents now attended the Mount Vernon Church on Sunday mornings but went to hear the fashionable Phillips Brooks at the Trinity Church in Copley Square in the afternoon. Ned, however, preferred the High Anglican Church of the Advent, then on Bowdoin Street. "I must go where the church sang and prayed, and the preacher waited his turn."[16] When a schoolfriend, whom he calls Lucy, was preparing to be confirmed in the Episcopal church, Ned devised for them both elaborate forms of prayer and calendars of devotion, which quite bewildered the other boy.[17]

We can take the adolescence chapter of Joyce's *Portrait of the Artist as a Young Man* as a guide to what Ned felt, with allowance made for the fervor with which Joyce ultimately embraced the ugly, including the ugliness of brothel sexuality, while Warren shrank away from it. Both aspirants expended much energy mounting guard against "impurity"—that is, sensuality. For both, love was idealistic. For Ned, it was also the love that dare not speak its name. And it was, therefore, furtive, as young love often was in those days—for Joyce too. But the furtiveness was doubled in Ned's case. He procured a photograph of a boy he liked and had a tintype made from it before returning it; he obtained this boy's autograph and carried it in an envelope with a transparent window, and he extracted the boy's discarded Greek exercises from the wastebasket.

Ned fell in love with a schoolmate—perhaps the same one—whom he watched from a distance playing football and studying at a window, and about whom he wrote a poem comparing him with Antinous. He described him as

> Clothed in the sweat of action, powerful, great
> With health and sinews mighty, born to live,
> To live and not to die, to seize the world
> Not vanish from it . . .[18]

This boy's power of action, and easy relation to the world, made Ned resolve that he too would try to love life.

Such aspirations naturally led Ned into conflict with his "Christian" feelings. He fell in love with the pride of life. In his *Defence* he writes, "Enthroning the virile, perhaps somewhat repugnant to him before, he became its jealous servant and defender."[19] He was upset by the psalm which said that the Lord "delighteth not in any man's legs." This was a conflict for him, but looking back as an aesthete, he was quite comfortable with feeling such a conflict. Aesthetes like Pater and Lionel Johnson blended pagan hedonism with a quite monastic piety, and the discord of the two gave the blend its flavor.

As for the other siblings, Sam was at Harvard through almost all of this decade. He began his undergraduate career there in 1871, at nineteen, and finished law school (cum laude) in 1878. Though he was thought haughty, he made a great impression at college and belonged to the Porcellian, the Hasty Pudding, the St. Paul's Society, and the Institute of 1770. Though not big, he was very strong, and a good athlete and sportsman as well as student, and he was for the rest of his life a member of the innermost circles of Boston society.

Sam was felt by his siblings to be "ambitious," which seems to mean a social ambition. He had these feelings on their behalf as well, worrying about his family's good name. These feelings could also be described as a strong sense of responsibility, but since he was a tense, shy, and irritable man ("not a clever hand," as Ned said), his expression of that sense of responsibility was often unwelcome to them. Even Cornelia, the sibling most sympathetic to him and least sympathetic to Ned, seems to refer in her novel to an early alienation between Sam and herself. The hero, Arnold Robertson, sounds rather like Sam. At college he had wanted to write history, but he has—though he takes no great interest in business—given up that ambition to look after his family's fortune and to guide his younger brother and sister. However, they do not welcome his guidance; though there is respect between him and his sister, Mary, there is no great sympathy, the novelist tells us. (Mary seems to represent Cornelia; like her, she is busy at good works, and she too has inherited her father's definiteness of belief and delight in action.) The brother and sister are somewhat alienated from each other. But this interpretation of the novel and of Cornelia's attitude toward her brother is hypothetical. More certainly, one can say that the brothers were usually out of sympathy with Sam.

Admitted to the Bar in Suffolk County in February 1879, and then to the U.S. Court, Sam looked around for a way to make his name. On January 20, 1879, he wrote, "I think, that is, I have half a mind, to write on the subject of the tying up of estates." That is what most young lawyers were thinking about then, but it was an ironic idea in light of the later *Warren* v. *Warren* suit. The passage comes from a letter to Louis Brandeis, his great admiration and friend.[20] Sam had graduated second from the law school, Brandeis had been number one. The latter went to work in St. Louis after graduation, but in May 1879, Sam persuaded him to return to Boston and to become his partner. They began in a very humble way, taking a third-floor room at 60 Devonshire Street for $200 a year. Their greatest extravagance was hiring a messenger boy for $3 a week. But they were soon to be successful.

Louis Brandeis

According to Alfred Lief, Brandeis's first biographer, Brandeis roomed with Sam in the Pinckney Street extension of the Warren house in his third year at Harvard Law School, 1877–78. But a later scholar, Philippa Strum, says he didn't move in until the fall of 1879. In either case, Brandeis must have been like another son to the family, being almost the same age as Henry. He and Ned were on a first-name basis until the fatal suit that made them mortal enemies; Cornelia and Fiske were also Brandeis's friends. He was legal counsel to each of them and even drew up Mrs. Warren's will and Ned's will of the mid-1890s.

Brandeis invested money in S.D. Warren and Company and "studied" the company, Lief tells us.[21] He became a businessman's lawyer and an adviser of businessmen in his early years, and the Warren company was the first one he knew intimately. For instance, "That company was a source of business education, one of the first in the country to install a cost-accounting system," and Brandeis therefore mastered the science of accounting.[22]

He was, in a way, a super-Warren; as much in love with empirical fact, analytical clarity, and above all, *numbers* as was Mr. Warren himself. Oliver Wendell Holmes saw that "the man of the future is the man of statistics and the master of economics,"[23] but Holmes himself remained a man of letters. Sam Warren referred all questions about bookkeeping to Louis. It was the latter who put Holmes's idea to work. Moreover, Brandeis's love of fact and practice and business was also moral and spiritual, as was Mr. Warren's, and his whole appearance manifested that. The Warrens must have felt like an Old Testament family in a Bible illustration, entertaining an angel unawares.

Brandeis was a tall and slender man, his head erect and well poised. He had large blue eyes set in very large orbits and a scroll-like, sculpted mouth. Gentle and aloof, serious and hard-working and austere, he gave up playing the violin and smoking cigarettes so as to concentrate on important things. He was visibly destined for greatness.

His friend, Professor Shaler of Harvard, told Brandeis that he was too sensitive for legal practice, but he had qualities of force and ambition too, all summed up in his goodness (that old-fashioned word is right in his case). He was to become a civic hero and to refuse fees when the cause was the public good. He liked to transcend ordinary legal categories; asked who he was counsel for in a complicated case, he replied "counsel for the situation."[24]

A later biographer, using a skeptical vocabulary, calls him "extremely rigid in his beliefs and controlled in his emotions."[25] Using a friendlier vocabulary, a contemporary witness said that Brandeis, having changed his mind about an issue, had a luminous look, as if he came from wrestling with the devil.[26] Exasperated cartoonists drew him with a halo, and editors complained of his self-righteous sermons. Probably Ned Warren did too.

It was Mr. Warren's side of the family to which Brandeis attached himself. Lief speaks of his "admiration for the remarkable abilities of his partner's father."[27] He does not seem to have had any strong aesthetic interests that might have drawn him then to Mrs. Warren or Ned; he was certainly untouched by the aesthetic movement and ritualist religion. "He spurned metaphysics. He preferred practicality. When Felix Adler later proposed that he become the Boston leader for the Society for Ethical Culture, he declined; the world did not need ethical preachers so much as ethical doers."[28]

Sam was of course the one who most appreciated him. He wrote on September 7, 1901, "My Dear Old Man, The best thing I ever did was done in 1879—when I induced you to come to us in Boston. You have been, I think, inexpressibly valuable in all our lives beginning with father's—'a very present help in time of trouble' and a sure adviser at all times. I cannot think of the family and its doings since that time without including you as a most influential part. You have encouraged our right impulses and criticized our faults with an unbiased discernment which could only come from outside."[29] Perhaps Ned's later resentments were fostered by the perception that Sam's attitude toward him was inspired by this revered friend.

In a more immediate and mundane way, Sam could do a lot for Brandeis. It was through Sam that he met, for instance, Oliver Wendell Holmes; for Sam began his law career with Shattuck, Holmes, and Munroe.

In practical and financial terms also, it was Sam's contacts that brought the young partners their first opportunities. Brandeis wrote, "Already he has quite a number of small claims with a prospect of some larger ones."[30] In a letter dated July 12, 1879, he wrote that Sam had "push"—"the same bulldog perseverance and obstinacy which brought me here will, I think, pave a way which he seems determined to make."[31] Sam, he said, was more practical than he himself was.

Because Brandeis played an important role in the lives of all the Warrens, we must make some detailed acquaintance with his mind. Born in 1856 in Louisville, Kentucky, a youngest child, he was early seen to be intellectually brilliant and to live in the world of ideas. Max Lerner says the earliest influence on Brandeis's thought was the romantic liberalism that his parents had brought with them when they left Prague for the United States in 1848. They were driven out by the political repression that followed the revolutions of that year. So was the Goldmark family, whose daughter Alice he later married. This liberalism was fostered in Louisville, where the uncle after whom he was named, Louis Dembitz, was a well-known Republican lawyer, author, and thinker.

Dembitz wrote for *The Nation*, the journal edited by E. L. Godkin, which spoke for the conservative conscience of the country. Felix Adler, the founder of the Ethical Culture Society, who was to become Brandeis's brother-in-law, belonged to the equivalent group in New York City. German and Jewish thinkers were prominent in this world.

Thus, in Brandeis's early years, he was in effect a German-American idealistic liberal. The German-Americans had played a part in the Civil War that left them, at its end, in some sense the Union's favorite sons. Their virtue was in part military: German-Americans enlisted in droves—in excess of other immigrant groups, it was said. And it was in part ideological: Many German-American editors wrote against slavery and for Republican policies and were rewarded by Lincoln with diplomatic and consular posts. (Louis Dembitz edited *Der Beobachter am Ohio* and translated *Uncle Tom's Cabin* for it serially; he also named his second son after Lincoln.)

This was especially true of the "48ers," the immigrant wave to which the Brandeis family belonged. One of their spokesmen was Carl Schurz, whom Lincoln sent to Spain and who much impressed Brandeis. (It was much later that Brandeis began to think of himself as Jewish rather than German.) He was an enthusiast for abolition, for peace congresses, independent voting, personal freedoms, and party- and civil service–reform.[32] And these tendencies were attractive to Sam too.

The two were to become Mugwumps together, and this was at no cost to their Boston respectability. Mr. Warren did the same thing at the same time. Even later, Harvard was one of the sources for Mugwump reform ideas and for anti-imperialism. But their partnership was also a brilliant coup for Sam whereby he lassoed a phenomenal young talent and ran side by side with it.

It is clear that Sam was deeply excited by this relationship, which satisfied romantic feelings in him. He wrote Brandeis on March 29, 1880 [about a case Brandeis was defending in Providence], "My dear old Man . . . the faint praise you allow yourself is, I know, to what you deserve, as dawn to sunrise . . . the C.J. [Chief Justice] wants you, but I wrote you are engaged before the Supreme Court of Rhode Island (toney, eh?)"[33] In 1890 he sent Brandeis some lines from Euripides' *Bacchae,* which became, Strum says, "the keynote of Brandeis's public life."[34]

> *Thou hast heard men scorn the city, call her wild*
> *Of counsel, mad; thou hast seen the fire of morn*
> *Flash from her eyes in answer to their scorn!*
> *Come toil on toil, 'tis this that makes her grand.*
> *Peril on peril! And common states that stand*
> *In caution, twilight cities, dimly wise—*
> *Ye know them, for no light is in their eyes!*
> *Go forth, my son, and help.*

And on July 23, 1891, Warren wrote, "Your life is very largely before you—with a great lead over all contemporaries. . . . Consider whether or not you will direct your course towards public life. I think you are fitted for it. This would not mean to seek office or place, but to command the leisure for public service as opportunity presents."[35] Clearly he infused a powerful charge of confidence and calling into his friend.

Sam yearned to see Brandeis become a great man, a public figure; a yearning that was obviously (and quite honorably) for his own sake as well. That is a difference between his wooing of Brandeis and Ned's wooing of Berenson, at almost the same time. The idea of greatness is public or political in the one case, private or aesthetic in the other. But both were right in their intimations of their friends' destinies; Catherine Owen Pearce's biography of Brandeis is one of a series, which also includes Franklin D. Roosevelt and Woodrow Wilson—American public heroes.

The relationship was psychologically important to Sam, and quite openly so. On November 9, 1878, he wrote that Brandeis *must* come to Boston because he, Sam, needed a kindred spirit with whom to discuss the law: "The strong feeling of need I feel in this respect is rather of a revelation of the extent to which the desire for sympathy in its etymological sense is mixed up with the intellectual as well as the moral departments of our ego . . . together we could make a more gallant fight against the whole army of heresies and fallacies of which the law must be purged."[36]

Sam's enthusiastic sense of his friend's talents was not unique at the law school. A fellow student of both, William E. Cushing, wrote in 1878, "My friend Brandeis is a character in his way—one of the most brilliant legal minds they have ever had here . . . believed to have some Jew blood in him, though you would not suppose it from his appearance. . . . Is supposed to know everything and to have it always in mind. The professors listen to his opinion with the greatest deference."[37] Another classmate wrote, "Mr. Brandeis had scarcely taken his seat in our classroom before his remarkable talents were discovered and his claim to immediate distinction allowed."[38] Probably the same thought occurred to other young Boston lawyers, but it was Sam Warren who made the decisive move to capture this phoenix for himself—for the Warrens.

Henry and Cornelia

Henry Warren also attended Harvard during this period, but he did not go in for social life. He wrote in his Harvard Class Report of the class of 1879 in his exquisite plain prose—he was the finest stylist of the family—"When I was about two or three years old, I tumbled one day out of the carriage (it was I believe one of the old-fashioned bobbing chaises) which my mother was driving. I struck on my head and soon after I grew hump-backed, and ever since I have been excessively delicate and always ailing; and at present I am only about five feet high." A short time after the accident, he says, his life was despaired of, and then came dyspepsia. "It was only in my sophomore year that I gave up the practice of lying down in the daytime. I have not been able to take part in athletic sports or even to be social—so that I am a non-society man." After his time at Harvard he spent five years at Johns Hopkins (except for a few months in his father's office in 1881) studying Sanskrit with Professor Lanman, whom he followed back to Cambridge sometime after the latter moved to Harvard.

Henry's life in the family home was rather isolated. Cornelia explains that he was so handicapped that he needed to devote every minute to his studies. Too much of his time would have been taken up if he had shared in the daily routines of the family. He had to work with nagging perseverance, often stopping to change his socks (we don't know why) or to take medicine or to rest his back. He could not, in later life, sit down to study, but must either stand (leaning on crutches) or kneel.

He had read Plato, Kant, and Schopenhauer at first at Harvard, and became a protégé of Professor Palmer, the philosopher. He also studied chemistry and botany, and even later worked with a microscope and kept an aquarium. He used to explain a nitric acid burn on the back of his hand, acquired at Johns Hopkins, as Warren nitrate. But his major interest was languages: He knew German, Dutch, Russian, French, and Spanish, and began Sanskrit with Professor Greenough at Harvard. Finally he fixed on Pali, the sacred language of South India, in which the sacred texts of Buddhism were preserved; and he became a world authority. (It is worth noting this likeness between several Warrens: Sam's devotion to Brandeis, soon to be paralleled by Ned's devotion to Berenson, another brilliant Jew, and Henry's self-identification—in a somewhat different sense, to be sure—with a remote language and religion.)

The legend is preserved that Henry maintained a library somewhere near his parents' home. It was supposed to have pulleys and runners in the ceiling so that, in a harness, he could be attached by a hook to a cable and thereby lifted from shelf to shelf, right up to the ceiling. By a similar mechanism, apparently, he could give lectures in New Lecture Hall, Harvard, and would, when excited, swing out toward the audience. The servant who looked after him, and got him into the harness, was the large black manservant who took Henry on his long trips to California and, later, to London.[39]

Cornelia's life was more absorbed into, or shaped by, her
mother's. Like her parents, she was painted by Alexandre Cabanel
in 1871, when she was thirteen. She is wearing a riding habit and
carrying a whip, and is in something of a Sir Joshua Reynolds
posture—stature as status; the artist's way to claim hereditary aristocratic rank for her. She often went to France with her mother and
spent some time there studying music. She spoke French fluently
and became an accomplished musician. She also studied with Na-
thaniel Hooper, and passed the college entrance examinations devised and administered by Harvard in 1876, but she did not go on
to college. She said (apparently as an explanation for not going) that
her interests were in social service and philosophy; she did study
privately, for three years, with professors from Harvard (George
Herbert Palmer) and from M.I.T. (George Holmes Howison). Perhaps her not going to college was also her mother's wish; at least
her brother Sam in later life spoke of her having sacrificed her life
to their mother.

Since Henry Warren too had been a protégé of Palmer, the latter
was something of a family friend to the Warrens, and he seems to
have joined in the family effort to rescue Ned from the lures of
aestheticism. Ned tells us, "Professor Palmer had asked me to read
some poems of Swinburne to him and had, for correction, referred
me to George Herbert. . . ."[40] Ned sums up this correction as yet more
New England moralism.

Palmer married Alice Freeman, the president of Wellesley, which
became something of a spiritual home to Cornelia, who became a
trustee of the school. Her charitable causes were predominantly the
same as Alice Freeman's. Cornelia's novel, *Miss Wilton,* was written
in a style that reminds the reader of the Palmers at every turn. Its
distinction is the frankness and force with which conflicting moral
ideas are expressed and related to each other—most notably Christian and anti-Christian ideas, or those of orthodox and heretical
Christianity. Alice Freeman was physically and temperamentally of
the type Cornelia made her novel's heroine, Bessie Folsom—that is,
she was small, dainty, animated, blending force of mind and will
with a childlike spontaneity and gaiety. And she was of the type
other people also saw as a heroine; her husband's hagiographic
biography of her sold fifty thousand copies.

Professor Palmer was born into a Massachusetts family much like
the Warrens, which he described as puritan, and remained loyal to
it in his conduct while he liberalized its system of ideas. Having

suffered from ill health, partly of a nervous nature, he seems to have invested his ambitions in other people—in his pupils and, in some notable cases, in women. He was married twice, both times to brilliant and sickly women whom he cherished. He married Ellen Margaret Wellman in 1871, when it seemed she had not long to live, though in fact they had eight years together. (It is significant that he made a hero of John Stuart Mill and took an interest in the Mill marriage, Mrs. Mill's feminism, and Mill's profound deference to his wife.)

Palmer was, moreover, a very successful tutor, and successful at teaching women whom he took as private pupils as well as at Harvard. This tutoring, through which he knew Cornelia Warren, seems to have been a serious enterprise. In 1872–73 he tutored the daughter of Nathan Matthews and was paid $2,000 for the year's work. Since he was paid only $500 for a course at Radcliffe, one assumes that the tutoring meant something more than elementary work for an hour a week. In 1899 another Boston businessman, Edwin H. Abbott, gave Palmer $1,100 in railroad bonds in appreciation for all he had done for Abbott's son. He himself spoke of teaching as the only fine art in which he was expert. It seems clear that he set his stamp on Cornelia Warren's mind too.

In his autobiography, Palmer tells us that he realized early on that he could never be a system-builder, or a man of encyclopedic learning, like some of his philosopher colleagues, so, "Criticism became my sacred word. . . . I need something to begin with and improve. This ethical sense of a better, in alliance with its twin sister, the aesthetic, trains practical judgment and makes one a generally useful person, resorted to for advice."[41] This applies well to Cornelia's life, but criticism, as he uses the word, also seems to mean the delicate justice done to, and balancing of, contrary moral principles, which we find in her novel. It will remind us of George Eliot.

He, Mrs. Palmer, and Cornelia Warren were literary people. Cornelia wrote poetry all her life, though none of it seems to have survived. Mr. Palmer published Mrs. Palmer's poetry after her death. Art, Mr. Palmer tells us in his *Autobiography of a Philosopher,* early became for him a close ally of philosophy and religion.[42]

As examples of the quasi-heretical side in their debate over traditional—that is, Christian—ethics, let us take one passage from Mr. Palmer and one from his wife. "But there is danger in the religious temper. For some persons the light of eternal things casts a shadow over the temporal. . . . This danger even besets those who are predominantly moral. They become narrow, heedless of what cannot at once be related to law; while momentary matters, chance, facts, the mere happenings of our hurly-burly world, do not joyously engage them. This is the same as to say that such persons frequently lack humor and spontaneity. . . . A saintly minister of my acquaintance, on being asked why he was going to Europe for the summer, wisely answered, 'To de-moralize myself.' "[43] This suggests the very qualifiedly (but in matters of conduct still severely) Christian atmosphere of Cornelia Warren's book. She was described in an obituary as a "liberal Congregationalist."

From Mrs. Palmer we can take this passage: "Religious people now feel that they have no right to waste time in hearing pious nothings uttered by men who will not take the trouble to do any thinking. I fancy that nowadays many stay away from church conscientiously."[44] In both passages there is much to remind us—in style as well as substance—that Palmer was a colleague of George Santayana. On the other hand, the day began with public prayers, at Harvard and Wellesley, for both Mr. and Mrs. Palmer, and she, and he in a different way, was active in temperance campaigns. Together they present as fine an example as could be found of "high-toned," and highly intelligent, Boston culture at that time, balancing an extraordinary variety of moral and amoral imperatives one against the other. But we should not, because of the "aesthetic" likeness between Palmer and Santayana, overlook the gulf of difference between the two, a gulf that was felt in the Warren home between Cornelia and Ned.

While Ned went off to Oxford, took a homosexual lover, and made plans to subvert sexual orthodoxy through Greek sculpture, Cornelia stayed at home, engaged in charitable work, or went shopping all over Europe with her mother.

Mrs. Warren was an energetic traveler. Cornelia describes how, when the two of them alighted from their carriage at some Flemish inn, her mother said, "You get rooms and unpack—I saw an antique shop a few streets back."[45] As another example, on the day they were to leave Seville, Mrs. Warren went to the cathedral "to see an exposition of St. Ferdinand's relics before catching the train."[46] This can serve to remind us of the energy of achievement and ambition bred in the bosom of the Warren family, and passing from one to another of them.

Ned at Harvard

Lastly, let us return to Ned and his experience of Harvard. He was a freshman in 1879, so his time there should more logically be discussed in the next chapter. But his experience of Oxford, which followed immediately after, was so different that it seems proper to put them in separate chapters.

Ned was not happy at Harvard, partly because Sam had cut such a swath there and partly because he was forced, or induced, to worry about his social status all the time. His class, he tells us, consisted of two hundred men, but only seventy or eighty counted socially, and of them only forty-five were in the innermost circle. His chief desire was to get into the Porcellian Club, because Sam had done so; but Ned was an unlikely candidate because of his eccentric slouch and absentmindedness. In some aspects of his dress, he was very smart ("Ned was known for his neckties," he says of himself) but others were neglected.

He found that at Harvard all friendships were superficial and worldly.[47] No sort of ideal love was understood. And the immorality of the other students shocked him; the 2:30 and 3:30 A.M. streetcars from Boston (and its brothels) were always full. His own behavior in the relationship he tells us most about, with a Southern student named Charlie Perrin, prefigures his later intense friendships. When Perrin got diphtheria, Ned nursed him; made up a bed on the floor of his room and slept there; allowed someone else to take over once, but found that the invalid relapsed, and so he reinstated himself from then on as irremovable. Perrin was a passionate, romantic, and unreasonable type; Ned had to bully or trick him into studying.[48] One day, when Perrin didn't arrive at Mount Vernon Street as promised, Ned went into Harvard and listened at Perrin's door, heard him talking, and realized that he wasn't going to come. Ned stole softly away and went home, but he couldn't find anything else to think about to distract himself, so went again to Harvard, listened again at Perrin's door, and returned home again.[49]

In the winter of 1881–82 he felt the stress of passion, he tells us, and his Harvard life began to be fruitful in love and melancholy.[50] He read Shelley, in whom what he loved best was the sense of pleasure fainting from its own excess. The "Hymn to Intellectual Beauty" was his creed. Sam, he tells us, also liked Shelley's *Prometheus Bound,* but thought that "it was no use knocking your head against everything in that manner."[51] Presumably this is told to show us Sam's philistinism.

When Wilde came to lecture in Boston in 1882, and Ned was enraptured, Sam told him not to seek a personal interview and took him to meet Holmes instead—who explained that Wilde's poetry was all borrowed jewels, and that Wordsworth was the greater poet. (Ned observed that Wordsworth had "nothing to do with what I was after,"[52] and *did* seek out Wilde's acquaintance later in New York.)

The side of Wilde's imagination that resembled, and probably influenced, Ned's is well illustrated by the former's fairy story, "The Young King." The hero is sixteen years old, a bastard brought up as a commoner, and a brown woodland faun in appearance. But from the moment he was recognized as heir to the throne, "he had shown signs of that strange passion for beauty that was destined to have so great an influence over his life."[53] A cry of pleasure broke from the young king when "he saw the delicate raiment and rich jewels that had been prepared for him."[54] He flung aside his rough leather tunic and coarse sheepskin cloak, and was much preoccupied with his coronation robe of tissued gold.[55]

It is clear enough what kind of identification both Wilde and Ned would make with such a figure. They were both very keen on tints and textures, and there are in fact some striking resemblances between this story and some of Ned's writings, notably "The Prince Who Did Not Exist" and "Alcmaeon." But what makes the similarity most important is the social conscience allied to the aestheticism in Wilde's story as in Ned's life. The young king has three accusing dreams about the weavers and galley slaves whose lives are being sacrificed to make his royal robes. As an act of conscience he renounces his throne, but a miracle turns his resumed rags into gorgeousness. Ned too, we know, had a social conscience; it was as quixotic and fairy tale as Wilde's, but he did try to act on it.

Sometime in the academic year 1882–83 he met a freshman at Boston University, Bernard Berenson. Five years younger than Ned and a Lithuanian Jew, Berenson had been a star pupil at Cambridge Latin School and already had a reputation for brilliance as well as charm. He was, however, disadvantaged—far more than Brandeis was—by his own poverty and Boston's prejudice. Ned and he, and George Santayana and their friend Charles Loeser, had a great deal in common in their strong feeling for art and all the values associated with art and their hostility to the mood of the day. They had all learned a lot from Charles Eliot Norton's Harvard lectures on art, but had gone further along the route of aestheticism than he had. Berenson was unhappy at Boston University, and Ned sponsored him at Harvard; more than that, he tried to "annex" Berenson, to use a term later applied to him, in the way Sam had annexed Brandeis.

In their correspondence, Ned and Berenson cite a text that has an inspiring function for them parallel to that which Euripides' *Bacchae* had for Sam and Brandeis; but this is a very different text, Walter Pater's *Marius the Epicurean*. The story of Marius' musings in Antonine Rome justifies and inspires the private life of meditation and aesthetic appreciation, while the lines from the *Bacchae* celebrate the austere pride of public office and public service. Sam's protégé, Matthew Prichard, later sent the same lines to Mrs. Gardner—a different kind of public figure. Berenson was rereading *Marius the Epicurean* for the eighth time during World War II, sixty years after his first reading.

From Wilde, Ned turned to Swinburne; saying to himself, "He is corrupt [in poetic method] but I like him." He knew that in this poet he had met "the master of my soul."[56] Swinburne "carried intensity to its legitimate extreme"; and Ned used "intensity" to mean a category of experience that was the opposite of the sublime—associated with down rather than up, with hell rather than heaven, but attractive and valuable. "The love of God, the love of beauty, the love of love, the love of passion, the love of intensity,—Cotytto,—these were the natural succession . . . my fellow-worship with Swinburne was nothing short of self-sacrifice."[57] In both this taste, for Swinburne, and this vocabulary, of intensity, Ned was a typical member of the aesthetic movement.

He had maintained, or increased, his religious fervor during the early years at Harvard. During Lent of 1880 his brother Henry, himself giving up Christianity, grew alarmed at Ned's piety and gave him Matthew Arnold's *Literature and Dogma* to read. (Henry too had been George Herbert Palmer's pupil, we should recall.) He was afraid that Ned was going to end up a priest. But in this winter of 1881–82 there developed a conflict between that piety and what the poets were teaching Ned, and at Christmas he found that the Christ child meant nothing to him anymore. He then "passed out of faith with pomp and rejoicing," and wrote himself down as an infidel in the college questionnaire when he graduated.[58] ("Infidel" was not a category the questionnaire recognized, so he never knew how—

among whom—he was counted.) Presumably it was also around this time that he wrote on his bedroom wall at Cedar Hill, "Man should not be separated from his mother, Nature. It hinders equal development."[59]

Swinburne was *the* poet for most members of the aesthetic movement, including Santayana. When the latter met Frank Russell at Harvard, at the beginning of the most important of Santayana's personal relationships, the occasion was sealed by Russell reading aloud to him all the choruses of *Atalanta in Calydon*. (This was Earl Russell, the older brother of the philosopher Bertrand Russell.) Swinburne provided the litanies of aesthetic/erotic rebellion.

Santayana and Berenson both felt as alienated from Harvard as Ned; all three found what they wanted at Oxford. From there— from Ned's lodgings there—Berenson wrote back to Mrs. Gardner in January 1888, "Poor Harvard, and its men, it's not fair to compare it and them, especially them to Oxford men. These are all—as far as I can see, very clever, brilliant, serious even although without too much gravity, and well-taught, just the men whom I admire and even adore. There is something so crude and vulgar, and stupid about many if not most Harvard men."[60]

There was certainly nothing crude or stupid or vulgar about Berenson. Around this time he was described as "This beautiful and mysterious youth . . . for whom nothing in the world existed except a few lines of poetry which he held to be perfect, and the pictures and music he held to be beautiful . . . I felt like a dry sponge that was put in water." And the writer who quotes this adds that "all his life Berenson was to have this kind of exhilarating effect on most of the women he met, and on not a few young men."[61] One of those young men was Ned Warren, and his exhilaration was intellectual and moral as well as emotional. Berenson embodied the values Ned believed in—values the opposite of Brandeis's—and was Ned's inspiration as much as the other man was Sam's.

It was Ned who arranged for Berenson to enter Harvard in 1884, where Mr. and Mrs. Jack Gardner probably paid his fees. Others in their circle were Santayana, Charles Loeser, and the writer Logan Pearsall Smith, the last according to the scholar Colin Simpson a proselytizing homosexual even then, and involved in scandal.[62] They had all listened to Charles Eliot Norton lecture on art. But they represented a different kind or further stage of aestheticism. Norton was a friend of Ruskin's; they were devotees of Pater. The story went that Norton had told Berenson that Pater's *Studies in the Renais-*

sance was a book "you can only read in your bathroom." The Palmers, and Cornelia, stood with Ruskin; Santayana and Ned preferred Pater.

To the younger men, even Harvard's "advanced" ideas seemed feeble: Santayana speaks scornfully of the readings from the Upanishads that replaced a funeral service in Concord for one of his friends who died young. And its general tone was vulgar: He describes Harvard and its environs as "A red-brick world, mean and shabby-genteel, with an atmosphere of whimsical, ineffectual Bohemia" and compares it with Joyce's Dublin.[63] "Science was a mighty word, the great future of industry loomed vaguely but magnificently before you, and any ulterior rebellion against it, though Ruskin might prophecy it, was put aside as unthinkable. Unthinkable was a favorite word in those days. Wealth and Morality dominated the scene from their granite pedestals, like ponderous Victorian statues. . . . "[64] These were the idols the aesthetes meant to pull down as they purified the temple of the mind.

Santayana also describes a Beacon Hill home in a way one guesses would fit 67 Mount Vernon Street. At the imposing door a young visitor rarely dared to pull the door bell hard enough to be heard the first time. "Within, all was solemnity and hush: thick carpets drowned your footsteps. Here and there a gas-jet, turned down low, marked the long distances, or dimly revealed the shining surfaces of black walnut monumental furniture, Chinese vases, and gilded picture frames. The tables seemed heavy and fixed like sepulchres, and the armchairs grew in their places like separate oaks."[65]

4

The Aesthetic Movement

1880–90

*It seems to me that Mrs. Gardner has brought back to
us all that is really best of Rome and Italy and has
considerately left the rest behind. A visit to her Fenway
Palace really suffices to show one everything. The head of
Aphrodite is superior to everything I have seen in the
Vatican. I also think that we have by far the better half
of the so-called Ludovisi Throne.*

—J. P. Marquand,
The Late George Apley
(George Apley is supposed to have been born on Mount
Vernon Street in 1866.)

Henry Warren and Beck House

During this period Henry Warren established himself at Harvard
and as a scholar of Pali. He traveled to England in 1884, the year
he returned from Baltimore and Johns Hopkins, carried from one
mode of public transport to another by his black manservant. The
purpose of his trip was partly to visit Ned at Oxford and partly to
meet Rhys Davids, secretary of the Royal Asiatic Society and a
leading Pali scholar, in London.

In his report to the American Oriental Society in March 1894,
Warren described how he had begun ten years before to translate
some Buddhist scriptures. He had then borrowed Davids's palm leaf
manuscript of the Visuddhi-Magga ("Way of Purity" or "Way of
Salvation"), written by Buddhaghosa, simply to read it as an aid to

his translation work. Eventually, he found himself engaged in a full-scale translation of this manuscript and the editor of the English edition.[1] He borrowed several of these manuscripts from the India Office in London. Ned, living in England, acted as Henry's bondsman when it was necessary to give the English proprietors some surety.

Warren lived mostly at home from 1884 until 1888, when he bought 12 Quincy Street, a house on the edge of Harvard Yard, where the bulk of his later work was done. He was then thirty-four years old. We don't know much about the staff who worked with Henry on his translations, but among the letters preserved in the Massachusetts Historical Society are several written in the 1890s by a Sarah W. Brooks, who worked at 12 Quincy Street and refers to it as "the shop." These letters are gay and chatty—in a mild way, flirtatious—and so suggest a different side to Henry's personality than the one his family reports. Three or four other women who worked for Henry are mentioned in letters, or write themselves, and others are recommended by members of the family—also one of Sam's brothers-in-law, who had a drinking problem, but seemed to be over it. But exactly how many there were at any one time it is impossible to say.

In 1884, Warren had already published in a Providence journal a translation of a Buddhist story from Pali. Brown University had some Pali texts, and so took an interest in that area of scholarship. The study of that South Indian language was, necessarily, also the study of Buddhism, and nearly everyone in this generation of the Warrens, or to be mentioned in this story, even the peripheral figures, were for a time proto- or would-be Buddhists.

The study of Pali was developed in nineteenth-century Europe, by Danes in particular. But with the foundation of the London Pali Society, there was a shift in the balance of scholarly power to England, and then America. Warren, with the backing of his Harvard friend Charles Lanman, was entrusted in London with almost irreplaceable texts.

Lanman (1850–1941) went to Yale as an undergraduate, studied at Tuebingen University in Germany, and became professor of Sanskrit at Harvard in 1880. He was a fully qualified and accepted member of the small community of Western Sanskrit scholars and was well known in Paris, Berlin, and St. Petersburg. He edited thirty-eight volumes in the Harvard Oriental Series (begun by him and Warren in 1891) and two dozen other books—some of them grammars.

Lanman is said to have practiced yoga and to have loved the hedonism of Omar Khayyám, but the outlines of his personality, as reported, were bluffly American, nineteenth century, and manly. Historian Samuel Eliot Morison described him as "a forthright and vigorous gentleman."[2] He was one of the characters of Harvard, but of the native-Yankee variety, and thoroughly respectable and reassuring. His and his wife's relations with Henry Warren were apparently important to both men; when Henry's family wrote to him, they habitually asked about, or referred to, the Lanmans; but those relations seem (from what little we know) to have been conducted within conventional limits of the time. Lanman's portrait of Warren is also blandly conventional, saying Warren had "a moral character of singular purity, unselfishness and loftiness" and "a profoundly religious nature."[3]

During this decade Henry Warren had tried various modes of independence from his family, living alone at Cedar Hill for a while, transferring to Johns Hopkins, and briefly trying California. Ned speaks of the queer herb dishes Henry's manservant had prepared for him at Cedar Hill. (Henry is listed, in the Waltham Directory for the late 1870s and 1880, as the only Warren living at Cedar Hill.) But in 1888 (the year his father died, and he came into money) he bought the Beck house on Quincy Street, on the edge of the university.

Built in the 1800s, this house had long been the residence of Charles Beck (1798–1861), a professor of Latin. Beck was an ardent Abolitionist and had made the house a stop on the Underground Railway for escaped slaves: He had a trapdoor and a secret room put in the floor at the top of the stairs, and iron spikes, to serve as footholds, in the sides of a well going down into the basement. These are still to be seen, together with modifications made by Henry Warren, because the house has been preserved as the home of the English Department at the university.

Because of his scientific interests, Warren added an aquarium. At the end of a miniature balcony in a large upstairs dining room, he installed a small glass room in which he slept. He also had an elevator put in (there was much discussion in the family letters of these alterations) presumably because stair-climbing was difficult for him. And because an ordinary bed gave him so little comfort, he installed a "roomette"—as in a railway coach—with a rolling wood curtain, such as a rolltop desk has. He breathed through a tube that introduced cool outside air into the room. Despite his disabilities, Warren would have no servants sleeping on the same floor as himself.

Molly Osgood's father, who was a family friend of the Warrens, took her to visit Henry, to inspire her with a sense of how much could be achieved by someone who suffered from severe disabilities. It does not seem that either she or Henry was able to help the other. It was his strong-bodied intellectual comrade Charles Lanman from whom Warren was able to draw comfort.

In 1888, from Port Said, on his way to India, Lanman wrote his pupil and friend about his idea for a Harvard Oriental Series, which he had discussed with leading Oriental scholars in Europe, and which they had encouraged. The series was to make available "the incomparable lessons the Wise Men of the East can teach us: concerning the simple life, moderation, repose, the search after God."[4] Christianity was to be strengthened by the study of other religions. Warren's *Buddhism in Translations* was third in the series, and his enlightened funding of the whole project, Lanman said (writing during World War I), "seems to have been an almost prophetic anticipation on his part of a great political need."[5]

Lanman seems to have not only taken the place of a hypothetical wife or lover for Henry Warren, but to have supplemented his actual brothers and parents, giving him emotional as well as intellectual comradeship. (There is of course also the enigmatic figure of the black servant who did so much for Henry, but we have no grounds for speculating about their relationship.) Lanman was himself a hearty man, the father of six and a vigorous oarsman all his life—he logged twelve thousand miles on the Charles (on his seventieth birthday he rowed to Waltham and back). He ascribes to Warren a simple faith in religion in general, and in Buddhism in particular, and its power to end imperialism, materialism, and the woes that man is born to.[6]

One is inclined to join Ned Warren in his skepticism as to this reading of Henry's temperament and the motives for his lifework. In an essay of 1927, Ned said that Henry had chosen Buddhism as his topic because he disapproved of the simpleminded uplift that was then being taught in Boston under that name. "He desired to show that that was not the genuine thing; but I never observed any tendency to believe in the genuine thing. 'The heathen in his blindness' interested him as contradiction of the blind tradition of New England. His impulse indeed was sceptical reaction."[7] We might well suspect Ned of twisting Henry's motives in order to make him seem another ally against Boston. But the epigraphs Henry chose for his volumes do stress the ontological and epistemological negativism of Buddhist piety.

"Whether Buddhas arise, O priests, or whether Buddhas do not arise, it remains a fact, and the fixed and necessary constitution of being, that all its constituents are transitory."[8] There are three sequent sentences on that pattern, all ending differently: In the second one, the constituents of being are *missing,* and in the third they are *lacking in an Ego.* Warren seems to use Ego to mean a separate or separable being. Thus Sections 15, 16, and 17 are entitled "There Is No Ego," "All Signs of an Ego Are Absent," and "No Continuous Personal Identity"; while later we find a section, "The Colorless Life," and another, "The Body Is an Open Sore." It is obvious enough what sense such ideas could have made to a man in Henry Warren's situation. Santayana drew a character like him in *The Last Puritan,* and I have taken a few lines for the epigraph to Chapter 5.

Molly Osgood Childers says that Henry was "repulsive-looking [and] not friendly . . . personal expressions and exchanges demanded too much. . . ." Mrs. Childers goes on to describe his intense suffering and his difficulty in breathing. "The room was kept at about 90 degrees and the windows shut." She does not say whether she was able to learn anything from his heroic triumph over his handicaps, as her father hoped. "He did not welcome me, but knew why I came and tolerated my visits because he realized I was myself learning to overcome physical lacks by will-power."[9] He told her that any man could become an expert scholar in any subject in three years, if he set his mind and will to the task. For Henry Warren himself, that was apparently true.

Mr. Warren's Death and the Mills Trust

Mr. Warren died on May 11, 1888, and the flag was flown at half-mast at the Cumberland Mills. The funeral service was held in Boston, but it was in Westbrook that his passing was a major event; that was where he had been king. And it was fitting that the special bodyguard at his funeral was composed of four of his nephews, not his sons.

A meeting was held in the evening of May 11 in the Westbrook Library to decide how to pay him due honor. The church was draped for thirty days and the bell tolled seventy times; on the afternoon of his funeral the seven schools were all closed. A large photograph and a crayon portrait were displayed in the church, and a three-foot-tall floral tribute entitled "The Gates Ajar," with "Our Employer" spelled out in dark flowers against white ones, was sent to Boston.

At the three-hour service (hymns, prayers, Scripture readings, tributes, and sermon) every seat was filled. A text cited was, "Know ye not that there is a prince and a great prince fallen this day in Israel?"[10] Despite his modesty, the congregation was told, Mr. Warren was such a prince, who had established morality and righteousness among his people. There were several references to Lincoln and to the shock caused by *his* death; Warren was seen as another Lincoln. He had also been a steward of God, developing and promoting the highest principles of manhood.[11] At the same time, of course, he was held up as a successful businessman, and the mystery of Providence merged into the mystery of "success." (In the later *Highlights of Westbrook History,* he was compared with Edison and Ford.)

Mr. Warren's children used their own rhetorical styles, differing from each other but all of them differing from that of the memorial service; some of them may well have winced at some of the phrases used. Ned at least did not think of businessmen as having so much political or spiritual authority. But it made a difference to their sense of Mr. Warren and even of themselves that they had heard their father called a prince in Israel.

The memorial service was held the Sunday after the funeral. This time Mr. Warren was compared with the aged Jacob who blessed his sons as he died. He was a figure of strength and that strength was threefold: He was strong (1) to labor, (2) to plan and execute, and (3) to keep to puritan ideals. This was puritanism, they were told, not in the hard, narrow, restrictive sense, but in that larger sense—of the will to resist temptation—in which puritan seed gave New England her preeminence over the United States and over the world, and made Massachusetts what it is. The post–Civil War generation of New Englanders laid complacent claim to this refurbished puritanism—except for those New Englanders most in touch with modern aestheticism, like Santayana and Ned Warren.

Mr. Warren's will, dated May 1882, was simple compared with those his children were to draw up. He left his wife his Boston houses and all his pictures, plate, porcelain, bronzes, statuary, art, and furniture. His sisters got bequests of two, five, or ten thousand dollars; and some money went to his brothers or their heirs. Of the residue, one-third went to Mrs. Warren and two-thirds was to be divided among the five children.

One of the will's most notable features was that, perhaps saddened by the reluctance of any of his sons to work for S.D. Warren and Company, Mr. Warren suggested that the family might want to sell it. The executors (the widow, the oldest son, and Mortimer Mason) were to continue the business for eighteen months while the decision was taken. However, he wrote this in 1882, and by the time of Mr. Warren's death in 1888, both Sam and Fiske *were* employed there, though Fiske was in a very junior capacity. And in the following year the family decided to continue the firm, through the agency of a trust, which distributed the profits to Mr. Warren's six heirs (his widow and five children) and leased the mills to certain partners, who were in fact Sam and Fiske and Mortimer Mason.

The company employed eight hundred workers at this time, and Mr. Warren left an estate worth $1.9 million. According to author Lewis Paper, the company was making between $300,000 and $400,000 a year at this time, though the profits went down somewhat immediately afterward.[12] (For the first six months of 1888, Mortimer Mason rendered an account to the company of $174,844.10.) There were very bad economic conditions in America in the early 1890s, and a comparable fall in S.D. Warren receipts perhaps made at least Ned think that his father had indeed been a prince in Israel, while his brother Sam was no substitute.

In May 1889, therefore, what was known thereafter as the Mills Trust was set up, to run for thirty-three years or until the death of all the heirs. Its design was largely Brandeis's work; he acted on behalf of both the heirs and the partners, even though the two groups' interests could not always coincide. (As we know, he liked to transcend conflicts of interest.) Partly for that reason, the provisions of the trust were to cause, or to be the occasion of, a great deal of trouble in the years to come—to Brandeis as well as to the Warrens.

The heirs conveyed the mill property to John E. Warren, and he conveyed it to the trustees (Mrs. Warren, Sam, and Mort). Then the trustees conveyed it to Brandeis; and he of course conveyed it to the partners. At least one of the trustees was always to be a nonpartner heir. The profits were to be distributed in the proportion of five-fifteenths to the widow and two-fifteenths each to the children. The partners were allowed to create a reserve fund and to make improvements in the mills costing up to one-third of the net income, which of course diminished the income the heirs would draw.

The Mills Trust was to play an important role in the subsequent history of the Warrens, and it must be understood in its historical setting. The trust device is one of the great success stories of Anglo-

American law after the Civil War, according to scholar Lawrence M. Friedman, but it has in fact been much more American than English and is particularly associated with Boston.[13] There are several kinds of trust; the one in question here is called "dynastic." It is similar to the more common caretaker trust, but different in that the trustee of a dynastic trust is allowed much more freedom in investing the money under his control. This freedom was defined in a "prudent investor" rule originated in the case of *Harvard College* v. *Amory* in 1830. (In other parts of the country "legal lists," drawn up by the courts, prescribed to trustees what stocks they could invest in and those they could not.)

The prudent investor suited Boston, Friedman says, because of the genteel and frugal traditions of Boston's mercantile families. Indeed, "the Boston trustee" is a semi-mythical figure in the history of the law, or at least something more than a resonant phrase, and it seems legitimate to apply that label to Sam Warren. Taken literally, this would not be quite correct; the Boston trustee was a professional who took on many clients, to most of whom he was not related; but taken metaphorically, the phrase seems appropriate because of the special powers and prestige of Boston trustees, semi-moral, semi-practical, so like those that Sam assumed vis-à-vis his siblings—autocratic powers.

Thus, on May 31, 1889, he wrote to Ned that he was not sending him a detailed account of the trust, first, because such figures might "go astray," and second, because he had had so much explaining to do to "the other children" that he knew it would be a great effort to make Ned understand them.[14] Sam habitually referred to his siblings as the children even when they were thirty years old and older.

In *The Proper Bostonians,* published in 1945, Cleveland Amory talks about the "spendthrift" trust (another version of a dynastic trust) as a clue to the history to upper-class Boston. The Massachusetts Supreme Court's interpretation of such trusts forbids heirs to borrow against their inheritance, or to receive any income from it, against the trustee's judgment. As long as the latter remains a prudent investor, his rule is absolute.

One effect of the Mills Trust was to tie the Warrens together for life, financially and therefore in other ways, and to make them dependent on each other but above all on Sam. This was exactly what dynastic trusts in general did, as they spread, very quickly, in Boston between 1880 and 1905; they installed the trustee in almost absolute power. A decision of 1889, in *Claflin* v. *Claflin,* declared that even a sole beneficiary could not terminate a trust once it had been set up. The trust, and the trustee, was supreme.

There was plenty of criticism of this arrangement. In 1883, John Chipman Gray denounced dynastic trusts in *Restraints on the Alienation of Property;* he said they were essentially paternalistic and against the spirit of free enterprise. Frederick J. Stimson, a Massachusetts lawyer, denounced them in his autobiography, published in 1931, calling them the most notable cause of Boston's commercial decline. "Immense wealth had been accumulated in Boston in the first sixty years of the republic; instead of trusting their sons and sending them out at their own risks . . . they had them all trusteed. . . . Perforce they all became coupon cutters, parasites, not promoters."[15] When Ned Warren sued his brother in the first decade of the twentieth century, he drew on these ideas.

Ned Warren and Oxford Aestheticism

The 1880s were the decade of Ned's happy self-discovery at Oxford. He took what one might call the eastward route of escape from the constraints of Boston culture. A friend, he tells us, went out to Texas to cure himself of his problems and wrote back, "I had no idea a man could be so healthy or so dirty."[16] (This Western or seagoing route had been followed by attorney Richard Henry Dana, historian Francis Parkman, and Theodore Roosevelt.) But Ned felt that for him to follow that example would have been "to forego my last chance of culture."

For the rest of his life, Ned Warren measured Harvard against Oxford, to its disadvantage. He saw Harvard as a university at the service of a philistine middle class. In his 1918 essay "Classical and American Education," for instance, he takes a very satirical tone about what it had to offer him. The standard, he says, was the commonplace, though the young men were socially privileged and exclusive. "They were men of the world, content with its tenets. . . ."[17] Though exclusive in matters of dress and manners, they thought that "opinions not dominant in Beacon Street or Fifth Avenue were obviously fads." Of course, a New England literary tradition still lingered, but it was one that he found comic. "Emerson still lectured to ladies, though he forgot the order in which he had intended to read the pages of his manuscript and remembered to take other people's umbrellas as far as his next stop; Longfellow appeared, like a harvest moon, at symphony concerts; Whittier's 'thees' and 'dosts' were to be heard in Mount Vernon Street; Holmes read verses at dinners . . ."[18] In the 1880s, Warren's taste had of course turned away from such mild nineteenth-century humanism to the daring poetry of the aesthetes.

His own early poems (first published in *Itamos*, 1903) show him strongly influenced by Swinburne in his preference for themes of death and dreams and love in some vague and exalted sense, and by Poe—number 15 is dedicated to "E.A.P.," and says

> *Yet none salutes my soul of right*
> *Like thine, O poet of mysteries.*

And behind Poe and Swinburne stands Shelley. It is a familiar mixture.

In 1883, Warren went to Oxford, to New College. He chose to avoid Balliol, recommended to him as the college of contemporary ideas, because he already knew he wanted old-fashioned ideas; he wanted the Oxford of Shelley and Newman.[19] (It was someone who admired Sam who recommended Balliol to Ned—Balliol was Sam's kind of place.)

Any idea defined by "the Oxford of Shelley and Newman" may seem to us a strange jumble in itself, but it would have been an intelligible, a natural, phrase to many aesthetes of that time. In their creed a strong devotional influence had combined with aestheticism and even immoralism, from the earliest days of the Pre-Raphaelite Brotherhood. (Even in the pious verse of Christina Rossetti, it was the beautiful in religion, not the ethical, that was stressed.) Newman and Pater seemed twin spirits. So did Shelley and Blake. And it was as "an aesthete of those times" that Warren went to England. Though he may have thought he was being old-fashioned, he was also joining in the swim. In 1882 the first book on the movement, entitled *The Aesthetic Movement in England,* was published. Written by Walter Hamilton, it starts from the currency given the phrase by Gilbert and Sullivan's satiric opera *Patience,* but the book is not uninformed about or unsympathetic to its subject. (There are chapters on the Pre-Raphaelite Brotherhood, on Ruskin, on a number of poets, including Morris, and so on.) So though Warren was seeking the past, he was also joining a movement of the moment.

It was a diverse movement, and Warren did not belong to the more extreme branch, which attracted scandal in the 1890s. "Maquillage" and "Morbidezza" (poem titles by Arthur Symons) were not slogans for Warren. In the matter of furnishings, for instance, he seems closer to Morris than to, say, Lionel Johnson, the poet. Santayana tells us that Johnson had a jug of whiskey on his table, between *Les Fleurs du Mal* and *Leaves of Grass.* That was not Warren's style. W. B. Yeats describes Johnson's rooms as papered in brown, and with gray corduroy curtains at window, door, and bookshelf. Warren favored a bare effect, with a minimum of curtains and carpets, as Morris came to do. This is unexpected because in other matters—notably in sexual matters—Warren and Morris were so dissimilar. But aesthetically they were closer to each other on the whole than Warren was to, say, Wilde. For instance, in the Greece Warren loved the central city was the archaic Thebes, and Athens stood for a kind of decadence; Wilde loved Athenian art and thought Thebes stood for a kind of stupidity or primitivism.

Anyway, Warren found in Oxford what he had sought in vain at Harvard, including young men's open appreciation of each other's youthful beauty. The students sometimes addressed each other as "beautiful creature," he says, but there was no immorality.[20] The bordellos were farther away from the colleges than they were at Harvard, and the students were happier and less (heterosexually) immoral.

In fact, one homosexual scandal that must have come to Warren's attention involved the sending down, in 1885, of Lord Russell from Balliol because of his sexual relations with Lionel Johnson at New College. This was not publicly acknowledged at the time. We know about it from Santayana and because of the connection between those two men and Santayana two years later. Warren knew Johnson quite well, for the latter was president of the New College Essay Society, to which Warren belonged. When Berenson came to Oxford, Warren brought him together with Johnson.

In *A Defence of Uranian Love,* Warren talks, though obliquely, about his discovery of his own sexuality in his adolescence. Such a boy as himself is, in his spirituality, he says, "ready for ecstacies, and treads lightly on the earth. But he foresees, dimly, that his love, once developed, will weight him and bring him down to earth."[21] Then he comes to positively value his sensuality. "He has known so many pure who are not warm and loving . . ."[22] (This presumably refers to Warren's own family, among others.) He meets "an older lad who appears to him to have the beauty of a Greek statue, and a solidity and stability which he misses in himself."[23]

The idea that in some men the concept of manhood becomes glorious because they are like or *are* statues, is one Warren often refers to, and it obviously bears on his passion for Greek sculpture. While the fact that the connoisseur collects fragments of statues, handles them, and puts them together again, must also have imbued the work of the collector with an erotic glamour for him. There is a photograph of Warren nursing a handsome male torso, in marble, slightly smaller than life-size, on his lap at Lewes House. As collector-connoisseur he has power over these forms that before had power over him.

Something comparable is the "Attic pelvic line" that he and Marshall discussed: a way of recognizing Attic sculpture, distinguishing it from that of other periods by the way it represents the male pelvis and pubes. Here again the intellectual activity of the connoisseur coincided with the voyeuristic pleasure of the homosexual; the mind legitimized the imagination's intrusion into the forbidden, into the secret places of the body. But this came later than the 1880s.

In *Uranian Love* we are told that older lads, by natural law, have younger followers and exert authority over them. They are admired and happy. The younger boy's "ideal will be the youth of twenty, already possessed of the full virility which, to him, carries with it some awe, but not yet disfigured by maturity. He is worshipping what he himself would become."[24] The younger boy then needs to be drawn quickly into manhood (which, Warren implies, did not happen to him). He needs a worthy lover "to console and fortify him, to gratify his longings, and to shout to him at football."[25] There are many references to the bitter experiences that befell Warren himself because he was not sent where he might find this fellowship—to an English public school, for instance.

The same ideas constitute an element in his retelling of the Greek legend of Alcmaeon. Alcmaeon himself loves Parthenopaeus, who is the son of Atalanta, and who teaches him to ride, to wrestle, and to box—in short, to be a man.[26] Parthenopaeus is a free male spirit, not entangled in family relationships. But Alcmaeon has to learn also to be a king. When he visits his subjects in villages far from the capital, many of them look hostile, and "A girl's eyes seemed to say: 'You have everything and I have nothing.' "[27] (In literal fact, in 1888, when Ned inherited $20,000 a year under his father's will, a skilled worker for S.D. Warren and Company earned $2.16 for a twelve-hour workday, and a common laborer earned $1 a day.) Alcmaeon blames his mother for this. "This then was his mother's pride; her golden vessels and soft raiment were given to her by the poor wretches. . . . "[28] And he is outraged when he sees her, shortly after, fingering greedily a costly new silk with a gold border. His father's ghost commands him to slay her.

Yet she is a devoted mother, like Mrs. Warren. It is *for him,* Alcmaeon, that she wants everything; that is why she is glad of the death of his rival for power, Aegisleus, whom Alcmaeon loved. The main theme of the story in fact is her will to destroy—for her son's sake—men of various ages, including boys. (Warren's book is dedicated to "Master T. Warren"; the boy, Travis, whom Warren had adopted in 1911.) After the war on Thebes, the ghost of the father he has never loved lays on Alcmaeon the command to kill his mother because she means harm to another young boy, Cyanippos.

It is worth noting that despite this pagan cult of virility, Warren was still very interested in Catholicism, and sought and was granted an interview with Cardinal Newman; and in Paris at Christmastime 1883, shortly after naming himself an infidel as he graduated from Harvard, he spent hours in Notre Dame listening to services and attending every function, he said, where he was likely to meet a cardinal.[29] Later he wrote to Marshall that he was hiding from his loneliness in his Roman breviary, though he was interpreting that work in his own sense.[30] "I believe in the devotional life, meditation and vain repetition."[31]

Indeed, Part III of his *Defence of Uranian Love* contains many notes on the missal, the Bible, Dante, and Aquinas. He acknowledges the theological virtues, which include purity, penitence, poverty, humility, chastity, obedience. All of these he appreciates, as feminine virtues of the sublime, though he regards them as no substitute for the masculine virtues of the noble. This rather bizarre blend of tastes and emblems was of course fairly typical of the aesthetes. That is why Buddhism was of such interest; the theological virtues were what people then saw in Buddhism; even Lionel Johnson had his Buddhist period. Thus Warren's mixture of tastes is to be found again in many aesthetes, like Wilde and Pater and Johnson; and Berenson converted to Roman Catholicism, the religion to which Santayana remained very attached.

The Aesthetic Movement

The first of Warren's aesthete-protégés, Berenson, came to Oxford as his guest for the Lent term of 1888. He shared Warren's rooms, on Holyoke Street, and later traveled in Europe on Warren's money.

When he sailed for Europe, Berenson saw himself, and was seen by others, as a man of letters. Historian H. A. L. Fisher, who met Berenson at New College, says that he then knew nothing about Italian art. But like Warren, he was turning away from literature (the preferred art form of nineteenth-century humanism) toward the visual arts.

Warren was already recruiting men of talent to devote themselves to the "Hellenic idea," which was best to be served by the study of Greek art; but Berenson did not yield to that direction. In 1889, however, Warren gave him a retainer to help him live—and find works of art for his patron to buy. This was on condition that he go to Greece before surrendering himself to his "beloved Italians." "Before you begin to see," Ned wrote, "the veil must be lifted." This is an allusion to Walter Pater's novel, *Marius the Epicurean,* the bible of the aesthetic movement, published in 1888. In that novel, Pater writes, "The veil that was to be lifted for him [the hero] lay over the works of the old masters of art in places where nature had used her mastery."[32]

It is above all Chapter 9, "The New Cyrenaicism," that is full of indices to Warren. "It was intelligible that this 'aesthetic' philosophy might find itself . . . weighing the claims of that eager, concentrated, impassioned realization of experience, against those of the received morality." Marius "seemed to be living so intently in the visible world! And now, in revolt against that preoccupation with other persons, which had so often perturbed his spirit . . ." he developed "a thirst for experience in exquisite places."[33] The aesthetic, the exquisite, the visual, the perturbation of spirit caused by personal relations: these are all themes to be played out in Warren's life—and in Berenson's.

It is worth trying to imagine the Warren family's anxiety at Ned's enterprises at Oxford. Having contributed to Berenson's traveling scholarship, he then gave him $800 for another year abroad, and then the retainer. Whether or not he was infatuated with the other man, and whatever the terms in which they referred to his sexual susceptibility, they must have been suspicious. And then there was his lordly scheme of founding a new college at Oxford. It is no wonder that Cornelia, as she later confessed, thought Ned was "going crazy."

Santayana also came to England and to Oxford. His father, an old-fashioned Spanish liberal, had loved the idea of England as the moral avant-garde as well as the industrial workshop of the world.

The philosopher son, on the other hand, loved its opposite side, its "intense poetic, sporting, and religious life . . . the cult of splendor and aristocratic ways of living and feeling [that] endured" there.[34] Being a foreigner (and an aesthete) he saw England the way Kipling saw it—the first among modern English writers to do so—and took pride in it not as the home of liberals and progressives but as the home of soldiers and sportsmen.

Santayana's novel *The Last Puritan* was hailed, when it was published in 1936, as the truth about a generation of Harvard men. It can remind us often of the Warrens, and in fact Santayana saw a lot of Ned in the early 1920s, while he was writing it, and talked to him about Boston. In the novel, Oxford, and then Italy, are offered as the antidote for Boston idealism, and many of Santayana's insights into American character were shared by the other exile.

Warren of course devoted his energies to classical studies, especially in art and archaeology; it was into these or other branches of the academy that some of the best energies of many aesthetes went. A whole moral philosophy was implicit in classical studies. In the second volume of *A Defence of Uranian Love,* Warren wrote, "Now the Dorian blood, defending itself in hill-fortresses, among those stony heights which cover Greece with their severity and produced its hard health, that blood, martial by birth, breeding and necessity etc., found its last prophet in Pindar."[35] And in the third volume he says that to fortify ourselves we must turn back to Greece: not to Greek conduct, unless it be to the Spartans; not to Greek thought as developed in philosophy, but to "the common beliefs which preceded Pindar." This needs a conscious effort, because, "Whereas we live daily under the influence of some dilution of Christian feeling, the lesson of Greece has well-nigh perished."[36] The Greeks loved manly men, he tells us, not feminine ones. Danglers after the divine—one example is St. Augustine—make a sublime feminine cry out of their lives; a quote from Nietzsche follows.[37]

Thus both Sam and Ned Warren were preoccupied with the idea of heroism in this decade. Both wanted to make heroes possible again in their time. Sam wanted to be the friend of a great man—Brandeis; Ned wanted to imprint the idea of greatness on young male minds. But for Sam the possibilities of heroic action were determined by the conditions of nineteenth-century politics and statesmanship. For Ned they were embodied (and body was the word) in the ideal images of Homer's and Pindar's poetry and the sculpture of their place and time. That opposition, of the aesthetic idea of the masculine to the political one, was at the heart of the aesthetic movement.

Eighteen eighty-five saw the beginning of Warren's classical collecting and donating. He had decided that the Hellenic idea was unintelligible without art—meaning above all Greek sculpture, but also vases, coins, intaglios, and cameos. To ally the appreciation of such art to the study of classical literary texts was to be the work of the graduate college he planned to found at Oxford.

H. A. L. Fisher was an undergraduate at Warren's college, and in his autobiography describes meeting him.[38] Warren was Fisher's second American acquaintance, the first being James Russell Lowell. He describes Warren as being sturdily built, with a shy pale face and a retiring manner, and well read in the silver Latin poets.

Warren had found a site for his graduate college, opposite Magdalen College across the river, and had consulted Alfred Robinson, a New College academic statesman, about business tactics; but he was outbidden by a foundation that was to establish the Magdalen College School on the site. (According to Goddard, Ned's scheme was opposed by conservatives at Oxford, by landowners, and by the Warren family.) From other sources we gather that the work of Warren's college was intended to correct the "platonizing" bias of Greek literature and to give a franker idea of what Greek culture had been like—how virile it had been. Warren never gave up the project of replanting the Greek idea in Oxford, where it was so well suited to flourish.

Of course, if Warren had gone to Cambridge instead of Oxford, he would have found almost as much to suit his needs. The social world E. M. Forster knew at King's College would have welcomed Warren, as it did Santayana a little later. In fact, among the King's dons, Warren did come to know Oscar Browning (who is referred to as an old friend whom Warren saw in Rome in 1911) and Lowes Dickinson seems to have sent him friendly messages about his poetry. The ideas and tastes these men dealt in were aesthetic in the same sense. Indeed, Warren's friend and official biographer, Osbert Burdett, was one of that circle; in his biography of Dickinson, Forster cites Burdett. Perhaps Oxford was more central than Cambridge only to the decadent part of the aesthetic movement.

Whatever the reason, however, Santayana too spent his most impressionable time in England at Oxford. After Harvard he had gone to Germany to study, where he found that "what counted was

Greek ethics."[39] But from Germany, a place to study, he went to England, a country to fall in love with. He wanted to discover and understand "original or charming persons. And where were these more likely to be found than in England?"[40] This was Warren's and most American aesthetes' vision of England.

In a famous passage in *Character and Opinion in the United States*, Santayana says, "The luckless American who is born a conservative, or who is born to poetic subtlety, pious retreats, or gay passions, nevertheless has the categorical excellence of work, growth, enterprise, reform, and prosperity dinned into his ears: every door is open in this direction and shut in the other; so that he either folds up his heart and withers in a corner . . . or else he flies to Oxford."[41] This applies very well to Warren.

As we know, Santayana had met Frank Russell at Harvard, and he was an embodiment of this aristocrat's England. Orphaned early, he was the second Earl Russell, the older brother of the philosopher, and he lived according to an aristocratic code of free self-assertion. Santayana says that Russell "moved deliberately, gracefully, stealthily, like a tiger well-fed and with a broad margin of leisure for choosing his prey . . . he suggested a latent capacity to leap."[42] Santayana confessedly felt an irresistible attraction to Russell, even though he got into a lot of trouble through him. One of his professional problems at Harvard was that he had been mixed up in Russell's scandalous divorce suits—which were scandalous partly because he was accused of homosexuality.

Santayana spent the spring of 1887 in Oxford, where he met Lionel Johnson and other young men to whom Russell had referred him. In April he wrote, "I like a man to feel his worth, just as I like a man to feel his beauty, otherwise the splendour is taken out of both. . . . Nothing is more exhilarating than to see the fit man come to the front in full consciousness of his divine right to lead."[43] One feels there the affinity to Nietzsche, and the distance from Harvard moralism. In 1900, William James wrote to G. H. Palmer, Cornelia Warren's mentor, about Santayana's *Interpretations of Poetry and Religion:* "It is refreshing to see a representative of moribund Latinity rise up and administer such reproof to us barbarians in the hour of our triumph."[44]

Santayana refers to Russell on occasion as "a young god," and clearly he felt about him the way Warren felt about the violent Greek heroes—Achilles, for instance. The two Americans wanted Englishmen to be of a type complementary to themselves, to be gentlemen. They defined that idea in aristomilitary caste terms. "What is a gentleman?" Santayana asked. "A gentleman is a man with a valet; originally he also had a sword. . . . To be a complete gentleman, he should also have a horse."[45]

That is why there were so many horses in Ned Warren's establishment at Lewes. He himself kept falling off, but he had friends like Fothergill who rode bareback. Santayana had Russell, who flaunted his physical agility; he took Santayana boating on the Thames, and made him walk along a pole and fall off. Santayana saw England as a country of athletes, a country that had escaped the American scruple about appearing naked.[46]

Russell sent Santayana to Oxford to meet Johnson, and that meant seeing or hearing about Warren and Berenson. The Americans all knew each other; Berenson and Santayana had been at both Cambridge Latin School and Harvard together. Johnson wrote Santayana that Berenson had charmed Oxford for a term—he was too misanthropic but always adorable—and he, Johnson, would teach them both never to set foot again in Boston, "that Holy and self-satisfied city."[47] Boston was generally taken to be the opposite city to Rome—and to Oxford—those cities of the Renaissance.

Warren's parents, on their visit to Oxford in 1885, presumably did not know all that was going on, but they pressed him to return to Boston the following winter. He resisted his mother's arguments, but when his father said he needed him there, Ned gave in. He was, however, feeling critical of his mother. He described how his father, on that visit, "sat helplessly in his chair while Mamma and I shopped."[48] She told Ned, in his father's presence, "He finds it hard to make a decision, and used to find it so easy." Mr. Warren had been told by a doctor to rest but that there was nothing wrong with him. Yet when they went to the seaside resort of Folkestone, a doctor diagnosed a severe retention of urine. Ned reports all these things with the implication that his mother was at fault, and he reports that Henry said she left their father alone too much, and "I don't see how she can reconcile it with her conscience."[49]

Warren was unhappy in Boston, as we saw from his acid descriptions of 67 Mount Vernon Street, and from sentences like this, out of a February 1887 letter to Marshall: "Do you know, my Neo-paganism seems here like a dream of the past. [His happy years at Oxford had been like the life of ancient Greece.] . . . Here with cold winds and snow, the traditions of Puritanism, the ugliness of the men and the absence of aesthetic sympathy, all Greece is frozen out."[50]

Because of his bad eyes, Warren could read for only four and a half hours a day. He made a point of asking his father each morning what he could do for him; thus demonstrating that there had been no truth to the plea for help that had brought him to Boston, which he attributed to his mother.[51] Once back in England, he was reluctant to leave it. When Mr. Warren died in 1888, Ned refused to go home, alleging reasons of health, and when the family trust was set up the following year he signed the papers Sam sent him without asking any questions.

He had kept in touch with Berenson, as we saw, but—no doubt in part because Berenson was not homosexual—it was another man, also highly gifted as a connoisseur of art, with whom Warren was to make his main alliance in life.

John Marshall

Already, in 1884, at New College, Warren had met John Marshall, also an undergraduate there from 1881 to 1885. Marshall was witty, talkative, very clever, but also moody, capricious, and demanding to be amused.[52] After Marshall's death Warren said that he had always thought of Marshall as a faun, thoughtless and irresponsible, "innocent and forgetful. I am more consistent and aware of my actions"—and so to be judged more severely.[53] Surviving photographs of Marshall do not show him looking all that faunlike. But "the faun" is a well-known psychological or sexual identity: the merry, narcissistic, naughty youth who tempts the more responsible type into the bushes—or out of the closet. There are passages in Marshall's diaries and letters where one can see him playing that role; laughing to himself as he eludes Warren's anxious affection or possession. But this identity was the obverse of, the denial of, painful early experiences.

Ned Warren said that Marshall took his tragedy in his daily life and his comedy in literature; the second clause meaning that his taste as a reader was for Sterne, Falstaff, and Aristophanes. (J. D. Beazley, the archaeologist, another member of their group, cultivated a taste for Surtees and French farce.) The first clause referred to his family history. Marshall's parents were both pious (his father was a Liverpool wine merchant) and John went up to Oxford expecting to enter the church. While there he turned against both that vocation and its obvious substitute, the academic life; turning away when he discovered that his sexual preference was "abnormal."

Marshall's father was silently but profoundly angry at his son's change of vocation, and Marshall was wounded by that anger. Warren noted that *his* family ties were far from being that close, but one may doubt if he could have lived as he did later if his father had been alive.

Apparently reading Shakespeare's sonnets was an important step in Marshall's making these life choices—a step toward homosexuality and away from the church. At about the same time, Oscar Wilde too was proposing a homosexual reading of the sonnets. His "Portrait of Mr. W.H." appeared in 1889. Certain of those poems had for the young undergraduate Marshall a secret but unmistakable meaning. "For a long time I never dared mention those sonnets: those who knew them I thought would know my secret."[54]

There were of course also "respectable" texts that people like Warren and Marshall quoted to each other. One is a passage from Sir Alexander Grant's standard mid-Victorian edition of, and commentary on, *The Ethics of Aristotle,* which is cited more than once in Burdett and Goddard: "All here is broadly human, and yet the idea of Friendship is purely Greek. The Romans imitated it. But in modern times it has been much superseded by the idea of sympathetic marriage. Christianity ignores Friendship; and theoretically, it now exists only as a temporary advantage for the young."[55] To reinstate that idea of friendship in all its glory could sound like a blameless endeavor, but of course Warren and Marshall meant it to cover homosexuality too, which could not be publicly admitted.

Finding himself an outsider, Marshall for a time contemplated a life of reckless license and even crime (the "life of tragedy"). In an autobiographical sketch that he wrote at Warren's request, in 1889 or 1890 he speaks of "going to the dogs" and "stopping on the verge of the uttermost ruin."[56] At that time his life had been "horrible and sluggish," in a moral paralysis like that produced by drunkenness.[57] From this fate Warren rescued him with an offer of sexual friendship and cooperation in classical studies.

Marshall was in a situation like Wilde's when he was seduced by Lord Alfred Douglas, but in his case the seduction led him in the opposite direction, toward prudence, sobriety, and respectability. Part of the imaginative history of the aesthetic movement is the number of men who turned toward self-destruction: besides Wilde, Simeon Solomon, Lionel Johnson, Ernest Dowson. But these men belonged to the Decadence. Others, like Warren and Marshall, followed a different path, and they are also part of the movement's history. For instance, though somewhat differently, E. M. Forster and D. H. Lawrence found their own ways to avoid the disaster of decadence but still to become artists of the aesthetic movement.

Warren got to know both Marshall and the current object of the latter's affections when all three were undergraduates. He watched the last-named turn away from Marshall toward marriage, and then made his own offer, which was after long hesitation accepted. Only in 1889 did Marshall write him, "Now everything you say and do seems inseparable from you and from my love to you. That makes my judgment in the matter infallible."[58] Marshall made five drafts of his final letter of acceptance: "Dear Master: I like Master. I don't think Herbert loved it better, nor was his half so good. You have been my providence for a long while."[59] He was referring to the seventeenth-century poet George Herbert, who addressed God as Master in his poems.

Exactly what their sexual relations were cannot be said—certainly nothing like a chronological account can be given. It seems likely that other, younger men were soon more attractive to both of them. Yet it is clear that Warren also felt a great admiration and a long-lasting affection for Marshall—something beyond ordinary friend-ship—and that Marshall to some degree returned the feeling, allow-ing himself to be loved, and sometimes feeling irritated and cloyed and constrained by the situation.

Warren wrote their story down in the form of a novel, called *A Tale of Pausanian Love*, published in 1927. Its closeness to the facts is guaranteed by some of Marshall's papers now in the Ashmolean.

Pausanian Love

A Tale of Pausanian Love, according to Burdett and Goddard, largely written while in Naples in 1887, is strikingly like E. M. Forster's *Maurice* (also autobiographical) in its plot and setting. Warren's story is told in the first person by Claud Sinclair, a young man at Oxford, of partly foreign birth, whose father lives in Germany. (Sinclair's mother is dead, which is the novel's most significant departure from the facts of Warren's own case.) Marshall is called Byngham. One of the striking similarities between this story and Forster's is the small conspiracy between the hero and the other man's mother and sisters. For instance, Sinclair writes secretly about his friend's health to Mrs. Byngham and asks her not to mention his letters to her son.

The brilliant Alfred Byngham is like Sinclair in his intellectual tastes but unlike him in being a religious skeptic. He is the stronger mind and more reckless nature, and has gone to an English public school. Sinclair is self-doubtful and apt to believe in feelings that other people tell him they feel, or which they say *he* should feel. He is also—like Ned Warren—a fussy housekeeper who serves expensive Chinese tea in expensive porcelain and watches over his friends' health and happiness. (He nurses Byngham when he is sick, does his packing for him, watches his bedroom window to see what time he goes to sleep, and so on.)

They discuss Plato's *Symposium* and the theory of love there ascribed to the sophist Pausanias that there are two Aphrodites, of which the older is the daughter of Uranus and has no mother: She therefore symbolizes a love "of the male" in two senses, and a love not limited, as pederasty usually is, to an attraction to pretty boys. Byngham now scorns Plato as an idealist—that is, a self-deceiver— though "the Symposium was once my charter."[60]

The reader gradually gathers that Byngham is in love with Ralph Belthorpe, who is young, gay, ordinary, but very handsome. He looks like a moving bronze statue: "He never stood or stooped without the beauty of a plastic composition."[61] Sinclair too goes swimming with Ralph "for the beautiful sight of him," which repays him for all his earlier loneliness at Oxford. He makes a drawing of Belthorpe stripped, sitting on a chair arm, one foot on the seat and his elbow on that knee. Later Byngham declares that this drawing is better than Plato, better than Praxiteles, because firmer and harder. (Both Plato or Praxiteles, in their different ways, betray Greek virility by making it softer, sweeter, more ideal than it was.) Byngham and Sinclair want men to be heroes and agree that Shakespeare's sonnets are just as unsatisfactory as Plato's *Symposium* as renderings of manly beauty and the love it excites. Such a love "does not pass to the culture of strength, the beauty of the hero. We like heroes, we like strength. . . ." If we don't have heroes, our boy-love will remain merely soft and merely sentimental or sexual.[62]

The novel has no narrative tension, or indeed any other artistic merit, except in the climactic scene, which is ingeniously dramatic. Byngham, having renounced Belthorpe, is sadly holidaying with Sinclair when Belthorpe turns up "unexpectedly" (actually, with Sinclair's secret connivance). After they have eaten one of Sinclair's elegant meals together, Belthorpe goes up to bed, supposedly on the third floor, and is reminded to put his boots out to be cleaned. The other two stay up a while talking of different matters; they finally go upstairs, in the dark, to their rooms on the second floor, only to stumble over Belthorpe's boots. "Whose room?" Byngham asks, in desperate excitement; the reader of course knows that it is in Byngham's bed that the young Antinous is lying, but knows also that Sinclair is making this sacrificial gift to his friend. Byngham takes Sinclair's hand and puts it on his violently beating heart. The scene ends, and so does the first half of the novel, with Sinclair saying, "I passed into my room, as he opened the door into the darkness of his."[63]

The rest of the plot introduces Sinclair's dilemma: what he is to do with his own life if Byngham lives with Belthorpe, or indeed if he commits himself to self-destruction instead. If Alfred had chosen *him*, Sinclair would have felt that choice a direct call to live, with Byngham's help, the life of a hero.[64] Left alone, he would not have the strength to put into effect his great scheme to found a graduate college at Oxford or even to write his book about Greek love, a project that he had been able to conceive only when he saw that such a love was possible for him today. The climax of Part II echoes that of Part I, for it ends with a message from Byngham to Sinclair, as Belthorpe's wedding day approaches: "Come to me!" Sinclair's despair is, like Byngham's before, suddenly reversed into ecstasy.

The Cult of the Classics

The projects ascribed to the novel's two characters were in fact shared by Warren and Marshall. The graduate college was replaced by Lewes House, and the more extreme project of the two, *A Defence of Uranian Love*, was finally written by Warren. This was only a scandalous work in its day—to those who heard of it—and a forgotten one soon afterward. It certainly exerted no "influence," being far too eccentric. But to some degree the idea of Greek heroic virility, and of its rebirth in Edwardian England (the idea both projects served), inspired the whole generation to which Warren and Marshall belonged. At least R. M. Ogilvie, in *Latin and Greek,* says that about the period up to 1918. Take for instance the general preference in Edwardian England, which Warren shared, for Pindar and Homer, rather than for Plato and Thucydides. Pindar's principal surviving works, says Ogilvie, are "choral odes to be sung in honour of victories at the athletic festivals. . . . His themes are glory, beauty, nobility, freedom. . . . [He was] a Theban who lived through the great age of Greek success (c. 522–422 B.C.) and who was familiar with all the leading families and cities of the Greek world."[65] We see the likeness to Kipling and the Edwardian aristocracy.

The Victorians had concentrated on Plato and Thucydides, and it was left to the Edwardians to turn to Homer. Indeed, Ogilvie says, "the Edwardian age has all the marks of an heroic or Homeric age. . . ."[66] He is extending "Edwardian" to cover World War I and is thinking of the age of imperialism. "In Homer, the heroes owe their position to their prowess and they keep it only so long as they continue to display prowess. . . . Morality as such is practically absent from the *Odyssey* and the *Iliad.*"[67] Classically educated Englishmen then wrote about and appreciated each other in similar heroic language.

England, Ogilvie says, greeted Schliemann's excavation of Troy in 1877 much more enthusiastically than Germany or France did, because "The English wanted to believe that the Homeric scene was real."[68] Later, T. E. Lawrence took his copy of the *Odyssey* to every camp he was sent to. A whole generation (including its brilliant women, such as Margot Tennant and Diana Duff-Cooper) loved the Homeric qualities and tried to embody them. "The Great War was the fulfillment of the Homeric ideal. . . ."[69] Edwardian England welcomed war in 1914 in an ecstasy of self-fulfillment (see Rupert Brooke, Raymond Asquith, Siegfried Sassoon), because it extended them a rare invitation to acquire heroic stature. "For in Homer the hero was a warrior."[70]

But Warren's idea of Greece of course differed from this more generally popular one in the crucial matter of gender politics. That difference made his idea eccentric, and not to be openly welcomed as an ally by its more respectable cousins. But if one studies some of the men of letters among those cousins (Ogilvie discusses P. G. Wodehouse, John Buchan, and Dornford Yates at some length), they can make one feel that Warren was in fact speaking more frankly than they about a homoerotic motive that lies hidden below their surfaces.

Sam Warren and Louis Brandeis

To return to the other members of the family, the law firm of Warren and Brandeis went from strength to strength in this decade. Between 1879 and 1907, Brandeis made close to a million dollars, and he also earned a reputation as a lawyer and civic leader. For the first forty years of his life, the Felix Frankfurter book about him says, Brandeis was a successful lawyer and an idealistic leader, but in the later eighties he began to talk to labor leaders and to see labor issues from their point of view.

In 1884 he and Sam Warren both signed a declaration that appeared in the *Boston Advertiser* announcing the decision of independent Republicans to reject the Republican party ticket. The party had nominated James G. Blaine ("the Continental Liar from the State of Maine") and "Black Jack" Logan as its national candidates. The breakaways, who became known as Mugwumps after Charles A. Dana used that term, demanded good government and higher moral standards in politics.

Sam Warren declared himself an independent Democrat; he already belonged to the Massachusetts Civil Service Reform Association and the Massachusetts Reform Club. Both he and Brandeis belonged to the New England Free Trade Association, as did Fiske Warren (who entered S.D. Warren and Company employ in 1884). Blaine was objectionable to them as a protectionist as well as on the score of corruption. The Warren company suffered from high import tariffs, and Warren and Brandeis were of course the firm's lawyers. In 1886, Brandeis fought to have their raw materials exempted from certain duties, and in 1908 he again lobbied on their behalf in Washington on tariff matters.

Warren and Brandeis had no clients from the textile industry, which was the largest in the state and protectionist in sympathy. That industry was organized in large units; the average factory employed three hundred workers, three times the equivalent figure in shoemaking, which was the biggest industry that Warren and Brandeis *did* represent. This meant that they avoided connection with those employers likely to confront unions and to engage in the class war. (They represented merchants—Brandeis in particular often acted for Jewish merchants—and of course papermakers.) Their clients had liberal interests and tendencies.[71] In 1889, in a letter to his father, Brandeis praised the radical Henry George, later to be a hero to Fiske Warren, because he was a spokesman for free trade.

Their legal work therefore carried the excitement of progressive righteousness as well as that of profit. When Sam Warren withdrew from the law firm, at his father's request, it was with great regret, by the account of more than one friend. On February 7, 1889, Sam wrote Ned that he was going to get actively interested in S.D.

Warren and Company, but not to the entire exclusion of the law.[72]

Cornelia also began to move in liberal circles at this time, working on just the sort of causes Ned thought typical of woman-led Boston. (Fiske took up the further-left causes and ideas that were sometimes grouped together at that time as the New Life or the New Age.) Cornelia became one of the first trustees of the Boston Home for Incurables, in 1884; treasurer of the College Settlement Association, in 1892; and soon thereafter chairman of the Denison House Committee, in which Mr. and Mrs. Brandeis were much interested. Fiske Warren's father-in-law, Hamilton Osgood, was also on the Denison House Committee. The Osgoods belonged to another branch of the New Life, which experimented in Oriental philosophy and radical social and political ideas.

Brandeis, at this point, was a Progressive, not a radical, and came from a very conservative cultural position. He had arrived in Boston just early enough to be accepted in society, with Sam Warren's sponsorship—before anti-Semitic feelings were aroused. Brandeis was listed in the *Blue Book of Boston* of 1886 and *The Social Register* of 1891. But Warren's introduction of him to, for instance, Oliver Wendell Holmes did not develop into a friendship, and he was invited only once to the home of Henry Lee Higginson, a central Boston figure.[73] Though sponsored by Warren in the Dedham Polo Club, in 1887, and though he—like several Yankee aristocrats— bought a house in Dedham in 1900, he made no friends there.

In the background of these changes in Brandeis's social life (which helped move him from a Mugwump to a Progressive position) were changes in Boston society. The population of the city was 64 percent immigrant in 1880, 68 percent in 1890, 72 percent in 1900, and 74 percent in 1910.[74] Because the Irish had taken over the political machines, the Yankees closed ranks as a financial and social elite.[75] Brahmin fortunes were increasingly tied up in family trusts, run by blue-blooded lawyers and brokers. Lines of mutual hostility were drawn: The Immigration Restriction League was formed in 1894 and the Federation of Jewish Charities the following year.

Indeed, Brandeis's friendship with Sam Warren itself cooled after 1883, when Sam married. Brandeis was not among the hundred guests invited to the wedding, and Mabel Bayard Warren omitted him from her guest list whenever possible. She probably burned the letters from Brandeis to her husband, which were never found.[76]

Nevertheless, Sam continued to write warmly to Brandeis, supporting him in his advances toward a political career. In 1886, from England, he wrote that he himself could do nothing without Brandeis's equal, persevering, and courageous character to fall back on. "Certain it is that you without me would do better than I without you." The *personal* relationship, Alpheus Mason says, lasted till Sam's death.

When Brandeis became engaged to Alice Goldmark in September 1890, Sam's letter to her begins, "Louis's is one of the characters (I may say almost the only one) about which I generally keep silent for the unusual reason that I fear to appear fulsome in my praise of it. . . . What you do not know about him, you may trust to the future to develop with absolute confidence in the joy it will bring you.

"I know of no one else of whom I should feel like saying so much. I know of him in all ways except the one he is now about to enter with you, but I know that 'The bravest are the tenderest, the loving are the daring.' I know that his courage is high, his fidelity perfect, and his sense of honor delicate. . . .

"I sincerely trust that you may be in Boston before long, and that Mrs. Warren and I may have the *pleasure* of welcoming you to Boston, and to that important part of our lives which we have in common with Louis."[77]

In reply to a note from Brandeis of March 1891 announcing his wedding, Sam wrote, with some suggestion of reproach, "I thought of you on the 23rd and often since, and I got your short note. Life has become so full for you and for me too (too full I suggest) that it is only in these resting places that one has a chance to say any small part of what is constantly in mind. To you there can be but one message from me; and that by way of confirmation of what has gone before. I can think of nothing the years will change less than our friendship and my belief in you."[78]

In this period, therefore, both Sam and Ned found their life partners. Mabel Bayard was the daughter of the three-term senator from Delaware, Thomas Bayard (1828–98). He succeeded to his father's seat in the Senate in 1869; he became secretary of state in 1884 and was the first American ambassador to London in 1893. The family was Dutch but originally French. Senator Bayard was a leader of the new South, which fought back against the Republican reformers after the Civil War, and was more than once nearly nominated for the presidency by his party. Sam Warren worked in the senator's presidential campaigns.

He was therefore a prominent man, of distinguished family, and his daughters, especially Mabel, were Washington belles, admired by Henry James and Henry Adams, *inter alia*. Mabel Bayard attended private schools but not college; the same was true of Cornelia Warren, but whereas the latter remained a student all her life, the former seems to have adapted herself completely to social and family life. When Henry James visited Washington in 1882, Mr. and Mrs. Adams thought him socially promiscuous, but they approved of his getting to know the Bayards. He wrote his friend Isabella Stewart Gardner that the girls he met there, especially Mabel, were very charming; "with a désinvolture rather rare chez nous . . . happy specimens of the *finished* American girl—the American girl who has profited by the sort of social education that Washington gives." He described them to his mother as "Such as one ought to marry, if one were marrying."[79] In 1883 he declared he had sought her like in vain in the capitals of Europe.[80]

Sam and Mabel's wedding was held at the beginning of 1883 and Mrs. Adams wrote to a friend on January 14 that year, "I am told in confidence by a friend of the Warren family that Mrs. Warren is immensely elated at the Bayard connection."[81] Probably the curve of success of the Warrens reached its highest point then—or with the birth of the first of Sam's six children, in 1884—at least from Mrs. Warren's point of view. We can hear a similar exultation or arrogance in Sam's style at this time. He wrote to Ned in 1888, "Your letter on personal subjects is as clear as mud. Perhaps hereafter, say in some future life, you may have time and inclination to unbosom yourself to your affectionate brother."[82] Remarks of that kind he later paid for.

Mabel Bayard was a fashionable woman, and the new couple gave a number of entertainments at their home on Commonwealth Street. (They moved to 261 Marlborough Street later.) The newspapers are said to have reported these events, journalists insinuating themselves among the guests, dressed as waiters, and (allegedly, improbably) bringing cameras with them. The *Boston Evening Gazette* was held most to blame. Sam is said to have knocked the camera out of one man's hands; that is not very likely, but he felt an outrage that led him to his most significant contribution to the law.

Recent research by Lewis Paper and James Barron shows very little reporting of the Sam Warrens' social life. Almost the only thing is a note on the wedding breakfast they gave when his cousin Katherine Clarke got married. By Paper and Barron's accounts, it was rather the newspaper's mockery of Senator Bayard in 1889, as, for instance, "stolidly fatuous," that infuriated the Warrens.[83] In any case, Warren and Brandeis wrote an article for the *Harvard Law Review,* which appeared in December 1890, entitled "The Right to Privacy." (They had two other joint articles there, in December 1888 and April 1889, on an issue important to S.D. Warren and Company: factories' diversion of water for power purposes.) This was an important step in the development of this concept as a legal fact, and it was of course expressive of Warren's class and city at that time.

It is worth noting, for instance, that one of the sources they cite in their paper is a July 1890 essay in *Scribner's Magazine* by E. L. Godkin, the Mugwump editor of *The Nation.* And all five of the Warrens were at one in their resentment of intrusive publicity. The modern republication of the Warren and Brandeis paper edited by Morris Ernst describes it as "so splendidly conceived and executed that Dean Roscoe Pound was subsequently to say of it that it did nothing less than add a chapter to the law . . . it has imprinted all that followed with its brilliance, sensitiveness, and wisdom."[84] A very different attitude was taken by James H. Barron in a more recent article in the *Suffolk University Law Review.*[85] Barron thinks the authors' close affiliation with the Mugwumps distorted their view of the press-privacy issue.

Some of the earlier enthusiasm no doubt derived from the upper-class loyalties that many lawyers shared, and the elite sensibility that the paper defended. It was apparently Sam's idea; Brandeis seems to have been somewhat ambivalent about the issue. He told his fiancée, Alice Goldmark, that he would have preferred to write on the duty of publicity, not the right to privacy.[86] In April 1905 he wrote Warren that, as he remembered it, their inspiration was Warren's "deep-seated abhorrence of the invasions of social privacy." In the same year Warren unavailingly urged Brandeis to draft a statute protecting privacy for the Massachusetts General Court.[87] Barron speaks of the "hypersensitivity of the patrician lawyer-merchant."[88]

Sam and Mabel soon began to spend country weekends at Dedham. In 1887 he proposed to some twenty friends that they should play polo on a field there, a sport they had never before played and one associated with the English in India, with imperialism. It was to become Boston's elite-class sport. Four years later the Warrens bought an estate there, which they called Karlstein. They designed a polo field, a trotting track, and elaborate stables, and a social ritual was soon developed. A special train came out from Boston in mid-afternoon, the arrangements being made by Percival Lowell, the astronomer, and members were met at the depot by John Magee, who drove them to the clubhouse, where a steward had laid out their polo wear; they were then driven to the field. There were as many as forty to sixty ponies, led in strings by grooms.

The members were scions of well-known families: Cabots and Lowells and Maynards, Elliots, Cushings, Goodwins, and Welds. Sam was captain of the polo team and ranking back. They played as many as fourteen chukkas in an afternoon, on occasion against Harvard University. On Sunday mornings there were "larks": Men and women galloped over the countryside and then consumed huge lunches. Also there were escapades, in which Sam Warren often played a part. One of which had Warren and Percival Lowell in a midnight polo competition with mallets and a ball through the center of Dedham, to the residents' annoyance.

New Year's Eve was celebrated with some suggestions of naughtiness—a steeplechase on all fours, and a neat-ankled maiden leaping rows of candles at midnight. Predictably, there were comic poems about, for instance, Sam Warren's heavy drinking and wild bridge playing.[89]

The details all suggest the boisterousness of English country-house weekends mixed with hints of officers'-mess horseplay. Rudyard Kipling watched the Dedham club play while he was staying with the Stimsons and wrote what is said to be the best short story about polo, which he sent to his hosts to be checked for technical accuracy.

Besides Karlstein, Mr. and Mrs. Sam Warren had a house on the south shore, at Mattapoisett, like the financier Allan Forbes. According to one report, Mr. and Mrs. Fiske Warren had a house there too. Since they also had a house in Harvard, we get a sense of how their class was spreading its property wider and wider around Boston. The Sam Warrens' house at Mattapoisett was called Bohemia Manor; when one adds Fiske's Tahanto and Ned's Fewacres and Cornelia's Cedar Hill, one gets a sense of the Warrens as proprietors on the same scale as the Forsytes in contemporary London. A good deal of their money was invested in real estate. They were rentiers as much as industrialists.

Sam also built an L-shaped wharf on his Ned's Point property at Mattapoisett, and between 1888 and 1903 eight boats were listed by the boat club there as his property. Sam enjoyed manly sports, including hunting (in New Brunswick and North Carolina), and the social life surrounding them. "In this intimate circle Warren lost the shyness and diffidence which sometimes stood between him and the world at large, and became a boy among boys."[90] He loved the sea and the woods, and the free life of a sailor and woodsman.[91] When he died, his guide in New Brunswick and his Negro Stephen in North Carolina, who cared for his dogs there, were among his sincerest mourners.[92]

In some of these matters Ned was oddly enough quite like his brothers. He was hypersensitive in resenting intrusions on his privacy, and hated newspapers and reporters; he also approved—for others, but also for himself—of manly sports, and covering the hills with horse and hound. But there was a crucial difference, and the Yankee businessman-sportsman idea that Sam embodied was Ned's detestation. Intentionally, his collecting of antiquities was done in opposition to, for instance, the Dedham polo club. He once described his motives for collecting as "rebellion against Sam and against all to whom I had objected from youth, the worldly wisdom which was inconsistent with love and enthusiasm."[93] Again, "I have always said and believed that it was hate of Boston that made me work for Boston. . . . The collection was my plea against that in Boston which contradicted my (pagan) love."[94] He gave things to American museums not so much for the few who would love them, he said, as *against* the many who would not.

Cornelia

Cornelia Warren, meanwhile, had made friends with a group of women at Wellesley College (founded 1875). This may have happened through George Herbert or Alice Freeman Palmer, since Cornelia's particular friend in the group was Katharine Coman (1857–1915), who had followed Alice Freeman there from the University of Michigan. The group included Vida Scudder (1861–1954), Katherine Lee Bates (1859–1929), and Emily Greene Balch (1867–1961). Coman came to Wellesley to teach rhetoric, but in 1900 organized its Department of Economics. She wrote an *Industrial History of the United States,* published in 1905. She and Cornelia organized a working girls' club, called the Thursday Evening Club. (It was still in existence thirty years later.) Balch wrote about immigrants (for instance, *Our Slavic Fellow Citizens,* 1910) and her work for peace was rewarded with a Nobel prize. Scudder, who taught in the English

Department, introduced a course there entitled "Social Ideals in English Literature," which became famous, and she was, with Balch, a resident at Denison House. These women were all social radicals; though they went farther left than President Freeman, they were supported by and supportive of her.

Alice Freeman was born in 1855, so she was just two years older than Cornelia. Born into a much poorer family, she went to the University of Michigan, 1872–76, and came to Wellesley to teach history in 1879. She was immediately recognized as presidential material, even by founder Henry Durant, whom she challenged in certain ways. The college's most recent historian, Professor Patricia Palmieri, says she was a charismatic leader, in the strictest sense, with a feminine kind of charisma.[95] She became president in 1882 and transformed the place from a boarding school into a college. It was part of her charisma to be lovable as well as formidable, and lovable in conventionally feminine ways; so there was no incongruity in her becoming engaged to Palmer in 1887, though there was grief at her resigning the presidency when she got married.

This occurred after prolonged negotiations, for many people at the college did not want to lose her, and she did not want to lose the college. Nor did she: According to Palmieri, she continued to be, behind the scenes, effectively president of Wellesley until she died in 1902. And Mr. Palmer was her able assistant. Just how close the contact was between the newly married pair and the Warrens we don't know, but it was at least symbolically important that the Palmer wedding took place at 65 Mount Vernon Street, next door to where Cornelia lived, and that they lived at 11 Quincy Street, Cambridge, next door to where Henry lived. (President Eliot was also next door.) In 1892, when *Miss Wilton* was published, Cornelia's mind and imagination were, by all the literary signs, completely under the Palmer influence. And the Freeman-Palmer reform of Wellesley was a story that must have commanded her imaginative as well as her literal participation.

Wellesley stood for many things. Its founder, Henry Durant (1822–81), was a successful lawyer who had lost both his children. He was a romantic rebel against much in nineteenth-century culture—against business and the law and the city, in the name of poetry and nature and community. By the same token, he thought women morally superior to men and capable of purifying American culture. One of the women who inspired him was his childhood teacher, Mrs. Sarah Ripley, Emerson's aunt. Durant changed his name as an adult, taking two names from his mother's side of the family. His ideas about women's education were liberal in their intellectual and curricular aspect, and he appointed an exclusively feminine professoriate and administration—the only one in the country.

Mr. Durant had secured a charter for a female seminary at Wellesley in 1870. The name was altered to College in 1873, the first students arrived in 1875, and the right to confer degrees was granted in 1877. Mr. Durant, as long as he lived, kept what G. H. Palmer calls an almost despotic control over the college; requiring the girls to do some domestic work, to observe a daily quiet time, and to suffer his queries about the state of their souls. He would accost one on the grounds and ask if she were saved. G. H. Palmer spoke of the "Moodie-McKenzie" atmosphere—Moodie being the famous evangelist, and McKenzie a Cambridge minister on the board of trustees.

Alice Freeman, however, though a pious woman, had very different ideas and told Durant that to ask such questions was "an assault on the individual."[96] And since she inherited and, as her husband admits, "in her own way maintained" the founder's despotic power, she was able to change the college quite quickly and drastically after his death in 1881.[97]

Using the help of other graduates of the University of Michigan, and getting rid of many older faculty, she made the college aim at meeting the educational standards of men's colleges like Harvard. Another of the ways she accomplished this feat was by nominating as trustees reliable friends (or friends of her husband) like Cornelia Warren. In January 1887 we find G. H. Palmer recommending to her for that purpose both Cornelia and another person, as women of large experience and excellent judgment, who would not be "caught with religious chaff"; they were very devout, but they could see that lack of intelligence is no fit companion to piety.[98] To use Palmer's term, it was a de-moralization of women's education they were about, and a de-sacralization of puritanism. It was an important movement, especially for women, in which Cornelia was involved.

Alice Freeman Palmer and Cornelia Warren were not politically radical. They were not even suffragists. The former seems to have wanted the college simply to be a good college by academic standards; the latter was in some ways quite conservative—admiring her father's kind of social benevolence, above all. But they were both ready to support those on the Wellesley faculty, like Coman and

Scudder, who wanted to combine academic study with social work. One might legitimately object to calling their settlement house work "radical," but it was on the left wing of the options open to academics at that time.

In the late 1880s these women, with others from the Eastern women's colleges, all of them under thirty, founded a College Settlement Association. They were inspired by similar efforts in England; the word "settlement" seems to have been first used in this sense by Canon Barnet in an address at Oxford in 1883—an address that led to the founding of Toynbee Hall in London, the pioneer settlement house.

The part of Boston they wanted to reclaim was the South End, the population of which was estimated at the time to be about forty thousand. Tyler Street, where the Wellesley women settled, was in the South Cove; the houses were of brick, three or four stories high, built not long before for well-to-do families but adapted since as tenements—roughly or even "grotesquely" adapted. That is the word used by Robert Woods, a settlement house worker, in his book *The City Wilderness.*[99] This was Boston's equivalent of Greenwich Village in New York, though in Boston the Italian immigrants settled largely in the North End—and there was no artists' colony. In Howells's novel, the South End was where Silas Lapham lived before he moved to Beacon Street. The streets had been built for Yankee families, but by the 1890s, 6,700 of the South End's population were Irish-born, and 2,700 were Jewish, according to Woods. With the mass of the better-off Yankees having moved out, and social and economic conditions having deteriorated, the sensitive avant-garde, like Cornelia Warren's friends, moved in.

Vida Scudder heard Ruskin give some of his last, socially radical lectures in Oxford in 1884, and they made her realize her "plethora of privilege." (Ned Warren was in Oxford that year too, but his prime loyalty went to Pater.) She read Tolstoy's radical essays and developed a cult of St. Francis of Assisi. In 1889 she joined W. P. D. Bliss's Society of Christian Socialists and his Brotherhood of the Carpenter. When she wrote her *Socialism and Character,* she said, "The point of view of the book is that of a Socialist—a class-conscious, revolutionary Socialist, if you want—to whom nonetheless the spiritual harvest, the fruits of character, are the only fruits worth noting in any economic order."[100]

The book's dedication was written on a Tuscan hillside "sanctified by the Passion of St. Francis," and her socialism was Franciscan rather than Marxist. The others were not as religious as Scudder, and Cornelia was never so High Church, but several of them like Scudder joined an Episcopal monastic order of the Holy Cross. The men were called Fathers or Brothers; the women, Companions of the Holy Cross.

They felt some alternation of attraction to first the contemplative and then the socially active modes of the religious life, but at the end of the eighties, Scudder says, the social hope revived. In February 1889 the first appeal went out for a College Settlement Association; that same year a Settlement House was opened on Rivington Street in New York, which was followed immediately by Hull House in Chicago. In 1892 such houses opened in Philadelphia and Boston. The last, called Denison House after an English pioneer social worker, was made possible by Cornelia Warren's generosity with both her money and her efforts. The story of Denison House will form part of the next chapter, but we may note here that Cornelia was thirty-five when she began this boldest of her ventures; as Sam was thirty-five, Henry was thirty-four, and Ned was thirty when they began the Dedham Polo Club, Beck House, and Lewes House, respectively—all around the year 1890.

5

New Enterprises and Establishments

1890–1900

He is a hunchback and a cripple, an enthusiast who has gone over to Rome and built a Benedictine Monastery at Salem in his old family orchard. . . . His grotesque, pasty features looked larger than human, and his head preternaturally broad, with its sad pop eyes and dishevelled hair; and he seemed fiercely ready to defend his poor body with those long monkey-like arms and bent legs, like some wounded colossal spider . . . all this headlong prosperity and activity will one day—perhaps very soon—collapse at a word, like the walls of Jericho; nor is any great blast necessary, mere time and mutation and inner loosening will do, by which dust is forever returning to the dust. Against that day of trouble and light I have established my monastery. . . .

—George Santayana,
The Last Puritan

Lewes House

In 1890, Ned finally found and bought the house he wanted to live in and to make the seed cell of his Uranian creed and cause. He wrote to Marshall on October 22, 1899, that he'd seen a huge and old house in Lewes in Sussex, near Brighton. It had three or four rooms that were sunny, and a goodly number that were at least large; old mulberry trees round a quiet lawn; a large kitchen garden;

a paddock; a greenhouse; and stables ad lib. Close to the town, and visible from the lawn of Lewes House, were the South Downs, and visible from there, green woody country and the sea. This was to be both his Fenway Court and his anti-Christian monastery. He was thirty years old.

In a book about D. H. Lawrence and his friends, John Carswell says that in the New Age, the period between Marx and Freud, England was a post-Christian Thebaid, with small groups of spiritual "seekers" to be found gathered in every town. Ned and Lewes House would probably have repudiated any connection drawn between it and the New Age—that was more Fiske's kind of thing—but in fact it can and should be seen in that perspective. This was an aesthetes' form of the New Life.

One of Ned's protégés, Harold Woodbury Parsons, adds some picturesque details, in a description of 1967.[1] He says that the house was, at the back, a perfect Queen Anne structure; the garden walls had vines and wonderful figs; from the Downs, where the young men rode every day, they could see the English Channel glisten like a silver shield.

Warren leased the house in April 1890 for £150 a year, later renewed the lease for ten years, and finally bought the property in March 1913 for £3,750 (after his death it was sold for twice that amount). Following a marked pattern in Warren's purchases, the house turned out to be both an extravagance and a profitable investment. He employed several servants, whose wages cost him £300 a year, and who seem to have been very faithful to him. He treated them in feudal style, keeping their wages fixed, but giving each one £200 and a piece of antique silver when he or she had been with him twenty-one years, leaving them money in his will, and no doubt helping them in their emergencies.[2] It was not unlike the way his father had treated the workers of Westbrook, but with archaizing touches like the antique silver. It seems to have worked well at Lewes.

This was the sort of house literary people wanted at that time. Henry James just a little later (1897) bought a not dissimilar Georgian house in nearby Rye. By an odd coincidence, James was assisted in finding his home by another E. P. Warren, the architect Edward Prioleau Warren, which has led some scholars to think there was a friendship between Ned and Henry James (who did of course know Sam and Mabel—indeed, he *knew* Ned). But the only reference to James seems to be a disparaging comment Ned made in 1892 about *The Portrait of a Lady,* calling it a large American canvas, weak in color. Ned thought the all-too-American idea of "a lady" had constricted the novelist's imagination.

There was an atmosphere of secrecy, an anxiety about security, concerning many things at Lewes House. Part of this had to do with the provenance of the antiquities and secret negotiations about them. Part had to do with the denizens of the house, of whom nearly everyone had some scheme for which he hoped to get Ned's backing and about which he wanted to keep the others in the dark. The silver had to be counted at night; at least Ned says Marshall got tired of doing that—perhaps a metaphorical expression.[3] His private key hung around Ned's neck; if it was mislaid it had to be restored to him as soon as found. There was also a tin trunk known as "the will-box," in which the ever-changing disposition of his estate was written down. The constant, partly playful anxiety, the atmosphere of conspiracy, the keeping of his keys, and the changing of his will, characterize one side of Ned's temperament.

In the main house were the Business Room, the Red Drawing Room, the Dining Room, and the Hepplewhite Bedroom, plus several less imposing apartments. The Dining Room had a big Tudor oak table; John Fothergill (one of the young men) said he bought this for Ned from George Justice, the Lewes antique dealer, for only £25. After Ned's death it was sold for £2,100.[4]

George Justice was one of the people of Lewes whose life was changed by Warren's arrival in the town. Formerly a jobbing carpenter, he became an employee of the Warren estate and a prosperous antique dealer. Another local firm that became largely attached to Lewes House was Bridgmans, the marble masons.

The young men sat around the Tudor table on pew benches bought from a church in Ormskirk. Over the table hung a brass chandelier, dated 1748, for fourteen candles; there were rattail forks and spoons, and Capo da Monte dessert dishes. One photograph shows a desk on which stands a statue of a naked youth, so placed that, working at the desk, you sat in the shade of his proudly rounded buttocks. Bronze vases stood on ten-foot-high pavonazzetto columns on either side of the fireplace, and for a time the Filippino Lippi tondo faced a Titian landscape drawing. At one time a very fine Cranach of bright red apples and a deer with wonderful antlers hung there; Parsons said he bought it for Ned in Cassel in 1906. (It too was a bargain, and later sold for much more than it cost.)

The house's only modern features, according to Parsons again, were a Steinway piano and a Dolmetsch clavichord. Ned played Bach, Mozart, Handel, and Haydn beautifully, as did his "delightful and handsome boy-friend, Harry Thomas, who was also an excellent horseman." There were studies and bedrooms for eight, and three Arabian stallions in the stables.

Most of these young men worked on the collecting, cleaning, reassembling, describing, photographing, insuring, and sending of Warren's antiquities. But they were distinct from the dealers and craftsmen from London who came to work there. (And on at least one occasion, three Greeks were brought over from Paris to work on marble.) The friends were not all, perhaps none of them were, ardent Uranians in Warren's sense. But they were homosexual or bisexual, and simply by virtue of their work at Lewes House, they were agents in Ned's enterprise.

They were quite various and came on various terms. Richard Fisher, Marshall's friend from before Warren knew him, who joined them in 1891, had some money and sometimes helped in the collecting. He was gentle and ineffectual, according to Burdett, but ran the stable and the household staff. G. V. Harding, who had been a solicitor, came in 1894; he took a contractual promise from Ned that he would be looked after financially till either his father or his mother died. Matthew Prichard, who had been a barrister and had some property, had a promise that Warren would give him a year's notice if he wanted to change their arrangement—that is, send Prichard away.

This last had been a member of Oscar Wilde's circle. In a collection of Lord Alfred Douglas's poems, printed in Paris in 1896, there is one dedicated to Prichard, datelined Capri, 1895.[5] According to Boston rumor, Prichard had been "picked up" by Warren in Rome, having had to leave England because of the Wilde scandal.[6]

Prichard cut a picturesque figure in Lewes. He had taught himself Arabic or Persian, answered when spoken to in this foreign language, and wore a fez in the street. He also taught the local lads to swim and photographed them while doing so; none of the Lewes House group wore swimsuits. (The bath and bathroom in the house was large enough for the men to bathe together, and this was apparently their practice.)

Prichard was very thorough and precise; he kept a register of the coins in the collection and studied chemistry to learn how to clean the vases. But he was also a philosopher and mystic; Mrs. Gardner referred to him, in 1906, as "the mysterious and mystic Prichard."

We have called Lewes House a pagan monastery. Burdett and Goddard describe it as being like the court of a small German princedom: designed on a comical smallness of scale, and remote from the larger world. (They liked the idea of "small kingdoms"; as the very opposite of large republics, like the United States.) The daily news was little read and less discussed.

There is no record that even the trial and imprisonment of Oscar Wilde were talked about at Lewes House, which must be a sign of the excessive discretion of the biographers. It is impossible to suppose that that household could have ignored such a major event in the history of the aesthetic movement and of the homosexual community. Of Warren's close friends, Fothergill, Prichard, and Ross were seeing Wilde immediately before and after his imprisonment. But it is possible that another event of 1895 had seemed more *their* kind of history: the publication of A. E. Housman's *Shropshire Lad.* Burdett says that in his *Beardsley Period* some of Housman has an antique beauty, like "a piece of Greek sculpture unexpectedly found in some uncrowded corner of a country house."[7] Burdett felt very strongly the charm of the Lewes House idyll (Goddard was more interested in Warren's ideas), and this phrasing hints at a connection he saw between it and Housman. He also says, "The most manful sight in the world to him [Housman] is that of a Greek statue."[8] The cult of Housman's verse, which was very widespread, was an ally to the Lewes House cult of Greek art; we hear of the young J. D. Beazley, later to be the great authority on Greek vases, translating Housman into Latin elegiacs at Oxford a decade or so later.

Most things in the house and on the estate were supposed to be common property, and the power to initiate events (for instance, to invite guests to dinner) was supposed to belong to all. Warren liked to be surprised by some guest or activity that one of the others had arranged. No doubt they observed the limits of his tolerance carefully.

Nevertheless, we hear of social and nervous strains. Marshall was irritable, and Warren himself is said to have found it hard to be cheerful during the first years. Both of them suffered from bad health; Fothergill says Warren suffered from neurasthenia and bad digestion; Marshall was thought to have heart trouble and also digestion problems. Both went to German watering places for cures.

Fothergill tells us that six men lived there in his time, which was between 1898 and 1910. Each had his own horse, dog, and study.

They went riding on the Downs, and some of them hunted with the local pack. No woman entered the house except as a servant, and the town was quite mystified by the establishment—or so the establishment complacently supposed. Few of them could ride safely, so it seems that the horses represented an aspiration or a theory. It was, according to Fothergill, a local industry in Lewes to catch and return strayed Lewes House horses, at 2/6 a time.

Fothergill himself, however, mounted without a stirrup and could ride bareback, even standing. Not all of Warren's protégés were scholars; some were athletes, others could be called playboys; some, like Fothergill, combined elements of all three. The house was a college, a place of dignity, but of course there was naughtiness too. One guest was bade farewell with the message, "We shall miss you from the bathroom"—because of their bathing together in the nude. And there was a considerable collection of obscene art, which was given to the Boston Museum in 1908.

On the whole, the furnishing style was plain but grand. There was never a tablecloth on the Tudor table or a cushion on the pew benches, and the house had few curtains or carpets. Beside the horses, there were St. Bernard dogs, fox terriers, and a boarhound. Surtees was a favorite author. And Warren and Marshall saw the English country squire as a comic cousin of the Greek hero. This is the side of their sensibility that links them with Kipling (in stories of his like "My Son's Wife" or "An Habitation Enforced").

Parsons says the regime was monastic in its quietness and regularity, like that of I Tatti, Bernard Berenson's villa outside Florence, another aesthete establishment. Ned took a great interest in his friends' health, and prescribed diets, exercises, rest periods, and so on. There was a brief siesta after lunch and then a gallop on the Downs. After dinner everyone retired to his room to read, unless there were guests. Neither Warren nor Marshall cared about society (in that way being unlike Berenson). Fothergill confirms that "After dinner we retired, rather relieved, each to himself, or singly to talk to Ned."[9] This reminds us that Ned was the center—after all, he owned the house and everything in it. But also he had chosen the others; they had not chosen each other. (Marshall, for instance, seems to have rather disliked several of the younger men.)

William Rothenstein, an artist and friend of Fothergill's, talks about Lewes House in his autobiography, *Men and Memories*. He says it was "a monkish establishment, where women were not welcomed. But Warren, who believed that scholars should live nobly, kept an ample table and a well-stocked wine-cellar. . . . There was much mystery about the provenance of the treasures at Lewes House. This secrecy seemed to permeate the rooms and corridors, to exhaust the air of the house. The social relations, too, were often strained, and Fothergill longed for a franker, for a less cloistered life."[10] Fothergill says, "I myself, out of nervous inhibition caused by this monastic-scholastic life and high living, practised all sorts of tricks of horsemanship."[11]

Fothergill gives us several vivid anecdotes, though they don't sound entirely trustworthy. "At about ten o'clock Ned's trousers were beginning to slip down over his neat little paunch as he talked and walked to and fro, which was a sign that he was soon off to bed, whatever or wherever the discussion, and by the time he had slithered across the polished landing and into his room they had fallen altogether."[12] The Lewes House maid allegedly complained of the violence he did to his buttons, wrenching his clothes off. (But other witnesses do not mention what surely must have been a striking eccentricity.)

John Fothergill (1876–1957) is rather an important witness to Lewes House. In *My Three Inns,* he says that his "amicological tree" (his series and sequence of friends, his equivalent for a genealogical tree) grew out of Robert Ross; its two main branches being the Rothenstein brothers and "E. P. Warren and twelve years of Greek archaeological study and surroundings." To this tree he can trace all his "chief relationships and interests."[13]

His great friend and patron, therefore, who determined his course in life, he said, was this Ross, a close friend of Oscar Wilde. (Robert Baldwin Ross, 1869–1918, was the grandson of a prime minister of Upper Canada and the son of an attorney general, but he early scandalized his family by openly asserting his homosexuality.) According to Richard Ellmann, in his biography of Oscar Wilde, it was Ross who seduced Wilde, so beginning his career of active homosexuality, in 1886. He also helped Wilde write his Shakespeare theory, "Mr. W. H.," and was the literary executor who published the collected works of Wilde in 1908. He was one of those most faithful to Wilde after his disgrace and regularly wore a big green scarab ring that had belonged to Wilde. After he died, Ross's ashes were buried with those of his friend.

Wilde addressed him, in verse, as "O heart of hearts! O friend of friends!," and that phrase was generally taken up about Ross. "Friendship" has a special pathos among homosexuals of course.

Burdett speaks very highly of Ross in his autobiography, *Memory and Imagination* (1935), and Fothergill names Ross as the one person outside the Lewes House set with whom Warren corresponded regularly. He seems to have visited Lewes House in the summers, and perhaps they also met in Italy, where Ross stayed with Reggie Turner and others of the Wilde circle, who lived in voluntary exile like so many English people whose lives had been touched by scandal.

This is especially interesting because we have an account of those friends in Florence from D. H. Lawrence, and a major novelist's account is always worth having. In *Aaron's Rod* (published in 1922) Lawrence describes James Argyle (Norman Douglas), Algy Constable (Reggie Turner, a close friend of Ross), tiny Louis Mee, and Walter Rosen. Spiteful and amusing, the last three snap and rattle at each other, teased by the more virile Argyle; and the themes of the conversation are ideas that engaged Lawrence as much as Lewes House—the idea, for instance, that in the modern world sexual desire begins with the woman, not the man, of a couple.[14]

Norman Douglas was an embodiment of the bold manliness Lewes House cultivated, and he also associated that manliness with ancient Greece and modern Italy—and with homosexuality—in the same way. His theme in this conversation in *Aaron's Rod* is that there is too much chastity in the world. Lawrence talks of his "wicked whimsicality . . . he must have been very handsome in his day, with his natural dignity, and his clean-shaven strong square face. But now his face was all red and softened and inflamed, his eyes had gone small and wicked under his bushy grey brows. Still he had a presence."[15]

Even more interesting, perhaps, is Lawrence's other account of Douglas and his friends in his "Introduction to *Memoirs of the Foreign Legion*." The author of these memoirs was a religio-aesthete named Maurice Magnus, and Lawrence describes the relations between him and Douglas in ways that would apply well to Warren and Marshall. Douglas was "decidedly shabby and a gentleman, with his wicked red face and tufted eyebrows."[16] Magnus, on the other hand, was very polite, anxious, and "knowledgeable"; an American, like Warren, he "knew all the short cuts of Florence. Afterwards I found that he knew all the short cuts in all the big towns of Europe."[17] He was also, like Warren, very secretive, and was always locking things up. He was "a great epicure, and knew how things should be cooked."[18] He "was like a little pontiff in a blue kimono-shaped dressing gown, with a broad [sash] of reddish purple. . . . So he minced about, in demi-toilette. . . . A very elegant little prayer book lay by his bed—and a life of St. Benedict."[19]

Magnus was a rabid woman-hater, but he had a "curious delicacy and tenderness and wistfulness" about his men friends.[20] He looked after Douglas, the way Warren looked after Marshall and others. "So it always was, Magnus indulged Douglas, and spoilt him in every way. And of course Douglas wasn't grateful. Au contraire!"[21] Fussy is Douglas's scornful word for him. Magnus was unhappy in the modern world and always on the point of entering a Benedictine monastery, but he never did and never would, Lawrence says. He had found his life in *friendships*, a word on which he lays a special emphasis. And he is always acid against women, "Not because of their sins, but because of their virtues," says Lawrence, "their economies, their philanthropies, their spiritualities."[22] All this is strikingly like Warren and Lewes House. (Magnus's life, however, ended in suicide; in Warren's case, the other man, his enemy, died; Warren was tougher.)

Fothergill wrote a series of semi-autobiographical books in the thirties and early forties that throw an interesting light on his own psychology, and so on at least one of the types that gathered around Warren. He never mentions his father, and his anecdotes of school are unhappy. He had met Reggie Turner and Robbie Ross when he was nineteen, and they presented him to Wilde. He was a student of art at the Slade School and attended the London School of Architecture. Wilde grew fond of him, and Fothergill was one of those to be given an inscribed copy of "The Ballad of Reading Gaol," when Wilde emerged from prison.

In *An Innkeeper's Diary*, Fothergill tells us, "Fifteen years ago I was the best-looking and worst-mannered gentleman in London."[23] His bad manners seem to have been largely a matter of a complacent but ill-regulated aggressiveness. He was a more self-doubtful Norman Douglas. "I started life with fear as my only companion. I don't know why or how he came, but fear has brought about my jealousy, harshness, lovelessness, violence, self-consciousness. My youthful affectation was 'No time for love and no sympathy.' "[24] Describing a quarrel he was involved in at Lewes, "I felt elated, I felt like a God for strength and the righteousness of my cause . . . [the other man was] wondering whether this young man was a god or whether he, Goliath, had suddenly met his David."[25] Afterward Fothergill felt correspondingly ashamed.

It seems clear that these swings of mood were in some loose sense neurotic, and made him need soothing counsel and reassurance, which Ned gave to him as he gave them to Marshall and several other habitués of the house. Fothergill had some problems with the concept of manhood: "I don't like calling myself a man, there's something child offending, corrupt, hairy about a man."[26] His love for children and for beauty stood in opposition to "manhood."

Harold Woodbury Parsons, the connoisseur-aesthete, by his own account grew up in Boston, living with an indulgent grandfather on Commonwealth Avenue. His uncle John Woodbury was a Harvard friend of Sam and Fiske Warren, and he invited Ned to dinner to ask his advice about Harold's desire to go abroad to study art. Ned having given his approval, Parsons went to Cassel and then Dresden for a year, and then joined Lewes House. In a 1906 letter to the president of Corpus asking for a place for Parsons there, Warren described him shrewdly as witty and quick, but not accurate; and as "like an Englishman." Parsons's description of Warren was also fond but sharp-edged: He said Warren took little interest in art outside his classical specialty, except for the medieval cathedrals.[27] He also said Warren did not have Berenson's curiosity about aesthetic theory, or politics, or remote places and civilizations. While Warren tried to get Parsons to study Greek at Oxford, the latter, like Berenson, preferred to travel and look at paintings.

Parsons suffered from Marshall's scorn, as we shall see, and of this heterogeneous group, the principal person, in Warren's eyes and heart, was John Marshall. Fothergill tells us that Warren composed an epigraph for himself in the form, "Here lies Edward Perry Warren, friend to John Marshall . . . the finest judge of Greek and Roman antiquities . . ." with the date of Marshall's death, and not his own, inscribed.[28] J. D. Beazley says that Warren always spoke of Marshall (over generously) as in a class much superior to himself as an archaeologist. The relationship was intellectually and emotionally unequal. But there was some reciprocity, as well as this one-sided adoration. Each called the other Puppy, and in their later years, according to Burdett and Goddard, they came to resemble each other, looking like twin Punchinellos walking arm in arm together.

It was understood between them from the first that together they would, as part of their life's work, write the essay already described on the Greek idea. They also planned to write a homoerotic interpretation of Shakespeare's sonnets, like Wilde's, and indeed of some of Shakespeare's plays. (The appeal of this idea is obvious; if the aesthetes could annex Shakespeare, they might establish a vantage point overlooking all of English high culture.)

One such interpretation we know was of *As You Like It;* it is rehearsed in the form of a dialogue in a book of essays by Osbert Burdett, *The Art of Living.* De Guerin, who represents Ned Warren, explains that Rosalind/Ganymede, as played in Shakespeare's time, was not a girl pretending to be a boy, but a boy pretending to be a girl pretending to be a boy; so that the title's meaning is that the audience can choose to think of Orlando's lovemaking as aimed at seducing a girl, or a boy, as they like it. (The stress of this theory falls on literary indeterminacy as much as on sexual "perversity.") In his preface to the book Burdett says he included the dialogue in tribute to the great old scholar whose whim the theory was—that is, Warren. And modern theory, in the age of Roland Barthes, has taught us that "whim" is not simply a modest and recessive term. Whim can now be taken to be at the heart of all assertion.

Burdett wrote a partial autobiography that gives an interesting account of his relations with his father, a man in public office whom he refers to always as "the great man." He describes accompanying his father on a visit of inspection to a huge Manchester hospital— this was after he himself had graduated from Cambridge—but he was soon exhausted by the tour while his father strode on tirelessly. Mr. Burdett had perfect health and perfect self-confidence, while the son was funny-looking and feeble. (The image is more German than English: Mr. Burdett was a Teutonic paterfamilias, and his son wilts in the heat he emits.) The great man was as deep in chest as his son was wide.[29] "He really had the shoulders of an Atlas, while the only muscles of his youngest son were tailor-made," says the youngest son.[30] The latter's only defense against this formidable father was verbal impudence and flippancy.

It will be seen that an unsatisfactory relation with their fathers troubled many of the Lewes House men. I have mentioned the moral and emotional wound John Marshall received, and Warren's own case, and Fisher is said, in Burdett and Goddard, to have had his spirit broken permanently by his father's alternate petting and scolding.

We know nothing so striking about Prichard's relations with his parents, but his expressed attitudes toward women were equally characteristic of the group, though in a different way. "Men act; women are actresses. Man should approach woman as a king a servant, etc."[31] This sort of epigram must have been very acceptable to Warren and to the whole of Lewes House as we know it.

This did not mean that Prichard did not like brilliant and powerful women; he much admired the actual Mrs. Gardner and the legendary Jeanne d'Arc. His misogyny was perhaps primarily philosophical and historical. He seems to have drawn on the same German sources as D. H. Lawrence, like Nietzsche and Bachofen. He associated Woman with matter and the queen bee, and with the home, the hive. While Man he associated with creativity, with the honey made in the hive. Marriage seemed to him—as to Lewes House in general—a second-best option for the creative personality.[32]

Home and marriage were the slogans of the enemy. Burdett describes his home as typically Victorian—as if he had been born thirty years earlier than he actually was. Unhappy at school at Marlborough, he found happiness among the dandies and aesthetes of King's College, Cambridge, where, as he says, the nonsense knocked out of him at school was insinuated back in.[33] And from the homosexual groups there he made his way to Ross and the Wildeans, and then to Lewes House.

Though Burdett steers clear of professing homosexuality (and is therefore less interesting than Warren) he clearly belongs in the same camp. He is misogynistic; in his view, apparently gifted women always reflect or echo some man's energy or brains, and he associates the rise of women to power with America. "The moment man sacrificed his precedence, modern America was possible; America, the worst corruption, immorality, and vanity of which would contaminate a sty."[34] America means puritanism. In The Art of Living, "Thoughts on the Corset" looks back nostalgically to Elizabethan times, when virile men dressed to emphasize their hips and swell their chests. (Santayana plays with the same idea of masculine display in the opening of The Last Puritan.) Burdett had been a student at Cambridge from 1903 to 1907, and thus forms one of the links between Warren's group and the world of E. M. Forster—the latter being the novelist Warren should have read, the writer who could express all of Warren's best perceptions and velleities.

Aesthetes, Connoisseurs, Collectors

One of the reasons we should associate Warren with Lawrence and Forster rather than with the Decadents is that they were influenced by German rather than French thought. It is aestheticism as embodied in Nietzsche and Wagner that we find in these Englishmen and Americans, not the aestheticism of Baudelaire or Huysmans. It was Nietzsche above all who taught his readers to take the world as an aesthetic rather than a moral experience. And he was of course a professor of Greek, and theorist of the Greek idea. We should think of Shaw, classifying Nietzsche with Rembrandt and Mozart as three great artists.

E. M. Forster's novels of 1900 to 1910 are full of Nietzschean and Wagnerian ideas. To anticipate a little, we might say that the novel of 1910, *Howard's End,* tells of a conflict between two claims to set the values of English culture, acted out between the masculine businessman and the spokeswoman for art and ideas; a conflict like that which came to a climax for the Warrens in that year. Forster's Mr. Wilcox embodies an idea of the masculine (and the businessman) like Mr. Warren's; the internal strains in the Wilcox family are like those in the Warrens'; and the contrast between Mr. Wilcox and his son Charles is rather like that between Mr. Warren and Sam. Forster's embodiment of the feminine, as an opposite and finally triumphant force, in the Schlegel sisters of course finds no equivalent in Lewes House. But if Forster had written his *own* story, about the defeat of businessman masculinity at the hands of a nervous homosexual aesthete, it might have sounded quite like Ned's.

Lytton Strachey used to call Forster the *taupe,* the mole, because "he was drab-coloured and unobtrusive, and came up in odd places and unobtrusive circles. There was something flitting and discontinuous about him; one minute you were talking with him intimately, the next he had withdrawn or simply disappeared. He was freakish and demure, yet at times could be earnestly direct, as if vast issues hung upon simple truth-telling. And all the time there was something hapless or silly-simple about him. . . ."[35]

In all this there is much to remind us of Warren, including the ambiguity of his personality. "Was he [Forster] conventional or unconventional, mature or immature? He could laugh at his uncle's attempts to make a man of him. He played the bright little girl to his mother."[36] And Forster's own description of Gide in 1951—Gide is from this point of view a rather similar figure—applies well both to himself and to Warren. "Wavering, yielding, tempted, flustered, Gide nevertheless slipped through the meshes [of Paul Claudel's religious arguments] and continued his undulating course upstream.

Il se sauva."[37] Forster surely thinks of himself there—or at least allows us to.

Warren is to be understood partly by placing him in the brotherhood of such types, many of them connoisseurs. They were not all of the same temperament in, for instance, sexual practice, but in large cultural issues they were always on the same side. At just about this time one of Warren's earliest protégés, Bernard Berenson, was beginning his career as a connoisseur of Italian paintings—by his own account, inventing that career and that role. In a Bergamo cafe in May 1890, he says, he told his friend Enrico Costa, "You see, Enrico, nobody before us has dedicated his entire activity, his entire life, to connoisseurship." Morelli and Cavalcaselle, his precursors, were only part-time connoisseurs. "Others have taken to it as a relief from politics . . . others still because they were museum officials, still others because they were teaching art history. We are the first to have no idea before us, no ambition, no expectation, no thought of reward."[38] The reader perhaps remains skeptical about the "no ambition," but cannot doubt the writer's conviction that something new was happening. Berenson made a verb of the noun: He and his wife spoke of "conoshing" together.

This something was very close to the enterprise Warren was also beginning. In July of that same year, 1890, he wrote to the Boston Museum about a find of Berenson's, a letter that Berenson's biographer, Meryle Secrest, interprets as an attempt to win his friend a position as the museum's agent. Berenson had bought for him a 1561 Bronzino in Venice, which Warren had sent straight on to the M.F.A. to avoid paying customs, saying he was willing to take it back if they didn't want it.

Warren and Marshall began their collecting on a grand scale in May 1892 at the van Branteghem sale in Paris, where they bought Greek vases. Marshall went on from Paris to Italy, looking at, among other things, Count Tyskiewicz's collection of vases, glass, gems, and small bronzes. In 1894 they established a permanent base in Rome, in an apartment occupied mostly by Marshall. By that year Warren was overdrawn by $77,000 and had spent $40,000 of his capital. (In one year he spent $20,000 on three statues.) The family was much disturbed, and the following year he went to Boston to negotiate with them, which meant primarily with Sam. He was accompanied by Marshall; this was the latter's first visit to America.

The Warrens (seen here at their most Forsyte-like) thought Ned was throwing his money away—they thought of him as constitutionally imprudent and impractical—and were even more upset when he spoke of turning his hobby into a limited company. Several of *them* collected works of art and gave things to museums (especially the Boston Museum), but they did not think antique dealing could be called a reliable or respectable business. (In the Senate hearings on Brandeis in 1916, Sam's attorney, McClennen, said that Sam "did not believe very much in the antiquity business, and Ned Warren maintained that there was money in it, and I think has since maintained that he proved his superior judgment to Sam's in the outcome."[39]) Indeed, they failed to recognize Ned's shrewdness and Marshall's expertise. The two were to have a joint career as dealers that was very successful, even when judged by financial criteria. And in the course of being scolded by Sam, Ned's fraternal resentments seem to have been exacerbated.

His true brothers were his fellow connoisseurs. In 1894, Berenson dedicated his *Lorenzo Lotto* to Ned and hoped his friend would persuade Mrs. Gardner to help buy a Crivelli pietà for the museum; when she wouldn't, the Warren family put up the money, and Marshall made the deal in 1900.

This was the moment when Mrs. Gardner and Mrs. Warren were in competition. In 1896, Lord Darnley let it be known that he would sell Titian's *Rape of Europa* for $100,000. Berenson offered it to Mrs. Warren and then to Mrs. Gardner.[40]

On January 9, 1896, Ned wrote to his brother Henry how much he enjoyed this work: "As we get behind the scenes, and into the intrigues—for the antiquity business is full of intrigues—we have something to laugh at every day. We learn the polite evasive answer—the wily silence. . . . It is so entertaining that if we were dealing in pig-iron, instead of in beautiful things, the work would still be enjoyable. . . . Matt Prichard is a most excellent helper. He spots what is going on in other people's minds. . . . In point of taste and judgment, experience and Johnny are educating me. More book-learning I need."[41] This last is a concession to Henry's urging him to read more, but Ned goes on, in self-defense, to describe a man he knows, who though learned in art history has yet no eye for the art object.

Ned makes the distinction between collector and connoisseur in a letter to the director of the new Cleveland Art Museum, who had written to ask him to buy classical antiquities for them. The director thought he could probably raise a few thousand dollars for a shipment to arrive by November, when the building opened. Harold Woodbury Parsons had approached that museum, offering his services, but the director had consulted Edward Robinson in New York and Arthur Fairbanks in Boston, and they doubted whether he had "sufficient experience and judgment."[42]

Warren replied on April 21 to say he was too busy to do such work himself, and that "A collector is a connoisseur, not an archaeologist. He needs an archaeologist at times . . . he needs sometimes an expert in coins . . . but in the majority of cases he can decide for himself. His province is genuineness, beauty, and market value. His qualifications are alertness and dexterity in the handling of men and a quick eye. Ten thousand francs could easily be lost in a bargain by an archaeologist or an expert who was not quick to estimate an object and to judge people."[43] He himself would never have become a collector if he had been submitted to "all Museum tests" when he began. Warren clearly felt he was training young men like Parsons for such "active work"; something related to market values and to entrepreneurial skills; something pretty close to adventure when compared to the contemplative life of a museum curator.

How close is suggested by a report in the Marshall papers at the Ashmolean Museum; a report by Marshall dated 1908 of how he has been shadowed, and then cross-questioned, by detectives in Rome. He was under suspicion of buying something on someone else's behalf, though the actual detectives thought he was under suspicion of being an anarchist. "Mr. M."—presumably J. P. Morgan—was somehow involved.

And most of the connoisseurs were involved in that side of collecting—in various frauds and illegalities by which the works of art were discovered and acquired.[44] Ned had mixed feelings about this. Fothergill tells of him, after six months abroad, "intriguing for and buying antiquities for Boston,"[45] looking out of a train window in England and saying, "What a blessed sight, a man going across a field without intent to do harm."[46]

He was not at all ambivalent about another immoralist intent put into effect through this work: the subversion of sexual "normality" in America. His collection of erotica, for instance, was intended to break down puritan inhibitions and hypocrisy. But that was not of course for public exhibition. More immediately and subtly, his provision of sculptured and painted nude figures to American museums was intended to make male art lovers look at their own and their friends' bodies with a new appreciation. "The Museum," he said later, "was truly a paederastic evangel. It must be counted a result of love."[47]

He said this sort of thing not only in private to his friends, but, with some discretion in the phrasing, to museum directors. Thus at the very beginning of his work for the M.F.A., he wrote to the director, Martin Brimmer: "Art springs so directly from the life of man as it is that I have always had my doubts whether it was consistent with the moral aspirations which we of New England inherit. . . . All systems of morals which ignore the possible richness of man's life are fragile [so he wants to] store up in the Museum objects which may lead to a reconsideration of very intricate problems now currently regarded as settled."[48]

From early on, Warren's collecting was threatened by the museum's plans to build itself a new and larger home. This scheme was a concomitant of the rising prestige of art and a triumph for the aesthetic movement, in appearance. It could, however, also be an occasion for the philistine bourgeois types (the Soames Forsytes) to co-opt art and deprive it of its full being and its subversive effect; and from Ned Warren's point of view the new building turned out to be an occasion for Sam Warren to be the leader in doing so.

One of the issues was how the money available for art should be spent. Already in 1898, Edward Robinson, the director of classical antiquities, had told Ned that talk of a much larger building was in the air; and in 1899 it was touch and go whether there would be any appropriation for obtaining objects.[49] Ned said they could build later, that they should buy now, while he had the market at his command (the great museums of London, Paris, and Berlin being quiescent). Moreover, he had sunk a fortune in his purchases already.

The Family

He proposed various schemes of finance to the museum, several involving the Warrens as a family. In 1894 he suggested that the Warren family provide £1,000 a year for five years, and that the museum promise to match that, with which Ned could make purchases. On July 28, 1895, he convened a meeting of the family at Cedar Hill to set forth a new scheme before sailing back to England on August 3. On January 9, 1896, he wrote Henry how hard, and yet necessary, was the task of proselytizing Boston for art. "But what a vast amount of individual effort is necessary to make the Boston Museum without help from taxation rank with the Boston Public Library as a library? At present it is something as a Sunday school is to a real school."[50] And yet America particularly needs museums. (Public libraries, as we know, no longer aroused enthusiasm.)

He was not surprised by his siblings' lack of response. "I did not expect the family to show less posthumosity than the Museum." (This is the same letter.) He knew that they did not respond to his plea for three reasons: first, because of Ned's conduct and letters while ill (Sam's visit to Lewes could not have been worse-timed, he said); second, because the Warren family's view of life was centered on the Warren family—as distinct from public service; and third, above all, "the radical indifference of all members of the family, except Mamma, to art."

On May 14, 1897, Sam wrote Ned that Mrs. Warren was offering him a loan of $25,000, in five installments, six months apart—this to save him from the consequences of his extravagance. Ned had said he didn't want to die rich, and "all danger of this calamity is being fast removed." But Ned had to realize that the family was necessarily involved in everything he did; if he was ruined, the family would have to rescue him or suffer the mental anguish of not doing so.[51]

In 1892, Cornelia and Mrs. Warren had stayed at Lewes House over three weeks, and Cornelia sent Henry an account of the visit calculated to reassure everyone. She described the six fox terriers, the St. Bernard, the boarhound, and the horses. Ned had taken good care of her and her mother, and had exchanged visits with the local parson, whom they had met at tea. With surely a conscious primness, she added, "Ned is very fortunate in his friend, Mr. Marshall. They suit each other very well."[52] Almost palpably she had other thoughts she did not express, and later visits were not to go so well.

In 1894 the Warren family sent over two deputations, or at least made two visits—one by Cornelia and her mother, and one, slightly earlier, by Sam and Mabel (whose father was then the American ambassador in London). Ned simply panicked and ran away, protesting that he was too ill to see them. He went to London as soon as his mother arrived there and said that he had to go to Bad Kissingen posthaste, to take the waters. She and Cornelia went to stay at Lewes House, but he left the day after they arrived. Cornelia wrote to Henry, "He has suffered since Sam's arrival from loss of sleep at night and consequent nervousness by day. . . . It is apparently the mental effect of the neighborhood of his family."[53] Sam did not believe in Ned's illness (neither did Cornelia) and went to talk to Ned's doctor.

It is worth reflecting on the whole phenomenon of Ned's illness, because it was so intimately connected with his family relationships. In a letter dated July 21, 1897, Ned promised to have his doctor in London, Dr. Althaus, send a full account of his health to Sam's doctor, Dr. Cabot, in Boston. The document was preserved among Sam's papers. Althaus had treated Ned since 1891, and his word for Ned's problems was neurasthenia, which covered what we might now call, loosely, "nervous" troubles, plus physical symptoms affecting his urine, with recurrent kidney stones and bleeding from the bladder.[54] Ned himself told both Sam and Henry that what he feared was Bright's disease. There was no sign of it as yet, but he had to avoid worry, excitement, and insomnia.

Hysteria was one of the medical concepts invoked. He told Henry, "I feel all right—am never hysterical, have no neck aches. . . ."[55] But he had had severe stomachaches for the past two years, for which he took castor oil or mustard plasters, and he had to wash his bladder out with a catheter every second day.[56]

He later reckoned he had been ill, on and off, from 1885 to 1902, and had cured himself by various regimens of diet, rest, waters, and so on. Fothergill says (probably echoing Ned) that he had had many years of neurasthenia and irritability, but pulled through to a sort of Buddhist calm.[57] Fothergill associates this neurasthenia with the fierce intensity and awkward adventures of the collecting, and probably Ned would not have denied that connection, but it was in fact family anxieties and above all Sam he usually cited. Writing to Cornelia on July 30, 1911, he blames his kidney stones on the anxieties he had suffered since 1907, apropos the suit.[58] We must suppose, then, that Ned felt himself assailed, poisoned in his own body, by his brother, and that he consequently armed and armored himself in his own defense to feel no guilt or weakness, physical or emotional.

In 1894, Ned had found lodgings for his brother and sister-in-law in or near to Lewes. He then tried to get Sam to come stay at Lewes House, leaving Mabel free to be with her father in London. It is not at all surprising that Ned and the imperious Mabel did not get on; he wrote Marshall that meeting her would show him how American women took up room enough for two men without doing the work of one. (Marshall did indeed see Mabel as a dominant wife—"you feel she has not arrived, and Sam is looking after the luggage"—and Sam as "a fine, strong and tender man, unhelped, and with too much on his shoulders.")[59] But what sympathy could Ned have hoped to evoke in Sam for the life of Lewes House? One can only guess that he saw Sam as an oppressed husband, and more generally as a man oppressed by the conventional masculine roles, and therefore as susceptible, despite himself, to the attractions of the Lewes House enterprise.

Sam told Marshall, about Mabel, "You'll find that the only way to prove to a woman that a thing is impossible is to let her try it."[60] Obviously the remark was commonplacely jocular, and it may well be that Sam's feelings were so too, but there is some evidence that Sam was seen by others as generally a case for masculine sympathy, or mockery. He looked like a man under stress, in the sex war and in other ways. In *Uranian Love,* Ned says we always laugh at "The harmless, necessary husband," and Sam seems to have been a prime example of the manliness Ned mocked and resented; the culturally defined, wife-deferring manliness, given all the outer trappings of leadership, but morally impotent—essentially emasculated—leaving the important decisions to women.

In their discussions, Sam again urged economy, showing the low opinion he had of Ned's practical abilities, and the latter admitted that he was in a muddle financially. (Presumably his methods changed later, or else methodicalness proved not to be necessary.) Yet despite Sam's warnings, he was in fact just taking on two new "secretaries," Harding and Prichard.

Marshall had been sent to London to parley with the family envoys. He found Cornelia skeptical about Ned's illness and quite ignorant about the antiquities that absorbed the two of them. Mrs. Warren said she was sorry Ned was ill, but she had come a long way, and if her son wanted to see her again, he had better make a trip to America. (Marshall quite admired her.) Cornelia said that if he couldn't stand his family's company even on a visit, his medical treatment wasn't having the desired effect. But she admitted that she now understood his classical enthusiasm better than she had. Apparently, during his years at Oxford she had seriously thought him crazy. She and Sam agreed that he had always "had too much done for him." But she allowed—or perhaps accused—that he was "not fit to marry." (Ned, being in Paris with her and their mother in 1898, wrote to Marshall that "Women don't have much strength of imagination or delicacy of divination.")[61]

People did think that Ned was crazy—or perhaps more often used that word about him. His Harvard friend, Perrin, for a time did so; Mrs. Gardner and Brandeis used the word semi-seriously in 1910.

The idea seems to have been inspired by a set of bodily mannerisms as much as by mental behavior. For once, Burdett and Goddard serve us well; they describe his "short but well-shapen legs" whose toddling gait added an incongruous feminine touch to his bodily movement, his square and heavy fingers, and above all his prominent eyes that would start rolling or staring at any interruption or surprise.[62]

To this we can add something more behavioral. Berenson wrote to Mrs. Gardner in November 1897 that he had bumped into Ned, in Fiesole, and that he looked quite gray. "He would not tell me where he was going from here. He even dodged telling me where he was staying. He remembers you with terror as a person who had tried to get some secret out of him."[63] Mrs. Gardner, a powerful woman, probably incorporated all that Warren disliked, but the crucial points are the evasiveness and the terror. He was a deeply frightened man but also one always on the attack, forever thinking up new schemes, as his brother was to find out.

Of course the family tried to put the best face on things, even among themselves. In January 1898, Mrs. Warren wrote to Henry that they had just had a charming visit from Ned in Monte Carlo. She was proud of him—he had "won his spurs," which seems to mean that he had become a figure of reliable authority. She suggested that Henry could get some good advice from Ned about the alterations he was contemplating for his house.

But Ned felt a constant pressure of distrust; the family doubted his "wisdom," his projects, and his common sense; "that will never pass from Sam's mind."[64] He got no support, and so "Ned is left alone to carry on the most important undertaking (save the business) going in the family." (We should note his desire to involve the whole family.) But he is not going to give it up.

The Boston Fine Arts Scene

The undertaking he would not renounce was the establishment and empowerment of the world of art in Boston. But he met of course some formidable rivals, including his brother, his friend Prichard, and Mrs. Gardner. This last emerged in this decade as an important figure in, or on the edge of, the Warren story. She and her husband had been involved in the founding of the Museum of Fine Arts from the beginning, and her husband was treasurer of the museum when he died in 1898. In the 1890s, Mrs. Gardner had begun seriously collecting herself, or at least for her own purposes, and built her own museum, Fenway Court, to house her pieces. In 1891 she inherited $1.75 million (her fortune was thus of the same order of magnitude as the Warrens'), and in 1892 she returned from Venice with two Whistlers and a Rossetti, but also five old masters, including Vermeer's *Concert*. On her next trip, in 1894, she had Berenson's help, and thereafter he was her main adviser. (Like Sam's link to Brandeis, Ned's to Berenson was gradually superseded.) Over the next ten years, 1894–1904, roughly the years of Ned's buying for the museum, Mrs. Gardner purchased some fifty old masters; the basis of her collection. In 1898, the year of her husband's death, she began to build. She and Ned were similar collectors in certain ways: in their turning away from contemporary art, and away from what we would call modernism, and in their putting together a variety of art objects to make an environment. Lewes House was never on the same scale as Fenway Court, but at its best it must have invited a comparison. It is clear that there was rivalry between the two.

It is also clear that each was jealous of his or her autonomy and fearful of cooperating with the other as an encroachment on that. But on the whole it seems that it was Ned who made the advances and Mrs. Gardner who did the snubbing. A key figure standing between them was Berenson, also nervous about *his* autonomy and eager to keep on good terms with both.

At first there was some hope of cooperation, through Berenson. This is expressed in Ned's early letters to his friend; in June 1899 there is talk of whether Ned or Mrs. Gardner shall try to help "Bindo" (a young Italian) with his problems. On June 15, 1900, Ned might take over her "work" if she fails (this work seems to involve the procuring of Renaissance pictures for the museum). Later he proposed that she might take over *his* work.[65]

On November 1, 1901, she is to buy two brocade hangings from him, through Berenson, for £700 each. On December 29 of that year, Ned was in Boston and called on her to intercede on Berenson's behalf, because, it seems, Berenson had offended her.

Soon thereafter began the long tale of the Filippino Lippi, which ended by ruining all possible good relations between the two collectors. Even in December 1901, Ned was sure Mrs. Gardner didn't like him, but at that point he thought they might be able to do business, through Berenson. Indeed, in March 1902 he broached the idea that he himself might sever all connections with Boston and asked if she would then take over the collecting of classical antiquities "on my own terms." He said he was going to ask her that himself.

Berenson was working closely with Mrs. Gardner. He had found his direction in life sometime before. When he read the *Italian Pictures* of Giovanni Morelli, given him by Jean Paul Richter, a collector based in Florence, he saw how to make connoisseurship a profitable as well as a rigorous branch of knowledge. But she was never to invite him even to Fenway Court.

Having absorbed Morelli's books, Berenson made himself known to the author and won his confidence. From 1890 on he traveled through Italy, looking at paintings, armed with Morelli's lists and at first funded by Ned Warren and Charles Loeser. Ned always consulted Berenson about Renaissance art purchases, and Berenson charged him only 2½ percent of the price. He came, however, to work with Mrs. Gardner much more than with Ned; indeed, neither Berenson nor Mrs. Gardner, but his brother Sam, was to be Ned's main counterplayer.

Sam Warren had become a trustee of the Boston Museum in 1891, and the post was to bring him into "professional" contact and conflict with Ned. It was to be an issue, which of the two—which type of man, the frock-coated trustee or the aesthete in country tweeds—was to represent art to Boston. The appointment was part of the pattern of Sam's career: In 1896 he became trustee of the Massachusetts General Hospital. But the Warrens were above all a museum family; it was on that institution, more than any other, that they focused their energies—their *group* energies. Given Ned's proclivities this made sense; it even offered hope for family cooperation, though it also increased the occasions for family fights.

Matt Prichard, who came to know and admire Sam in the next decade, said he had no knowledge of museums or developed feelings about art when first appointed. "These subjects were foreign to him. But he had vitality. Life made a demand upon him and he arose and responded to it."[66] (This apotheosis of "Life" reminds us that Prichard had read Nietzsche and Bergson, and had gone farther down the path of vitalist ethics than the other members of Lewes House.) Marshall too had reported favorably on Sam after their meeting in 1894. In the long run, however, he could not be on Sam's side. He and Ned saw Sam as the man in the frock coat, the uniform of the managerial class.

Ned began to act for the museum, buying and evaluating on its behalf; and he tried to involve his family. In his way Ned as much as Sam aspired to be an elder of the Warren clan. Despite the siblings' need to diverge and separate from each other, they also wanted to act as a unit. Perhaps Ned wanted to imitate and challenge Sam's leadership in particular, but perhaps he was only, like Sam, taking up a vocation they had both inherited. Mr. and Mrs. Warren had both bulked larger than mere individuals, and if Sam was continuing their father's work, Ned was continuing their mother's. He saw the Warren art collection as being as much a family enterprise as the family firm was. But so, it seems, did the others, however philistine they were in his eyes. They were a museum family.

We have already mentioned the draft proposal (it is not clear that it was acted on) that the Warren family should jointly provide £1,000 a year for such buying, and the museum should match it. Whatever Ned bought that the institution disapproved, he would keep for himself. In the fall of 1894, Edward Robinson (the curator of classical antiquities) came to visit him in England and wrote back to Martin Brimmer (the director) on September 15 that Ned had developed greatly during the previous three years. Since Ned found that "the chances of getting these [sculptures]—I mean even original Greek works—is by no means so remote as we have hitherto supposed, he now proposes to devote all his energies to securing these, taking vases by the way as he finds them."[67] He needed to count on strong financial support.

Robinson went to work at the museum in 1885, became its first curator of classical antiquities in 1887, and stayed there nearly twenty years. He and Sam were friendly at first, but found themselves involved on opposite sides in the so-called Battle of the Casts, an argument over the museum's stocking of plaster casts versus the buying of original works of sculpture.[68] This was a battle that took place everywhere. Kevin Herbert says it was the work of a very few, between 1890 and 1930, "to make American museums repositories of original antiquities."[69]

Robinson was on the side of the casts. He had prepared the museum's Catalogue of Casts and later helped the Metropolitan Museum in New York to make its collection. He did, however, hope to have some originals, and substantial bequests began to come in during the 1890s; in 1894 the trustees began to use money from unrestricted funds to buy original works of art.[70] Thus the balance of power shifted in that direction.

In 1895, Ned went to Boston with various projects. One of them was for the museum to buy the Ludovisi Collection from the

Ludovisi estate in Rome. Many problems developed with this scheme and finally all that the museum acquired was the Boston Throne, marble panels that were displayed at Lewes House before they came to Boston in 1898.

Another of the museum's famous acquisitions was the Chios Head, which Warren bought for himself in 1900 and sold to the institution in 1910. Altogether, his gifts and purchases amounted to 90 percent of its classical antiquities. In 1925, Beazley says, the museum had 134 sculptures, of which 108 were acquired through Warren, and 96 of those between 1894 and 1905.

During their 1895 visit to Boston, Warren and Marshall went to stay with Charles Eliot Norton at his summer home and won his approval. This was very important because of Norton's general prestige in Boston as well as because of his position as teacher of fine arts at Harvard. Ned wrote, using Norton's characteristic language—which had, after all, long been familiar to him—"We are doing the work most needed of all works, supplying eventually the terrible gap that exists on this new continent, the absence of that which delights the eye and rests the soul."[71]

Cornelia

Meanwhile, Cornelia Warren's work was done in the realm of education and social relief, which had been Norton's sphere before he specialized in art and aesthetics. She especially promoted women's groups and institutions. Aside from her thirteen years as a trustee of Wellesley College, she also worked for Bradford Academy and the International Institute for Girls in Spain. (Bradford Academy was the oldest private girls' school in the United States, brought back from decay by the efforts of Alice Freeman Palmer.) Both Cornelia and Mrs. Warren gave them financial support. Cornelia also made gifts to schools situated as far apart as Tuskegee, Alabama, and Roberts College, Constantinople. She also provided picnics and drama festivals for the children of Waltham at Cedar Hill, and did church and hospital work. It was also now that Mrs. Warren, in advanced years, came to rely more heavily on her daughter.

Cornelia did engage in one large enterprise that could be called more playful, or more egotistic, and so comparable with those of her brothers: She built a famous maze at Cedar Hill.

This can be seen as a kind of art, a kind of toy or game on a large scale, and one that carried the values of taste and historical interest.

But in this period Cornelia in fact also wrote a work of literary art; her novel, *Miss Wilton,* was published in 1892. It has two separable plot lines, one of which, to do with the Willcoxes, has already been discussed. The other, to do with Lilla Wilton, might remind us of Edith Wharton's *House of Mirth* as much as the Willcox story reminds us of *Middlemarch.* (In fact, Wharton's story is *very* close, in certain ways.) To put it another way, this part of Cornelia Warren's novel is halfway between *Daniel Deronda* and *The House of Mirth* in theme and treatment as in date.

It is perhaps characteristic of the Warrens as a group that the way *Miss Wilton* differs from those other two books in theme is that the heroine's sin is more exclusively financial. The first thing we see her do is leave a hotel in Vienna without paying her bill, and later she borrows at excessive interest and fails to keep her accounts—the novelist gives us the precise sums and rates of interest. But Lilla is also, like her sister heroines, sexually (i.e., socially) bold and indiscreet and, when humbled, is ready to serve the poor in penitence.

Miss Wilton's ideas are in some ways radical. Christianity manifests itself above all as social radicalism, though there are some references to the value of suffering and to the writings of Madame Swetchine. (Sophie Swetchine, 1782–1857, wrote about religion, and the relations between Eastern and Western Christian churches, in letters and a journal that were published in the 1860s. Cornelia Warren's citation of her suggests that she was influenced by the Companions of the Holy Cross.)

Arnold Robertson, the man she is later to marry, tells Lilla of "the conditions of life among those whom the Bible chooses to consider our brothers and sisters. If one follows this clue but a very little way, it makes most of the interests of our lives shadowy and unreal, not to say heartless. True love shares much the same fate. Just think of it;—human researches, human attainments, human skill, have become the interests of a class, while humanity itself lies helpless under the wheels of the industrial Juggernaut car . . . [philanthropists] follow meekly this car with oil and wine for the mutilated victims. . . . It occurs to but few to change the industrial machine itself into something that does not send the able-bodied by slow steps into our almshouses and hospitals. . . ."[72] He says that our aestheticism and our Americanism both have to be quickened by our Christianity.[73]

This is the main thrust of the book, its main idea. But it is notable that contrary points of view also get sharp and clear expression. Of someone who lives a life of service to the poor, we are told, "She gets all their troubles, and they none of her pleasures. . . . If I were starving ever so much, I'd be glad to have somebody have a good time. . . . You must deal with realities, Arnold. They are always cheerful. . . . The world is not yet so abject that you are forced to throw yourself away on it;—certainly not in America, at least."[74] "You don't love others as you do yourself, if you think their physical wants are the greatest. What the world needs is yourself at your best, at your happiest."[75] The novel obviously reflects a long debate over these issues; the novelist has heard both sides of these intricate questions eloquently put.

The other man Lilla might but must not marry, Mr. Gardner, is a "successful man of business," a representative of Social Darwinism. He too is given some force, both as a man of ideas and as a sexual being. Indeed, he is better realized, in his attractiveness as well as his dangerousness, than the Christian Socialist hero.

The writer even shows some acquaintance with the vitalist ethic—at odds though that is with penitential Christianity. Arnold says it is not virtue he is after but life. "Life itself is a success, and the more it is shared with, the more it deserves the name of life."[76] Bessie even says, "Something in me rebels when a man mentions his religion. . . . My ideal is the manhood of the old days, when men thought themselves the offspring of gods." And a reference to William Morris follows.[77]

In the same way the feminism of the novel is strangely contradicted at certain moments. At the end we are asked, "Does it not seem as if women belonged to some nobler race and in the world cannot but be mismated?"[78] Earlier we have been told, "Everywhere, women of some breeding and some idea of gentle manners are marrying much commoner men."[79] This suggests the feminist doctrine against which Ned rebelled, and against which Lawrence and Forster wrote. But Lilla says, "I don't believe a thing if only women believe it,"[80] and it is not clear that she is being perverse. Other sympathetic women say similar things at times. The different voices in the debate are given very free expression, and in that way the novel is interesting, and much better than Ned's fiction. It may be that Cornelia was wrong not to persist with her writing.

She told Henry that Professor Palmer had written her a very good—that is, very flattering—letter about her novel.[81] It certainly shows the influence of the Palmers, who were centrally placed in the debate of those times between traditional religion and a freer, more aesthetic, morality; between both of those and the urgencies of social reform. Though Alice Freeman organized a Christian Association at Wellesley, she refused to affiliate it with other such associations, because they might be narrower. Hers was a college church, and she belonged to no other, her husband tells us. Moreover, she loved pictures and Greek art—even the fragments of sculptures— and he of course translated Homer.

They went to Greece and met Schliemann, the excavator of Troy. (Perhaps this interest of theirs caused a change in Cornelia's earlier indifference to what Ned was doing.) And Alice Freeman Palmer's main task at Wellesley was to dismantle the "evangelical" apparatus set up by Durant.

As for social and economic reform, neither the Palmers nor Cornelia was really active in such movements, though they did support the women of Denison House—and Cornelia in a very substantial way. Their creed was "education." Alice Freeman Palmer was one of the five who organized the Massachusetts exhibit at the 1893 Columbia Exposition in Chicago, and she made its main theme education. This was reported on ironically by Santayana, for the true aesthetes were hostile to this stress on education—and "idealism," a cognate word. That, after all, was the issue in the battle of the casts at the M.F.A.

In 1908, Mr. Palmer published a collection of essays on education, by him and his wife, called *The Teacher*. The first essay, "The Ideal Teacher," begins, "In America, a land of idealism, the profession of teaching has become one of the greatest of human employments." A little later, "It has moved from a subordinate to a central place in social influence, and now undertakes much of the work which formerly fell to the church." But this pride is complemented by humility, for of the four characteristics which a teacher must possess, the first is "an aptitude for vicariousness"; he gives birth to his pupils—not so much a scholar as a maker of scholars.[82] These formulas are especially well-suited to G. H. Palmer in particular, but the contrast between his altruism and, for instance, Santayana's egotism, must have seemed to the Palmer party to represent them as a whole.

We should not, just because nowadays more people read Santayana than read Palmer, assume that that contrast works entirely to the latter's disadvantage. Education was too moderate and central to be satisfying to people with new ideas, but it was, at its best, allied to a remarkably just and clear-minded appreciation of all the options. That is what can be seen in *Miss Wilton*.

It is of course an old-fashioned novel. We place it in relation to *Middlemarch* and *Daniel Deronda*. *The House of Mirth*, itself soon to seem dated, recognizably made a more wholehearted commitment than *Miss Wilton* to the aesthetic movement in the novel.

These degrees of commitment to the aesthetic are hard for us to see now, but they were crucial. Mr. Palmer, praising his wife's poetry, makes it clear that it is not like that of Swinburne, Rossetti, or Keats. To the modern reader, Mrs. Palmer's verse seems generically Victorian, and so perhaps does much of Swinburne and Rossetti; the only difference being that they are more talented. To Mr. and Mrs. Palmer, however, the difference was one of kind. They, and Cornelia Warren, belonged to a different *party* from that which included Santayana and Ned Warren.

In consequence, Cornelia's aesthetic and moral style was humbler than that of her brothers; more of her interest went into the practical forms of service associated with Denison House and Wellesley, or with keeping the books for various institutions. She was treasurer of the College Settlement Association from 1892 to 1900, and a figure in that movement, so important in that decade.

To some of the ardent young teachers then at Wellesley, and at other women's colleges, forms of Protestant piety like Mr. Durand's were unappealing. They cared much more about, on the one hand, Catholic spirituality and, on the other, social and economic change. These enthusiasms (which found expression in College Settlement work) represented a partial revolt against the values of, for instance, Mr. Warren and his company. For that reason, perhaps, it does not seem that Cornelia Warren embraced those enthusiasms wholeheartedly, but she did spend time with, and give support to, women like Scudder and Coman.

The latter pair determined at least to know, and if possible to help, the poor and immigrant population of Boston, which had swollen to huge proportions and which the regular institutions of government scarcely reached. In 1900, 35 percent of the city's inhabitants were foreign-born, and over 70 percent were of foreign parentage.[83] It was clear that the existing social institutions could not express them, enlist them, or deal with them. There was a need for new ideas and new social forms beyond those Mr. Warren had served so well—beyond capitalism and free enterprise.

Though the Wellesley women did not know about Jane Addams's work at Hull House in Chicago when they first planned their own house, it was a very similar enterprise. (In her autobiography, Scudder compares their work with that of Addams.) Bishop Phillips Brooks, the Boston philanthropist, was an early subscriber.

There were co-workers from other colleges. Scudder mentions Bertha Hazard from Vassar and Helena Dudley from Bryn Mawr, and others, all under thirty. But Wellesley's contribution to the College Settlement Association was larger than that of the other institutions over the twenty-five–year period after 1889; Smith gave nearly as much, but Vassar, Bryn Mawr, Radcliffe, and Wells significantly less.

The Settlement House in Boston, called Denison House, on Tyler Street, in a neighborhood at first Irish and then Italian, was bought with Cornelia Warren's money. It opened in 1892; Hull House and the New York equivalent opened in 1889, which was the year the association issued its first appeal. Author Allen F. Davis says, "The social settlement in a working-class neighborhood of an American city was usually easy to spot. It was often the only house with flower boxes and a brass plate on the door; and it usually had a stream of children moving in and out."[84]

Denison House was the first college settlement in Boston, and the third in the United States. Katharine Coman was the secretary, but she was not resident. Helen Cheever and Emily Greene Balch, dominant personalities at first, meant the house to be "neighborly—sympathetic, and kind"; and the women attempted to involve the girls who attended their colleges. Undergraduates spent their vacations there. Mary Kenney O'Sullivan, a labor organizer, when she worked at Denison House, took the students through factories and to the lodgings of their operatives. Gradually the original approach was broadened and given more force and structure by her and Helena Dudley.[85]

Begun at about the same time as Lewes House, Denison House was on about the same scale (at its most flourishing, there were twelve residents, but most stayed only a year), and both were social inventions and interventions. The work Henry Warren and his staff were doing at Beck or Warren House was not a matter of social intervention; though compared with most people's work, it had a similar inventiveness. Of course the intervention of Denison House was not in the life of the imagination, like Ned's, but in society; the women intervened in the interest of renewing social relations, repairing the fabric of life torn by the cruel competitions of capitalism and its inhuman rates of change.

These are the kinds of ideas we find in Robert Woods's *City Wilderness* of 1898. Woods also wrote *Zone of Emergence* and *Americans in Process* about the South End and similar parts of Boston. He worked at South End House, the male equivalent of Denison House, which opened a little later. These two, plus Lincoln House and the Wells Memorial Institute, were informal allies in the battle against poverty, crime, and disease in Boston. Woods calculated that the first two had about three hundred regular clients each, and that altogether more than 7 percent of the South End's population was directly involved. Denison House was especially active in bringing employers together with labor leaders and in setting up a Women's Club and a Teachers' Association for teachers at every level of instruction. In its map of institutions and meeting places, *The City Wilderness* shows Denison House surrounded by daughter institutions like a Home Library, a Tyler Street Day Nursery, a Tyler Street School, and the Old Colony Chapel—bought by Cornelia Warren to be made into a gymnasium for the neighborhood.

The idea of a settlement, as distinct from a club, was that the residents shared their life as a whole with their neighbors. On social occasions Cornelia played the piano there, and once at least Gretchen Warren and her sister Molly Osgood Childers played and sang there. There was also a proposal that the M.F.A. lend the house some pictures, and an exhibition of paintings held jointly by Denison House and South End House drew 1,500 visitors a day.[86]

Thus if it was a charitable and educational enterprise, it operated for the benefit of the volunteers as well as for the clients. Vida Scudder says that in Denison House she escaped her class prison of shyness and learned how to appreciate people who were generous, kind, and feckless; she had hitherto known only "hard self-respecting New Englanders, who believed in economies and paying one's debts."[87]

Scudder also says that some of their finest officers were Jews; and Woods, in his book, shows some of the fascination with Jewish culture that was to become general. But the women of Denison House had their greatest success with Italian immigrants—an aspect of their work that linked them to the aesthetes, for Italy was the imaginative home of Ned Warren and his friends.

They established workrooms in response to the economic crisis of 1893, and welcomed the visits of such A. F. of L. leaders as Samuel Gompers, George MacNeill, Henry Lloyd, and Jack O'Sullivan. Radical thinkers from England, like Patrick Geddes and Ramsay

Macdonald, visited the house when they came to the United States. The Women's Trade Union League was founded there, as was a Social Science Club in 1893. Scudder and Helena Dudley attended the Central Labor Union in Boston every Sunday and took part in two strikes. Scudder became a Socialist; Dudley didn't.

Dudley, born in Nebraska in 1858, attended M.I.T. and Bryn Mawr; she studied to be a biologist but gave up science for settlement work. Strikers and unionists met at Denison House, and though Cornelia does not seem to have engaged in its more radical schemes of action, she got as involved as, say, Louis Brandeis. (He had apparently advised Cornelia about some property she was buying for the house, and Mrs. Brandeis was on the house committee, which Cornelia chaired for some time.)

In 1893, Helena Dudley was made the head worker at the house; she became Cornelia's friend, though fairly radical in her sympathies, and when she retired in 1912 Cornelia built her a house at Cedar Hill. In her letters to Henry, Cornelia often gives news of Denison House, and in November 1898 she wrote her mother from Philadelphia, where she, Miss Scudder, and a Miss Yerxa were visiting the Settlement House.

Brandeis

Brandeis was getting steadily more involved with politics and after 1884 in ways hostile to big business, though his political alliances were still with those conservative reformers called the Mugwumps. That group included such Harvard figures as James B. Thayer and James B. Ames, who was to head the Anti-Imperialist Committee of Fifteen during the war in the Philippines. Through his longtime friend Elizabeth Glendower Evans, Brandeis became an ally of President Eliot ("the king of the Mugwumps") and William James ("the Mugwump philosopher").[88] It was young lawyers who belonged to that world or wanted to enter it—men like William H. Dunbar and his cousin George Read Nutter—who joined the firm of Warren and Brandeis. (Dunbar's father was professor of political economy at Harvard and a close friend of President Eliot.)

However, most Boston Mugwumps, like Moorfield Storey and Charles Francis Adams, had railroad connections and were protectionist in their economic policies. Brandeis's clients were on the other side of the free-trade dispute. In 1897 he and Edward Filene led the Public Franchise League against the Boston Elevated Railroad scheme, and in 1902 they won. They went on to fight other battles against monopolies and corrupt government. Brandeis devised a sliding scale for the price of gas that worked in the consumer's favor, reformed workmen's insurance laws, campaigned for better schools, and fought the New Haven Railroad Company. He was not always opposed by all the conservative forces in these campaigns. Lee, Higginson and Company, the conservative Boston financial house, and his future enemies, were glad to see him defeat the Elevated scheme because their New York rivals, the House of Morgan, were behind it.[89] The same was true of his fight against the gas monopoly from 1903 to 1906. But they came to distrust his populist rhetoric.

During the 1890s, Brandeis began the transition leftward from Mugwump to Progressive. At the same time Sam Warren moved toward the right, and so their friendship became more purely personal. A letter from Sam of September 7, 1901, shows him reassuring Brandeis that he still has Sam's approval: "In many ways you are a better example of New England virtues than the natives."[90] But they were in fact no longer comrades.

Moreover, Brandeis's unpopularity with the Yankee elite was compounded by the anti-Semitic feeling generally on the increase, which of course made use of other terms to express itself. "How, some still ask, could he score financial success as a big corporation lawyer only to become so fierce an opponent of bigness, monopoly, and the money trust? . . . How, with his heralded liberalism, could he maintain so lucrative a law practice and die a multi-millionaire?"[91]

For a long time he was supported by Sam, who in 1891 wrote him—obviously in reply to some request for advice—that public life was his destiny. Brandeis, he said, should not worry about the case in hand at that moment, but concern himself with his life policy. He must select "the objects to which you will apply your force."[92] He sent him therewith a biography of R. H. Dana, the fastidious aristocrat squeezed out of Boston politics—a precursor of the Mugwumps—and told him to ponder the lesson. (In 1868, Dana ran as a reform candidate against Benjamin F. Butler, who was almost openly corrupt, and got under 10 percent of the votes because he looked like a mere idealist.) This presumably meant that Brandeis must put all his force into a political career, for anything less would mean failure.

He talked with Irish unionist leaders and picked up many of

The father.

The home.

The daughter.

The nudist.

The suicide.

The bride.

The cripple.

The Uranian.

Lewes House, inside . . .

. . . and outside. (Matthew Prichard is standing.)

Ned and a statue.

their ideas. Through Mrs. Evans and Denison House he came to know Mary Kenney O'Sullivan, the A. F. of L. union organizer who came from Chicago. She was active in the strikes at the Homestead works in 1894, and later at the ones at Lawrence and Fall River. (Vida Scudder and Ellen Hayes went from Wellesley to Lawrence in 1912 to show sympathy with the strikers, and risked their jobs.)

O'Sullivan went to work at Denison House that same year, and she and her husband, Jack or John F. O'Sullivan, labor reporter for the *Boston Globe*, lived at Denison House for a time; one of their children was born there. Samuel Gompers of the A. F. of L. was a witness at their wedding, so theirs was a labor marriage. According to Allon Gal, the O'Sullivans educated Brandeis in unionism. He quotes Kenney describing how Brandeis listened to her husband: "If ever a man talked facts, it was Jack O'Sullivan. He was known for facts."[93]

O'Sullivan was president of the Boston Central Labor Union, where Single Taxers, among other radicals, spoke. This then was a center of New Age Boston, another opposite to Copley Square, in which Brandeis came together (in tendency; we don't know that they literally met there) with Cornelia and Fiske rather than with Sam. All the first three were engaged theoretically rather than practically, and were among the more conservative of this radical world, but their engagement was not trivial—it was enough to distance them from Sam and Mabel.

The history of Sam and Mabel Warren seems to have run more and more along the lines of the Yankee elite: the sailing, the dinners, the trusteeships—of the M.F.A. and the company, but also of McLean's and Massachusetts General Hospital—and, above all, the polo. In 1891, Sam bought 120 acres in Dedham, to the west of the city. It was land largely bounded by a curve of the Charles River. He named it Karlstein, in allusion to a castle in Bohemia and to the Charles. He bought adjoining land, and by 1900 the estate was almost 200 acres.

He also added to the eighteenth-century farmhouse on the grounds, almost tripling it in size, and laid out a polo field and a trotting track for the ponies. The stables and the barns at Karlstein soon overshadowed the house, and lots of the Warrens' friends came to Dedham on weekends to play polo. Brandeis joined the club in 1887, when it was founded, and bought a house nearby in 1900, but it was the elite Yankee families, like the Lowells and the Cabots, who joined Sam's team, and Brandeis was gradually made to feel unwanted.

Sam was becoming a leader in society. In July 1897 he was persuading his siblings that the family as a whole should contribute $500 toward the Harvard athletic facility on Soldiers Field Road. Boston as a whole was being asked to raise $25,000. Sam and Mabel knew of course the elite of Harvard. Letters from Sam Warren to Mr. and Mrs. Barrett Wendell survive in the Houghton Library.

It is interesting to note how often the word "high," or that concept, was used about the couple. Sam, the Senate was told after his death, stood very high in the community.[94] Mabel was a sensitive, high-natured woman.[95] Sam was an unusual man, with a very high sense of honor, and extremely unbending.[96] He was a dominant man in any situation in which he was placed, a leader in any course in which he was engaged . . . not over-ready to take advice.[97]

There are indications, by witnesses and by later commentators, that S.D. Warren and Company was not doing as well as it had done under Mr. Warren. Sam wrote to tell Ned in July 1897 that the latter's income had fallen by 25 percent from the £4,000 it had been, and he wrote much the same to Cornelia the following October— her income had been $33,000 and would be $26,000—and since prices were still falling, "We'll probably never see the large profits of previous years." The return she was getting on her property at its book value amounted to only 3½ percent; that meant, he said, that the property was not worth its book value.[98]

This may well have been simply a matter of the bad economic conditions in general; we have not enough evidence to make a judgment on why. We do know, however, that Fiske was gradually squeezed out of the partnership, and that Ned was growing dissatisfied with the income he got from the trust.

Henry

At the end of this period Henry Warren's painful and solitary life came to an end, at the very beginning of 1899, in his forty-sixth year. He was given a lengthy obituary in *The Nation* of January 12. (The article next to it was entitled "Imperialism vs. the Constitution" and took up the topic that was to bring Fiske to public attention.) Not only did Harvard lose a devoted son and benefactor in Henry Warren, *The Nation* said, but American scholarship lost one of its distinguished ornaments. He did not reproduce what Western scholars have guessed or supposed about Buddhism, but made the native Buddhist speak for himself. (Like Ned and their mother, he got rid of facsimiles and gave people the authentic, the original, experience.) "And now, especially, when so many facile tongues are wagging with half-knowledge or worse about the isms of the 'Land of the Rose-apple,' it is indeed well that some sober-minded scholar should undertake to find out for us what the wisdom of these wise men of the East really was." Some Buddhist ideas are startling in their modernness, and unlike the views traditional among us [this seems to be a reference to Schopenhauerean pessimism], but this man, so impressed by Buddhism, himself led a life beautifully near to the best ideals of the high-minded Christian gentleman.[99]

Henry's will was dated December 31, 1898, the day he heard that he was about to die, though it had evidently been drawn up sometime before. (Apparently he had thought he had two years more to live.)[100] Essentially, everything went to Harvard. He bequeathed to it Beck (now Warren) House and an adjoining house, and land on Quincy Street. (He had already given the university some very valuable land fronting on three streets around the Yard.) He also left the Dental School and the Peabody Museum $10,000 each, and the Sanskrit Department $15,000 for the publication of the Harvard Oriental Series, plus $100,000 for general purposes. Both the Harvard Union and the Harvard Varsity Club stand on land he gave. His share of the trust was divided among the rest of the family, and Ned got a bequest of $25,000. Lanman got his books and $10,000.

The family's responses to *Buddhism in Translations* are interesting. Cornelia read it and sent him a couple of pages of notes, queries, and comments. Mrs. Warren told him that Cornelia had read to her the Buddha's pronouncements on women: "It seemed to me that his views were quite mundane."[101] Ned was frankly controversial and contradictory in his response. He wrote, "I cure myself of ills by the sight of a Greek athlete which to the Buddha would have been a filthy nine-holed body, and Nietzsche teaches one the precise opposite of his *Lebensverneinung* and *Mitleid*. To read your book and follow its thought, I should have to be at the antipodes of my philosophical whereabouts, or to stand on my head in imagination."[102] The following year he offered Henry a seventeenth-century relief of Minerva and the Muses for his Quincy Street house, but admits that they may not quite suit "the cross-legged philosopher."[103] At this point, Ned and Henry embody a major dialectic of the aesthetic movement. At other points, Ned and Sam do; and Ned and Cornelia; and Ned and Fiske.

Buddhism in Translations had considerable success despite its esoteric subject, and Henry took an interest in the advertisements his publishers issued and in the efforts of friends to get reviews written. (A letter from Sam reflects the pressure Henry had put on him to promote the book.) The first printing was of only a thousand copies, but the seventh and eighth, both in 1922, were of two thousand each. In 1910, moreover, Colliers was to publish Charles William Eliot's Harvard Classics, which by 1922 had sold 225,000 sets of the fifty volumes. A large selection of two hundred pages from Warren's book appeared in volume forty-five. Of Harvard authors, only Emerson and Dana contributed more pages than Warren to the series. The book was also a success in the East; the third and seventh printings came out in response to requests from that part of the world.

Lanman wrote a prefatory note for the printing of 1922, saying that it was "the fruit of thoroughly honest scholarship—and what is that but an aspect of personal character? . . . long acquaintance with the book only increases my respect for Warren and for his temper of mind . . . always worthy of the attention of a serious and virile intellect."

For Lanman the issue was world-historical. About the Harvard Oriental Series, he said, "The central point of interest in the history of India is the long development of the religious thought and life of the Hindus—a race akin, by ties of blood and language, to the Anglo-Saxon stock."[104] Contemporary history was making people appreciative of that religious tradition. "The world war of today is a terrible warning for tomorrow,"[105] and we should recall the good-will the Buddha preached.

Warren's own, more acerbic voice can be heard in his general introduction: "The works composing the third and last Pitaka are, of all the Buddhist Scriptures, the dreariest and most forbidding reading, and this is saying a great deal. However, like the desert of Sahara, they are to be respected for their immensity; and when they are all printed, no doubt something can be made of them."[106]

Lanman tells us that Warren had good relations with President Eliot, a close neighbor, whom he invited to Warren House a few days before his death (perhaps when he knew his death was imminent). Eliot later spoke of Warren's heroic serenity and his unceasing intellectual work, and how much that impressed him. Lanman says Henry told no one of his imminent end and would not have a trained nurse. However, a letter to Henry from Aunty, dated January 1, 1899, implies that the family knew the end was near. It reads like a last letter, stating that she had just arrived in Boston and was going to 67 Mount Vernon Street the next day to see if she could call on him, but she knew a visit might only weary him. (Ned said Henry welcomed visits from his family and told them funny stories, but did not invite them.) "You are so heroically patient, dearest Henry, and you have been so happy in your industrious and useful life."[107] The letter presumably reached Beck House after Henry's death.

Lanman composed a poem in honor of Henry's memory; for his "loved and unforgotten pupil and friend." It begins with a play on different meanings of Way; both the Way of the Buddha, the book that Warren had translated, and his own Way through life:

> Long didst thou toil this rugged Way to clear,
> Patience thy axe-helve, learning keen the blade,
> Till sank thy weary body, comrade dear . . .

Then it goes on to speak primarily of Buddhaghosa, though with obvious reference to Henry Warren:

> Full fifteen centuries, a man of might,
> This monk hath been unto the morning land . . .

Fiske

Meanwhile, in this decade of the 1890s, Fiske Warren becomes a more definite personality to us than he has been. His interests were various: In 1891 he bought an electric automobile—one of the three manufactured that year—and made himself feared on the roads around Waltham; in 1893 he was amateur tennis champion of the United States, and in 1894 he published *The Warren-Clarke Genealogy*.

On the cover the name of the Reverend Charles White Huntington appears as the author, the husband of one of the Warren cousins. But in fact Mr. Huntington had only assembled the data, while it had been ordered and interpreted (according to an experimental new method) by someone who wrote a preface and signed it "one of the nucleus." This coy periphrasis conceals Fiske—the nucleus being the five children of Mr. and Mrs. Warren (Sam, Henry, Cornelia, Ned, and Fiske). The study covered all the nucleus's ancestors for six generations and all the descendants of the four pairs of "his" great grandparents. This nucleus is referred to as "he," and the degrees of relationship of the others to "him" are computed mathematically, with fractions, and "to the power of 2," and so on—$\frac{1}{8}$ + $\frac{1}{16} = \frac{1}{(2)2.4}$ = the 2.4 degree of relationship. (The book was reviewed as being "something new in its kind.") This is the most overt expression of the Warrens' sense of family identity and pride—an expression rather touching in its awkwardness. The genealogical passion does not usually go with Fiske's other, radical, interests, but it seems to have been strong in him.

In 1891, at twenty-nine, he married Gretchen, the oldest child of Hamilton Osgood and Margaret Cushing Pearmain. The former was a well-known doctor who had gone to Germany in 1873 to study with the famous Professor Virchow and later to France to study with Louis Pasteur, concerning himself with the rabies antitoxin, which he personally brought back to the United States. (This alone made Osgood famous.) But he was also interested in more speculative and controversial forms of medicine. One of his first interests was in semi-psychological phenomena like blushing, and he used hypnotism in his own cures. He was associated with the idea of "Mind over Matter" therapy.

The Osgoods claimed descent from Anne Hutchinson and John Quincy Adams and were proud of the part their ancestors had played in the American Revolution. The children were educated at home, not at a school, and the family talked ideas and art at a high level. They allegedly sang four-part Bach chorales together after breakfast and read aloud from the Bible. Mrs. Osgood collected folk songs and made an anthology of the *philosophia perennis,* worldwide spiritual literature. Both were published later, the latter under the title *City Without Walls,* with an introduction by the Irish mystical poet AE.

Gretchen was a beautiful and talented girl who had had the best teachers. She studied singing as a mezzo-soprano with Gabriel Fauré at the Paris Conservatoire. The family knew Liszt and Clara Schumann and had many friends in the Boston Symphony Orchestra. Later Gretchen studied diction and acting under Coquelin l'aîné at the Comédie Française. According to rumor, she could have had a stage career in France, but her mother would not allow it.

They also had reformist and even revolutionary political interests. Hamilton Osgood was on the committee of Denison House, and Mrs. Osgood's brother, Sumner Pearmain, was a sympathizer with the Irish nationalists who were determined to fight England's rule. He was a friend of John Boyle O'Reilly, the journalist, and this

Irish connection indirectly led members of both the Osgood and the Warren families to settle in Ireland. One link was through the Irish writer, soldier, and, later, freedom fighter Erskine Childers. In 1903, the year he published his famous novel, *The Riddle of the Sands,* Childers came to Boston, and met and the following year married Molly Osgood. Thus the Fiske Warren children had Irish cousins deeply involved in Irish politics.

The Osgoods lived in a big house on Beacon Street, and both daughters' weddings were reported in the *New York Times.* In a letter he wrote just before his marriage, Childers described the Osgoods as a "remarkable family . . . not religious in the Christian sense but [are] the most deeply spiritual people I can imagine, beneath a brilliantly gay exterior and much varied cleverness. . . . They are utterly unworldly; and truth and beauty are the only things they really love."[108] Fiske Warren he described as "very nice and in complete contrast to the impulsive Mrs. Osgood and Gretchen. He lives by reason and yet has a deep background of tenderness. He's an impassioned anti-Imperialist, and spends quantities on the cause."[109] Childers himself of course became a more famous anti-imperialist.

The Osgoods were interested in all the newest ideas, but recognizably Transcendentalist or post-Transcendentalist in their intellectual style. They summered in Dublin, New Hampshire, together with some of the doctor's former patients and friends: the Monroes, the Crowninshields, the Pampellys. These people belonged to those social and intellectual elites who practiced handicrafts and put on pageants. The Monroes were also friends of Samuel Morse and Alexander Graham Bell. Thus the Osgoods' attachment to the arts and spirituality did not preclude an interest in new inventions and discoveries in science.

It is perhaps significant that it was in the year of his marriage, 1891, that Fiske also acquired his electric road carriage, which carried eight passengers at speeds of up to sixteen miles an hour. The significance lay in his love of new technology, but also in his love of transport. Fiske was a great traveler; he was in Europe in 1890, 1892, 1899, and 1904; and "girdled the earth" in 1897, 1901, 1905, 1907–1908, and again in 1931. It was in such terms that he presented himself in his Harvard Class Reports. Later, when other people drove cars, he gave his up and took to the bicycle, a more New Age vehicle. (Cornelia also cycled, as did the Palmers.)

Gretchen also loved travel. It is a clue to the couple's relationship that in 1897 they traveled around the world. They took with them their young daughter Rachel, her governess (an ex-nun), and Gretchen's sister Molly. In the East they visited Ceylon, Singapore, Saigon, and Japan, where Gretchen bought a great many things. (Ned felt great scorn for the fashionableness of Japanese art.)

They owned a farm in Harvard, Massachusetts, called Tahanto, where they spent their summers, and Fiske apparently often described himself as a farmer rather than a businessman. He had designed his own house there—in typically eccentric style. It reportedly consisted of two buildings joined by a bridge over which the servants carried the food. Gretchen entertained widely, and her circle of guests was more distinguished or at least exotic than either Cornelia's or Mabel's. Over the years one could meet at her table Frank Sanborn, Sun Yat-Sen, Booker T. Washington, William James, AE, Alexis Carrel, Clarence Darrow, and Robert Frost, as well as the Single Taxers and the Filipino patriots with whom Fiske worked. (It does not seem, however, that Fiske played the host often; indeed, he and Gretchen were considered by their friends to be leading separate lives during at least the second half of their marriage.) Gretchen also corresponded widely with such professors and scholars as Sir Richard Livingstone, president of the Oxford College Ned endowed.

One of their guests who has left some description of the household was H. A. L. Fisher, who had known Ned before. Fisher stayed with the Fiske Warrens in 1909, when he came to Boston to give the Lowell lectures. He was therefore there during the climax of the family tragedy, but he does not refer to it.

"Mrs. Fiske Warren, gay, lovely, affectionate and gifted ... [took] the leadership among the clever women around her. . . . She could talk of the beauties of Peking and the splendours of Angkor and was well read in French and German poetry. A brilliant gift of mimicry helped to make her the most entertaining of companions." Fiske, on the other hand, was a Boston visionary. He lived for an idea; his deity was the Single Tax. "This quaint, utterly unselfish man, an expert, I believe, in the conduct of business, lived a saintly and dedicated life. The multifarious tastes of his beautiful Gretchen left Fiske entirely cold."[110] Fisher repaid his hosts in a prose better suited to a guest book than to an autobiography, and he is not to be believed implicitly (it does not seem that Fiske was much of a businessman), but one can glimpse the truth behind the flowers of rhetoric. Leaving Gretchen to lead her own brilliant social career,

Fiske pursued his lonely pilgrimage, deaf to the economists, convinced to the end that he had found the clue to the purifying of public affairs, not only in his own country but throughout the world.

There was a strain of nobility in him, but also a strain of the crackpot. Even in the Senate, when Brandeis's nomination to the Supreme Court was debated, the mention of Fiske Warren brought a moment of laughter. Sam's attorney, McClennen, described Fiske as a man who "had a great interest in accounting, who pursued it to a considerable extent. I remember he used to keep accounts with the different members of his family for ledger purposes, and it used to be one of the things we used to discuss—not with him but as a matter of comment among his friends—whether the expenditures on the birth of his children were to be charged to his wife or to the children. He pursued the accounting to a very extensive degree."[111]

Fiske was clearly eccentric in various ways; one way was in a then widespread and well-accepted style, associated with the slogans of the New Age and the New Life. In later life, when alone, he traveled everywhere second class, carried his food in paper bags, abstained from wine and meat, carried his own luggage, wore reformed clothing (his digitated socks, fitted to each toe, like a glove, became a legend in the family) or no clothing at all. (Public authorities had on occasion to ask him to dress and cease to cause scandal.) The family clearly found him something of a trial. Mrs. Warren wrote to Henry in 1894, "I think he [Fiske] is doing his level best. Perhaps he is encountering now more difficulties. He seems, however, to be taking much pleasure at Harvard with little Rachel."[112] The silences between the sentences are loud.

Gretchen does not seem to have been politically minded, but she was a student of philosophies and religions. In her youth she was, in principle, in sympathy with reformist movements, perhaps even revolutionary ones. Even later she practiced dietary experiments. Ned said of the couple and their prospective progeny: "I am expecting some grand reformer from parents who go in so much for high principles and theories. They will prove their poor old uncle to have been much mistaken in his old-fashioned ideas of life."[113] Ned must surely have been at loggerheads with Fiske and Gretchen in matters of principle and temperament, but in fact he and Fiske were to league together against Sam.

As far as public issues go, Fiske took action with reference to the Philippines and American imperialism. The wealth that Mr. Warren had piled up was a part of a new national wealth which changed the way America saw herself and was seen by other countries. That has already been implicit in our account of Ned's and Mrs. Warren's collecting, Fiske's and Mr. Warren's traveling, and indeed the activities of all the Warrens. But now we must look at the explicitly political and historical aspect of that change. America was becoming a world power, and the question arose, was it not now an empire? An excited self-consciousness led many to answer yes: They read the essays of Admiral Mahan, advocating naval power, and applauded the speeches of Theodore Roosevelt, advocating adventures in war and empire. But many people, especially in New England, answered no to that question, as a matter of sternest principle. America was a republic, founded for the pursuit of freedom and in the denial of empire. The Warren family held this opinion, but most of its members, as usual, avoided public controversy. Fiske, the one they took least seriously among themselves, was the one who took the family name into the public arena. (They seem to have felt that he bought himself importance with the debased currency of public activity because he could not make himself count with the real money, the sound currency, of private life.)

The anti-imperialist movement was strong in Boston. It originated there in June 1898. On June 2, Gamaliel Bradford wrote a letter to the *Boston Evening Transcript,* asking for a public meeting on the subject in Faneuil Hall. This meeting was held on June 15 and passed protests against America's adoption of an imperialist policy.[114] An Anti-Imperialist League was founded, many of the founders being sons or grandsons of Abolitionists. They tried to make this new cause seem a continuation of the old one and to rally other groups, black and Irish-American, to it; but it remained overwhelmingly a Yankee enthusiasm, linked to reform. Moorfield Storey, a leader of the movement (and Fiske's attorney in the Warren family suit), saw the cause of imperialist policies in municipal corruption at home. Edward Atkinson, in whose offices the constitution of the league was drawn up, was a Mugwump eccentric of the same type as Fiske. Born in 1827, he was a businessman but also a reformer, an experimental dietician, an amateur statistician, an inventor, a pamphleteer, and so on.

All the league's founders were members of the Massachusetts Reform Club, to which Sam Warren also belonged; and Mabel Bayard Warren escorted Fiske's friend, Clemencia Lopez, to Washington to see the president. Miss Lopez also stayed with Cornelia at Cedar Hill; and Aunty Ellen Clarke Hammond wrote to Henry on April 19, 1898, and told him how sad she was about the war with Spain: "Our nation has taken a step backward." There was no split in the family as to the principle at stake.

But there was disagreement over how to support it. Some members of the league defied the government quite recklessly. Atkinson, for instance, sent out "unpatriotic" pamphlets denouncing America's action, and when the U.S. Post Office confiscated them as treasonable, he sent them out again as serial publications of the league. There was bitter public feeling in many parts of the country against the "Boston school of slanderers." Roosevelt called them "simply unhung traitors." The Grand Army of the Republic called them "unworthy of the name of Americans." And it was to the extremists like Atkinson that Fiske Warren joined himself.

All this no doubt embarrassed the other Warrens. Fiske seems, indeed, to have caused embarrassment to his public allies as well—and amusement to his enemies. But the Anti-Imperialist League was supported by a good number of academics and men of letters from across the country. Imperialism was associated with the yellow press and its mass readership. Several political and economic conservatives were of the party: John Sherman, George Boutwell, George Hoar. E. L. Godkin, in *The Nation,* blamed his old enemies, Hearst and Pulitzer, the publishers of the yellow press, for imperialism. It was to some degree an issue of political *taste* for people like the Warrens: The American empire was a vulgar, cheap, gaudy idea, the opposite to the old-fashioned dignity of the republic.

But many anti-imperialists were far from simply conservative. They were idealists concerned with peace and internationalism: men like David Starr Jordan, Andrew Carnegie, Carl Schurz, Edward Atkinson, and Moorfield Storey.[115] And it seems clear that Fiske was more influenced by this idealistic element. He was president of the American Peace Society from 1903 to 1911. And he is said to have been one of those who induced Brandeis to take up the anti-imperialist cause.

In the history of America it was an extremely important issue. According to E. B. Tompkins, the main American debate about imperialism began in 1890, and the crucial decade was 1892–1902; the Anti-Imperialist League was founded in 1898 and Fiske joined the following year. The league's main concern was opposition to the annexation of the islands, even more than the war.

Fiske's policy was that the independence of the islands should be guaranteed by an international agreement. The anti-imperialists generally held that for the United States to occupy the islands would be imperialism and as such unprecedented, that there was a complete difference between this action and America's expansion westward across the continental landmass in the nineteenth century. The latter had not required large military forces, and the land was settled with American citizens who developed self-governing states. This was "normal growth."[116] The imperialist leaders (who included Theodore Roosevelt, Henry Cabot Lodge, and Senators Platt and Beveridge) denied this. They used the old slogan, Manifest Destiny, to cover America's current claim to the islands.

Fiske's link with the Filipinos was through Sixto Lopez. When Commander Dewey fired on the Spanish fleet in Manila Bay on April 25, 1898, he was in alliance with General Aguinaldo and the nationalist movement. Aguinaldo had led a revolt against the Spaniards that ended in 1897; and the following year had formed an alliance in principle with the Americans. When the war broke out, Aguinaldo and his friends began fighting alongside them on the islands. In January 1899, however, he set up a Republic of the Philippines and sent a committee abroad to win it international recognition. This was necessary because, the month before, President McKinley had (illegally) proclaimed American sovereignty over the islands.

The chairman of the committee sent abroad was Felipe Agoncillo, and his secretary was Sixto Lopez, who had met Fiske in London in 1899 and converted him to the cause. It was a romantic friendship for Fiske, not unlike that between Sam and Brandeis, or that between Ned and Berenson. Fiske was then thirty-seven, just a little older than Cornelia when she found her cause, and in the same decade as Henry and Ned and Sam. Lopez was, like most of the other nationalist leaders, of the *illustrado* class, well-to-do and educated, belonging to an anticlerical and freemasonic-style secret society. He spent several months in Boston and New York, in 1899–1900, under Fiske's protection.

Fiske suddenly began to make speeches, write pamphlets, and appear in the correspondence columns of newspapers, and indeed in the headlines. In 1901 he made a trip to the Philippines looking for evidence that the Filipinos were reluctant to accept foreign rule; William Howard Taft and the imperialists had been saying that the islanders *wanted* to be ruled by America. Fiske went to visit the

Lopez family in Batangas, the province at the heart of the revolution. While he was there, Sixto's three brothers were arrested, and Fiske was asked to accompany their sister Clemencia back to the United States, where she could appeal to the president and Congress on her family's behalf. He was energetic on both her behalf and her brothers'.

Thus, on March 30, 1901, a crowd at Faneuil Hall heard Sixto denounce concentration camps and the hiring of mercenaries. Later, Fiske wrote to the secretary of war offering a bond of $100,000 in guarantee of Lopez's behavior if he were allowed to stay in the Philippines. (He was being deported for refusing to take the oath of allegiance.) It was as a result of that friendship that Fiske sailed to the islands in 1901 and made headlines in Boston papers (who spread the rumor that he was carrying unpatriotic propaganda) because he was forced to take an oath of loyalty before he was allowed to land.

Fiske wanted Filipino and American anti-imperialists to join forces, and to that end he tried to persuade Carl Schurz and George Boutwell to follow that policy. But to such men it seemed politically dangerous to ally the league with a national enemy. In some ways Fiske's own position was rather conservative. In 1901 he and Elizabeth Glendower Evans and Charles Francis Adams founded the Philippine Information Society, a group whose main goal was to *inform* the public. (Brandeis supported this society.) For like all the ideologically conservative Yankees, Fiske believed in education rather than politics. Thus at least one of the society's pamphlets went so far toward apoliticism as to exonerate the United States of responsibility for the war.[117]

Again, in March 1903, Fiske met with activist Edwin Burritt Smith in Chicago and proposed a Philippine Independence League with no political affiliation except the demand for independence. This was in effect an accommodation to the position of Theodore Roosevelt, according to historian Daniel Schirmer; an appeal to loyal and patriotic Republicans. It was as a result of this move that Chicago dropped out of the Anti-Imperialist League, an action that killed the latter as a national organization.[118] Thus Fiske's politics were, from the point of view of the historian of radicalism, both idealistic and Americanist in an old-fashioned style. He betrayed the anti-imperialist cause, though unwittingly.

Our point of view is rather different. We note, for instance, that Fiske's sudden involvement in politics came through a personal relationship, and so was like Sam's beginnings in the law and Ned's beginnings in connoisseurship and collecting. In all three the Warren involved was attracted to someone of different blood and background. This was surely the mark of a bold and generous kind of imagination; the kind that, however mixed with baser elements, distinguished all the Warrens.

6

Mortal Combat

1900–10

*His face was not as square as his son's, and, indeed, the
chin, though firm in outline, retreated a little, and the
lips, ambiguous, were curtained by a moustache. But
there was no external hint of weakness. The eyes, if
capable of kindness and good-fellowship, if ruddy for the
moment with tears, were the eyes of one who could not be
driven. The forehead, too, was like Charles's. High and
straight, brown and polished, merging abruptly into
temples and skull, it had the effect of a bastion that
protected his head from the world. At times it had the
effect of a blank wall. He had dwelt behind it, intact
and happy, for fifty years.*

—E. M. Forster,
Howard's End

Since this is the high point of the story, it is perhaps appropriate
to step back from the family a moment and look at the arena of the
conflict, which was also the manifestation of all that was at stake.
I will suggest that Copley Square, the heart of the new Boston, was
that arena, with the great buildings of the Public Library (designed
by McKim, Mead, and White), Holy Trinity Church (designed by
Henry Hobson Richardson), and the Museum of Fine Arts (Boston's
version of the South Kensington museums in London). These were
three triumphant memorials to the Yankee struggle to create a new
Boston that would be theirs, in compensation for the old Boston of

City Hall, which was lost to Irish ward bosses. This new Boston was the city of culture, the world capital of the aesthetic movement. Of course, in Boston the aesthetic was still fused with an old-fashioned idealism and had not yet come to terms with the new eroticism. But in no other city in the world was the aesthetic movement such a dramatic event, because in no other city was it so obviously involved with politics and history.

It happens that in this decade two writers from England wrote a book each about a visit to America, and each devoted a chapter to Boston. These were Henry James and H. G. Wells. The latter titled his chapter "Culture" and described Boston as a city of plaster casts, especially of female figures like the Nike of Samothrace. "It is incredible how many people in Boston have selected her for their aesthetic symbol and expression. Always that lady was in evidence about me, unobtrusively persistent, until at last her frozen stride pursued me into my dreams. That frozen stride became the visible spirit of Boston in my imagination. . . . Next to that I recall, as inseparably Bostonian, the dreaming grace of Botticelli's 'Prima vera.' All Bostonians admire Botticelli . . . indeed, Boston presents a terrible, a terrifying unanimity of aesthetic discriminations."[1]

A good deal of Wells's chapter is devoted to Wellesley College and "a sunlit room in which girls were copying the detail in the photographs of masterpieces, and all around this room were cabinets of drawers, and in each drawer photographs. There must be in that room photographs of every picture of the slightest importance in Italy, and detailed studies of many." In his discreet and playful way, Wells is of course preparing to criticize this aestheticism. "Those drawings of photographed Madonnas and Holy Families and Annunciations, the sustained study of Greek, the class in the French drama of the 17th century, the study of the topography of Rome fill me with misgivings, seeing that the world is in torment for the want of living thought about its present affairs."[2] Wells, despite his stylistic apprenticeship to James, belongs to a very different party in the parliament of cultural theory. "We give too much to the past. New York is not simply more interesting than Rome, but more significant, more stimulating, and far more beautiful, and the idea that to be concerned about the latter in preference to the former is a mark of a finer mental quality is one of the most mischievous and foolish ideas that ever invaded the mind of man."[3] Wells's sympathies lay, we might say, with the old Boston, with Mr. Warren and Brandeis, and with Jack O'Sullivan—those who believed in facts and numbers.

James, on the other hand, though he had many ironies about Boston, was an aesthete. What he felt as he looked at the city in 1904 and 1905 was grief at the triumph of the businessman over the artist and humanist, and alarm at the threat to culture. He grieved to see the Athenaeum, "this honored haunt of all the most civilized," diminished and deadened by newer and bigger commercial buildings all around it.[4] He found that even the Public Library—"a Florentine palace"—"spoke more of the power of the purse and of the higher turn for business than of the old intellectual . . . sensibility."[5] But crossing Copley Square to the Museum of Fine Arts, he felt at ease at last. He even found that that museum's Aphrodite, although or because she was bereft of her natural setting, looked more like a goddess than most Aphrodites in Europe. On this trip James was taken out to Karlstein by Mrs. Gardner, where he dined with the president of the museum's trustees. Here, by implication, he gives the palm of aesthetic honor to Sam Warren.

As for the family, in this decade the story of the Warrens came to a climax in a hostility so strong that it led to an actual death by violence. Both Sam and Ned, it seems clear, felt themselves to be under great strain; at moments they felt they faced ruin—Sam in his business reputation and his work as trustee of great Boston institutions, Ned by the loss of his museum career and several people dear to him. Sam felt his family did not trust his handling of their finances and blamed Ned. The latter felt his family had "wasted" him. He was not "what a good, rational, warm-hearted family would have made [me]."[6] He blamed Sam.

He lost Matt Prichard (and other Lewes House young men) to Sam and the M.F.A., and he lost John Marshall to marriage and the Metropolitan. And both his private income and the museum money that had funded his collecting were doled out to him by Sam, in amounts that were, or seemed, increasingly inadequate. He began to resent the Mills Trust.

Mrs. Warren's death opened the question of who should replace her as trustee. Ned returned to America in 1902 in order to have his say in that matter as in others from which he now felt he had been excluded. He wanted to be a trustee himself, but he and Marshall knew Sam would never agree to it. They thought he might accept Cornelia, through whom Ned could perhaps have an influence. There in fact ensued a long interregnum during which no new trustee was appointed. It was felt (by Ned, but apparently by others too) that Mortimer Mason would not, could not, oppose Sam's wishes, and the same was true of Fiske, who spent more and more of his time traveling, and pursuing his political interests, so that Sam was in effect sole trustee, in control of both the trust and the partnership. Thus Ned set himself to find out more about just how the Mills Trust worked and about how S.D. Warren and Company was run.

In 1910 they were fifty-eight and fifty years old, respectively, but the hostilities of boyhood had grown greater, not less. Cornelia as we know was alarmed as early as 1902 by the bitterness between the two brothers. In his letter to her of July 28, 1902, Sam refers to Ned's hating him "—and yet he has had the last cent that ought to have been spared either by the Museum or the business as it seems to me. We are now (S.D.W. and Co.) on the point of loaning him $100,000, secured by his interest in the Trust property. Did you see he has begun on that?"[7] Sam would have liked to step out and let another take his place in keeping the family together. This is pathos, but it is anger that gets expressed indirectly and by transference to others.

The pathetic note can be heard in Sam's letter to Fiske of July 28, 1902: "With all my faults upon my head, I am still" eager to do the right thing.[8] He clearly felt himself the object of his siblings' joint resentment. But there were other notes in his voice; for instance, impatience and hostility. In a letter to Cornelia dated December 28, 1903, he went coldly over Ned's demands and wrongdoings—delaying the appointment of Fiske as trustee, borrowing a large sum from the company, which it needed back, and so on. He reminds Cornelia that Ned had been given a half share in the Filippino painting for only $9,365, while according to him the picture's true value was $50,000 or $75,000. But he ends by returning to the note of self-doubt, saying that if she and Fiske still think differently, he will reconsider: "Perhaps I am wrong. I feel as if my judgment would be better on my return than it is now."[9]

We hear this tone recurrently, for instance in a letter to Cornelia dated March 14, 1898. After talking of other matters, "My dear little sister, I am very sorry you have such anxieties on your hands, added to troubles of your own. It is more than you ought to be called upon to bear."[10] And again in September 1901, "I think your self-effacing devotion to mother in matters great and small these many years ought to afford you the truest satisfaction. I know some who have apparently done the same thing but I have never known such faithfulness and constancy to a trust in every thought and deed. I want you to know I appreciate this and put it very high in my estimates of virtue. I hope I may be something more to you in the future than I have been. Show me the way please—and I shall seek it for myself."[11] There is something of his father's winsome warmth and effusiveness in this, but we should not forget the other side of his personality. The warmth appears at moments of family guilt, which are frequent, and, outside the family, with people by whom he is impressed, for instance Mrs. Gardner, and above all Brandeis. (A letter to Mrs. Gardner, dated December 30, 1907, ends ingratiatingly, "Pardon this personal note, which probably will not interest you.")[12]

Mrs. Warren and Ned were drier in their emotional styles, and may have found that manner cloying. Sam addresses his sister as "My Darling Pussy"; Ned says "Dear Cornelia" and even signs a good many letters to family members "E. P. Warren." Ned, offering Henry some health advice, observes that his own experience has been quite different, and his tips "imply a very strong and not expansive heart, which is perhaps my character in mind as well as in body."[13]

A letter from Ned to Cornelia, dated September 13, 1908, is evidently written in reply to one from her in which she had said she felt forced by him to sign a document that would bring about the dissolution of the company. (Probably she means only the partnership.) He takes an implicitly tough tone, dismissing her fears that they are imperiling the health of their cousin Mortimer, who had been ill for some twelve months, and who was, technically, as much to blame as Sam for wrongdoing by the partners or trustees. Ned claims to be doing what their father would have done and says that things had gone so far wrong that drastic measures were necessary. Their father was the criterion by which they measured each other. Ned said Sam was continuing their father's policies in changed circumstances.

Mrs. Warren's Death

Mrs. Warren died in 1901. She had been ill for some time, her mind overcast and her judgment unpredictable, we are told. She had made some changes to her will in 1898, while on a trip to Europe, which upset Sam. She left $20,000 to Massachusetts General Hospital, $5,000 to the Peabody Museum, $10,000 to the M.F.A. (to constitute a fund to spend on caring for pictures given by the Warren family), and $5,000 each to three missionary societies, to Bradford

Academy, and to Williams College (Mr. Warren had been a trustee there). The M.F.A. was also to get $60,000 to buy whatever it chose of her collection, and she set up a Memorial Foundation in Westbrook, with a $50,000 endowment (plus $2,500 a year to give away) for the promotion of the arts and humanities there.

The house at 67 Mount Vernon Street was sold and its contents dispersed in 1903. Mrs. Warren had been collecting art to the last, and there was a big exhibition of her collections after her death. The porcelains, silks, tapestries, furniture, watches, fans, and old jewelry were auctioned in December in Boston, and the paintings, pastels, watercolors a week later in New York. The catalogues of both sales are preserved in libraries. Judging by the prices written into the Boston Athenaeum copy of the paintings catalogue, over $270,000 was realized, not counting the $60,000 of Mrs. Warren's bequest to the museum. (A Millet sold for $23,000, a Corot for $15,000, a Gérôme for $16,000.) The museum acquired two paintings by Sir Thomas Lawrence, a Gérôme, a Dupré, and, as a memorial gift from the children, a Wohlgemut.

She had made her last trip to Europe with a "consuming desire" to buy French pictures, but the family had agreed to set a limit of 150,000 francs on her expenditure. Ned had been called in to advise her, and at his request Berenson also came to Rome to consult. It was then that they bought for her the Filippino Lippi tondo (the Virgin and Child and St. Margaret), which was the pride of her collection. In fact there was not a single French work on the list Ned gave Berenson on October 22, 1898, of the pictures that had just left Italy. Besides the Lippi, it included the Wohlgemut *Death of the Virgin,* a "Titian" Brusasorci (a painting once attributed to Titian) depicting the bust of a lady against a landscape, a "Catena" Madonna, a Flemish Madonna, and a marine painting. (The paintings' subjects were almost exclusively women.)

The Lippi Tondo

The Lippi hung for a time at Lewes House and then was brought to Mount Vernon Street. It caused further dispute between the brothers and sister, and in a letter dated March 29, 1903, Cornelia backed a plan, originally Fiske's, of giving it or selling it to Mrs. Gardner. This was not to Sam's taste, but he accepted it. Cornelia had convinced herself that the picture was deteriorating in the climatic conditions of the museum.

The idea seems to have been intended both to ensure the picture's proper display and preservation—in Boston—and to avoid giving either Sam or Ned the victory in their quarrel. Other people did make Mrs. Gardner gifts of that kind, though it does not seem likely that they were on this scale. However, the scheme fell through, and Ned and his friends took a very hostile tone about Mrs. Gardner thereafter. Burdett and Goddard refer to her anonymously as "a wealthy woman" who lived in a setting of palm trees and singing birds. Marshall said—supporting Ned—that this other collector was only out for notoriety, and camels would have done as well as paintings for her.

The tondo is described by a Lippi scholar as by far the most important work of his in the United States.[14] Its Madonna is said to be comparable with Raphael and Botticelli, but its significance for us is rather different.

The painting is circular and contains five figures. Dominant is the Madonna, who rises above the rest, bending over the Christ-child and toward St. Margaret. The latter has her child on her lap, who reaches out toward the other little boy. St. Joseph is outside the domestic circle, an altogether older and rougher figure. The composition marginalizes him. In matters of feeling, Neilson speaks of the "gentle, faintly sorrowful sentiment" expressed.[15] It was obviously a very suitable picture to make the pride of Mrs. Warren's collection; perhaps in its nineteenth- even more than its fifteenth-century context, the picture is an adoration of woman in her motherhood. It is not surprising that Cornelia became very attached to it. By the same token, however, it was a very unsuitable, indeed an ironic icon to associate with Ned. As he told Berenson, he had been an undutiful son to his mother because he had rejected her faith, which Cornelia had inherited, that "all that is personal in a man can be submitted to the court of feminine arbitration." Filippino's sweet Madonna is not seen in the act of judgment, but his painting is just the thing to hang outside such a courtroom.

In July 1902, Ned wrote to Fiske in agitation about the cost of the painting. Berenson had said it was worth $50,000, but the museum was balking at that price. "It is asinine to suppose that the Filippino is not worth 50,000 dollars, and I believe that the Museum people are not so much doubting its value as aiming at other pictures. . . . What trouble I had to get the Crivelli into the Museum! What trouble I shall have, if any picture is to be got in! . . . I don't want to present money to the Museum, when I have to fold my hands and see picture after picture lost, knowing that it is no use to apply to the Museum or to the family."[16]

There was some hint of legal proceedings between the brothers. In September of that year Ned wrote to Sam that his attorney, Youngman, would call on him to make sure that there were no misunderstandings about the plans for the picture. On November 1 he wrote again to ask Sam to send Youngman copies of all the relevant letters. Sam, on the other hand, seems to have been very conciliatory, at least at moments; in March 1903 he suggested that Ned should sell the picture abroad for the $50,000 he said he could get for it and spend the money on classical antiquities for the museum.[17]

The offer was finally made on April 16. The Warrens were in fact represented by Fiske's wife, Gretchen. She was on friendly terms with Mrs. Gardner and had just had her portrait painted at Fenway Court by John Singer Sargent. (The fact that she and Sam had been in and out of the place made Ned's exclusion all the more pointed, as he told Berenson.)

Cornelia in a letter to Sam dated April 16, and Ned in a letter to Berenson dated May 7, described the scene. When the offer was made, Mrs. Gardner burst into tears and left the room, later explaining that it was the first time anyone had offered to help her. (According to Cornelia, she said she would remember the offer through life, being hounded and found fault with as she was so constantly.) However, having gone over the palace with Mr. Sargent, she had found no room to hang the Lippi, and she had to decline the offer. (Cornelia surmised that she was no doubt moved by the thought of the responsibility such a gift would bring.) Cornelia betrays no anger at Mrs. Gardner, perhaps because she was glad to get the picture back in her own hands.[18]

Ned's letter, however, is stiff with anger, and he says, "I heard that Mrs. Gardner has the greatest possible prejudice against me." (We should remember that Prichard was her close friend at this time.) He offers no explanation of why she refused, but he does tell how he and Cornelia had tried to investigate the conditions at the palace. He had talked to Potter, who was advising Mrs. Gardner at that time. (Potter's portrait of Prichard was a permanent feature on her writing desk.) Potter had told him what he could and then asked Mrs. Gardner if Ned could look for himself. She replied, apparently, that if Mr. Warren wished to see her house, he should apply to her, like everyone else. Naturally, Ned did not "apply."[19]

We can guess that Mrs. Gardner foresaw a series of such interferences and investigations. Perhaps she also thought that such an inquiry was designed to humiliate her, for the "conditions" in the palace were likely to fare worse than those in the M.F.A. if examined as anxiously as the Warrens were doing. The glass roof over the inner courtyard created a greenhouse effect, which must surely have been disadvantageous for paintings, especially with the damp air needed for the gardens. That is something Ned and Cornelia Warren must have thought about, given their interests, and something Mrs. Gardner could not want to be the subject of discussion.[20]

Thus Ned was defeated by Mrs. Gardner (and her friends) in the eyes of all Boston. Mrs. Gardner told Berenson, in a letter dated May 19, 1903, that she had not taken the Lippi (he had hoped to see it installed in Boston) because it really belonged in the M.F.A., Sam being the president, and besides the Warrens all adored it. Perhaps that meant she had visions of Ned and Cornelia haunting her halls, hygrometer in hand, unable to sleep because of their fears about deterioration. It does seem that it had become an obsession with Cornelia, which is appropriate, if it had that emblematic character of "feminine arbitration."

The Museum

The other great occasion of sibling conflict was of course the M.F.A. and its new building. Sam became chairman of the Building Committee there in 1902 and also president of the trustees. It was agreed that the museum's old quarters on Copley Square were inadequate, but Ned and Cornelia both favored retaining the Copley Square building in addition to whatever new structure was built.

Sam consulted Ned in 1899, and in a letter dated February 5 that year Ned replied. We can probably take his advice to represent a consensus at Lewes House; Prichard was still his friend, and Prichard's later ideas are not discordant with these. Ned suggested a new museum should be built on the edge of the city, in Longwood, on the borders of Brookline. This was because it must be independent, not built on city or state land, and it should be in a small park, with a one-story building consisting of a series of small courts, containing a variety of things, including textiles and architectural casts, and so on. Interesting old buildings also should be transferred to the park. An American museum should be a complete small-scale version of the Old World. The classical exhibits at least should be housed in a series of small rooms, to be seen and walked all round. The Copley Square building should be kept for casts and for the Museum School. Stave off the architects, Ned said, have no architecture inside, and the simplest kind outside. "Americans are given to architectural 'features' and fuss. They weary one (like Fiske) with their inventions."[21] Ned here aligned himself with Sam against Fiske, claiming to be one of the elders of the family.

The Building Committee, however, decided to have a new structure on a much larger scale, to reflect the increasing prestige of both Boston and art, but still near the heart of the city. They found a large new site, on Huntington Avenue and backing on to the Fenway, which seemed to be the last such piece of land available. In Copley Square their building sat on about 30,000 square feet (154 feet by 212 feet) and offered 26,000 square feet of floor. The new site had 518,000 square feet of land, and their plans called for 182,000 square feet of floor, plus a Museum School of 16,650 square feet, a Casts Building of 26,000 square feet, and open courtyards of 79,000 square feet.

This project we can consider as Sam's building, to put side by side with his father's Westbrook buildings. The plan accepted, drawn by Guy Lowell, was for a building shaped like the letter H, with the ends enclosed and with wings projecting toward the avenue. Thus courtyards with glass roofs at the second-story level occupied the centers and the open spaces of the H.[22] As you entered you faced a monumental marble staircase of four steps, leading to a rotunda. There light fell through a coffered dome, as in the Pantheon, and Ionic colonnades opened on to corridors: All the main exhibits were to be on this first floor, and the visitor with more advanced knowledge and interests found his needs met in rooms on the floor below. It was to be both a place of public education and a research center.

On the whole, the style was plain, though massive, but a four-column Ionic portico rose above the main entrance and each wing had two modest Ionic pavilions in cut granite. What Ned thought of the building we don't know, but probably his judgment was not unlike that of Matt Prichard, who wrote to Mrs. Gardner in 1906 that the building corresponded to *their* principles "save for a great slice of 'architecture' in the middle." Even that dismal feature, he said—dismal because it did not correspond to any true *feeling*—would have been eliminated if he had not been fired from the museum.[23] Walter Muir Whitehill implicitly agrees, saying that it is a testimony to the support Sam gave to Prichard and Benjamin Ives Gilman that there was only one such slice.

The project was Sam's, and he presented it in the M.F.A. *Bulletin* for June 1907. It was typical of many of his projects in that though it incorporated new ideas, it was also conservative—being a Yankee elite enterprise. The city contributed nothing to it. And the irony was that he had by then been driven to resign from the presidency of the board of trustees.

In addition to new ideas, aestheticism brought with it, actually and symbolically, new careers. In 1901, Matt Prichard and Richard Fisher came to Boston from Lewes and began to work for the M.F.A. Later, in 1929, William J. Young, who had worked at Lewes House, set up a research laboratory and became the man in charge of cleaning and restoration for the museum. The expertise of preservation, so "scientific" and plausible to Americans, became one of Ned Warren's weapons against his brother and his rivals, as we have seen.

Then Berenson of course worked with Mrs. Gardner on her collection and museum, and Harold Woodbury Parsons collected for the Cleveland and other museums. Thus several young men found their way into the American art world through Ned Warren's networks.

But this was not all triumph for Ned. In Boston, Prichard became great friends with Sam and Mabel Warren. Joining the museum in 1902, Prichard also transferred his loyalty to Sam, and Ned regarded him as a traitor. He told Berenson, in a May 11, 1903, letter, that Prichard joined the M.F.A. and Fisher entered Sam's household (as a tutor) as direct consequences of quarreling with him. He declared that Prichard and Sam were of the same "frock coat" kind. "I fancy that American men have got their frock coats into their nature." Ned's "Roman acrobatics," Burdett and Goddard say, could not be performed in a frock coat.[24]

It seems possible that another kind of jealousy may have been at work in Ned. Now that Sam was president of the trustees of the museum, Ned may have hoped, not unreasonably, to win his brother's recognition as a knowledgable adviser. In the 1899 letter about the plans for a new building, for instance, there is a note of eager hopefulness and a readiness to invite Sam's alliance in jokes at Fiske's expense. In a very early (1890) letter to the museum about sending the Bronzino, Ned asked Mr. Brimmer to show Sam everything he sends, "so he knows what I am doing."[25] If that was his hope, he may have felt that Prichard was taking the place in Sam's confidence he had wanted for himself, as well as feeling that Sam had taken his place with Prichard.

Prichard was appointed secretary and then assistant to Robinson, who became the director of the museum. Sam had been warned that the appointment would be seen by Ned as an unfriendly act, but he had insisted on it.[26] Prichard and Ned quarreled once again, and the former never forgave the latter for what he said at that time. Then, because of the battle of the casts, Robinson quarreled with Sam and Prichard. In 1905, Robinson resigned from the museum and went to the Metropolitan, where he offered Marshall the position of being that museum's agent in Rome. In consequence of the ill-feeling stirred up, Sam and Prichard had to resign from the M.F.A. the following summer.

The first "Communication to the Trustees regarding the New Building," in 1904, included an essay by Prichard on "Current Theories of the Arrangement of Museums of Art." A museum should contain, he said, "only objects which reflect, clearly or dimly, the beauty and magnificence to which life has attained in past times." Its aim is to establish taste: "this is the first and great commandment," to which all others are subsidiary.[27]

It is clear that Prichard's ideas had a great effect on Sam Warren and others. There were two other essays, in sympathy with his, in the same "Communication," one by Paul Chalfin, the curator of Chinese and Japanese art, the other by Benjamin Gilman. Walter Whitehill, writing in 1970, says Prichard's was "practically a blue-print for the planning of the new building and a foretaste of princi-ples that were to become general in museums. . . . Here is a mind nourished by the classics successfully at work upon a practical problem."[28] The aesthetic movement was finding its voice on the subject of museums.

The quarrel at the museum, however, was not only over ideas. It was also over personalities and alliances. Prichard and Mrs. Gard-ner, with Sam Warren's assistance, seem to have planned a palace revolution to take the museum away from Robinson and his sup-porters among the trustees. Prichard introduced prospective allies like Paul Chalfin to Mrs. Gardner, and she, by a flattering invitation to lunch, kept Dr. Bigelow (one of Ned's allies and Robinson's supporters) away from a meeting of the Building Committee. Their maneuvers sound, as Whitehill says, like the giggling conspiracies of comic opera, but we should not fail to take them seriously for that reason.[29] The sound of those giggles may have "given them away," but they also provoked intense resentment.

The ideas themselves seem innocuous enough now, but at issue was, among other things, the importance of plaster casts and education versus that of original works and taste. In September 1904, Robinson wrote a long public letter in which he "invoked the sacred name of 'education.' "[30] On November 1, Prichard replied, saying, as a good aesthete, "Joy, not knowledge, is the aim of contemplating a painting."[31] Casts are useful for teaching: "engines of education, and not to be shown near objects of inspiration."[32] They are a mechanism, the pianola of the visual arts, as incongruous at the museum as a pianola would be at symphony. This sounds more pointed when we know that Robinson taught a course with the use of casts.

Prichard also pointed out that the visual arts are handicapped in their appeal to the public by their lack of movement, and so museums ought to move things around from time to time—an idea that upset trustees like Dr. Bigelow. Prichard felt museums should have docent guides, lectures, and drama—for instance, Greek or Japanese plays—in the courtyards.

Benjamin Ives Gilman said, "The future Museum promises the city a new agency of spiritual well-being, not dedicated to discipline of mind or direction of conscience, like a school or a church, but, like the shrine of the Muses from which it takes its name, sacred to the nurture of the imagination."[33] Prichard and his friends gave elegant and lively voice to typical aesthetic ideas. He is one of the heroes of Whitehill's centenary history of the M.F.A., written so long after his death.

Prichard's gifts were not merely theoretical. He had an effect on the museum world, even in practical matters: He devised a system of museum cards (like library catalogue cards, but carrying a photograph), which was generally adopted.[34] But he could not survive at the M.F.A., even with Sam's support. In July 1906 they both resigned, and Prichard went to work on a Committee on Museums, based at Simmons College; its purpose was to persuade schools and colleges to make use of art collections, and it was chaired by President Eliot. But Prichard seems to have found it a cul-de-sac, and in 1907 he returned to Europe, though he kept up his friendships with Sam Warren and Mrs. Gardner.

Prichard stayed loyal to Sam and angry on his behalf. In April 1910, after the latter's death, Prichard wrote to Mrs. Gardner that before Sam's time the museum "was despicable and despised. A few families had a special cult for it . . . on weekdays the temple was closed to all save the initiated, who appeared to bully the director and oversee their family tomb. For it was recognized that one room belonged to this family and another to that."[35] He called it the last sanctuary of the Boston aborigines, ". . . frightened tradesmen endowed it with their millions that their descendants might be smiled upon by its popes and hierarchs. . . . Sam Warren opened its windows and ventilated it with the air of the world's experience." Sam was opposed because of his liberalism and his indifference to aristocratic tenure and prejudice.

Sam was opposed, Prichard continues, by a combination of the trustees, Boston society, and Boston artists. (When the question of buying the Lippi was in the air, such Boston artists as Edmund Tarbell, Frederick P. Vinton, and Joseph Windon Smith were quite hostile. Their favorite modern was Sargent, and their old master was Vermeer.) But Sam changed the museum's aim from cult to cultivation, from science to art, from investigation to enjoyment. Knowing little himself about art, he responded to the challenge life brought him, and "His infinite love, patience, and confidence carried him through." He was a great liberator. "He did not stop short of being great."[36] It is not easy to see what facts support Prichard's claim, but it clearly proceeds from conviction.

Still, the most important issue, as far as relations among the Warrens went, was that because of its building plans the M.F.A. had no money to spend on classical antiquities. The Copley Square property was sold for $1.8 million, but the museum still carried a deficit of $38,000 in 1900 and of $34,000 in 1901, which Sam was determined to pay off.[37] In 1904 he announced a purchase of antiquities that he stated must be their last.

One of the Coolidges suggested to the University Museum in Philadelphia that Ned might buy for them, since the Boston Museum could no longer finance him. Museum officers in Philadelphia wrote, and Ned agreed to find things for them too, laying down his terms of freedom of operation and one of his warnings: "All you people will I fear be in the field when the chance is gone. I flatter myself it is much diminished already." (That is, he and Marshall have already bought up the best things.) But in this same letter of February 1902 he hints at a readiness to transfer his services as a whole to Philadelphia: "The Museum here is in one of its periodical throes. Whether it will or can produce any more money or at least enough to go on with is very doubtful. Perhaps I shall have to sigh for new worlds to conquer."[38] He did in fact buy $2,000 of statuary for them (the money was supplied by Lucy Wharton Drexel) and remained a consultant until 1915; but it was Boston he bought for and gave to, much more.

The new policy was a major check to the collecting at Lewes House, though many deals remained in process; over the next two or three years items worth $300,000 piled up there. Gradually Ned accepted defeat and turned his attention, his aspirations, his ambitions elsewhere. He told Sam he was cured of his ambition to serve his native city.[39] Henceforth he would collect for his own satisfaction—mainly gems. (In fact, after Sam had been disgraced and no longer had power at the museum, Ned began again to sell and to give to its collections.)

Ned had not been denied all recognition in Boston. Far from it. On his and Marshall's trip of 1900, they gave speeches at dinners, after which the listeners promised contributions; and at one such dinner Charles Eliot Norton said of Ned, "There is not and never has been in America or in Europe a man with such capacities, will, and circumstances for collecting, and the Museum must be entirely dependent upon him."[40] This was surely public acknowledgment.

Collecting

Warren and Marshall were both excited by the work they found themselves doing, and by the practical qualities of patience, energy, self-control, and psychological penetration it required. Marshall, for instance, became very interested in the forgers of terra-cotta in Greece and wrote a paper on the subject, according to Beazley a fine piece of work. Apparently the Greek dealers were awed by the fierce energy he put into detecting such forgeries.

In Ned's case, it seems clear that he saw his work as being like (being as manly as) his father's and brother's. In a paper delivered to the trustees of the M.F.A. in 1900, he said, "A collector is thought to be a dreamer on days gone by, a loafer in idle lands . . . a leisurely grandee. This impression is a mistake. He is a commercial traveler, a forager. . . . He daily sees forgeries and futilities that he must on no account buy. . . . he daily weighs lie against lie to elicit the truth. . . . He receives with equal complaisance the idle intriguer, the petty huckster, the foolish and faithful adherent, the empty-headed grandee, the agent on the make, the cheating dealer. . . . With one he is adroit, with another soothing, with a third frank, with a fourth inscrutable. . . . He takes an interest in private affairs, illness and financial trouble, he sends salutations and writes constantly to those from whom he obtains one or two things a year. His letters must do him no commercial harm if shown, his agreements no harm if known. . . . He lives in a shower of letters and telegrams. . . . I myself have ridden four days over hill and dale through a Scotch mist to behold two antique bronze heads held together with screws of equal antiquity."[41]

The language of that last sentence reminds us of the connections between collecting and "adventure" as it was understood at that time—in the age of Robert Louis Stevenson and Kipling. The whole piece echoes the self-excitement of Anglo-American imperialism. A letter of Ned's dated August 1, 1914, reminds us of the element of straightforward violence in this work. He writes to Martin Gardner Lane at the museum about a marble lion available in Paris for 40,000 francs, perhaps of the fourth century B.C. It is in two parts, having been blasted apart in order to get it out of Greece, but it could be put back together without any restoration except of a drill hole.[42] This is reminiscent of the ways in which the aesthetes and scholars remained the cousins of businessmen and men of action, from whom they turned away. The world beyond their national frontiers was all "underdeveloped" and lay in need of exploitation.

Warren had also of course to deal with the Boston Museum itself, in negotiations that also required special skills. He described "paying through the preliminary stages a premium to the museum to induce it to accept a service—and only winning with difficulty to the point where its vehement desire to possess such things should break through the crust of prudent tradition."[43] He had to buy things that the museum would not pay for and hold them until they wanted them. "In some cases I thus passed into the Museum what had before been specifically rejected, for instance, the best of the Bourguignon vases, which are among the best in the collection. But there was another reason for being in advance of supplies. I could rely on them only if the general effect of the last sending had been pleasing—and there were many important objects which would not add to the effect. In choosing what was to be sent for the year, I was therefore obliged to combine, say, marbles with other things, say small bronzes—since these last, whatever their merit, attract less admiration. For this choice, an accumulation was necessary."[44] Thus collecting was a form of commerce, of entrepreneurship.

It was also of course a form of highly refined appreciation and analysis. Though Warren and Marshall were not primarily writers, we do have Marshall's piece on the Chios Head, reckoned one of the finest of essays on Greek sculpture, and an anonymously published piece by Warren entitled "The Scandal of the Museo di Villa Giulio." The first appeared in the *Roemische Mitteilungen des Deutschen*

Archaeologischen Instituts in 1910, entitled "Of a Head of a Youthful Goddess, Found in Chios." It was provoked by the skepticism of other connoisseurs as to the statue's authenticity.

Marshall makes considerable use of Rodin's essay on the head, which had been published in *Le Musée* in 1904: *'Il y a dans cette tête la vigueur, la santé, une santé étonnante même, et une force prodigieuse . . . les caractères essentiels [de l'Antiquité] sont la force et la santé. . . . Point de vague. . . . Grâce à lui j'ai compris Praxitèle, moi qui croyais que le Parthenon était le summum de l'art.'*[45]

It is notable that both connoisseurs were looking out for "geometry" in sculpture. Rodin says *"La géometrie, cette qualité divine, est entrée en lui avec un tel naturel"* and Marshall goes on to analyze the head in terms of ovoids and cylinders. Michelangelo's structures are anatomical, but this is geometrical—and that is better. The face is not a portrait.[46] They also share an enthusiasm for skill—understood as the power to deceive the onlooker—reminiscent of Kipling. The technique of the ears is an extraordinary piece of daring, Marshall says, which he is indebted to Rodin for explaining. Because the head was meant to be looked at from the front, the sculptor neglected the side view "in a quite astonishing manner."[47]

Warren's piece appeared in the *Monthly Review* of February 1902 and was an attack on the Italian government's intervention in the art market in an attempt to preserve the national patrimony. It was written on behalf of the international community of classical collectors, and with the cooperation of Wolfgang Helbig, the German scholar, and Fausto Benedetti, the Italian excavator. Warren declared that the creation and publication of the collection of the Villa Giulio was an archaeological fraud: "In no country but Italy would it have been possible for a small band of public officials. . . . The Government, as is well known, reserves all excavations for Italians. It is almost a crime to see any object come up out of the ground. Your presence gives rise to fearful suspicions. Doubtless you are meaning to spirit away 'the national patrimony. . . .'"[48]

The Ministry of Public Instruction was in charge of such matters, and Professor Felice Barnabei was at the head of the Museo di Villa Giulio, where the finds of certain sites were theoretically preserved. In fact, Warren claimed, the contents of different tombs were mixed up together and their provenance confused or falsified. In any case, these things are the *world*'s patrimony.[49] All kinds of corruption and carelessness are alleged. We shall never know the truth; Italians are grossly apathetic about such matters.[50] We must not expect from high-ranking officials in Italy the seriousness, dignity, and interest in the public good which we would find elsewhere.[51] "The intensely corrupt methods which to the Italian are synonymous with business, and which have invaded the public administration, are taken as matters of course."[52]

Readers today will probably be struck by the Anglo-American chauvinism of these remarks; one also notices a difference from Ned's attitude to the Germans in Rome, toward whom he is full of respect. (By his own hedonist and erotic criteria, he should have preferred the Italians; perhaps he did, in the field of hedonism and eros, but not when it came to scholarship and commerce, the world of work.) As for the chauvinism, it should be remembered that this journal was edited by Henry Newbolt, the poet of English imperialism, and Warren probably displayed such biases more prominently as he shaped his thoughts for that audience; at Lewes House, it seems likely, "high-ranking officials" of the American kind were not taken any more seriously than Italian ones. But demonstrably Ned did feel that he was himself displaying, in the field of art, the manly and Anglo-Saxon qualities he had long been called on to admire in his father and brother. His fellow collectors respected him as Sam's colleagues respected *him*.

Ned's Other Activities

Ned suspected that *Boston* despised him. The competition between the brothers was acute, and Ned felt he was denied "success." He wrote Marshall in 1902, "It comes to this, I think: we have arrived at that age when a man usually wins success if he deserves it. We have deserved it and we have not won it, because we are dealing with the new American world. . . . I have done as good work as he [Sam]: I deserve success as much: I don't get it."[53] This key word "success" had been used very freely in eulogies of Mr. Warren, and both brothers probably associated it with their father.

As we know, Ned described his main motive in collecting as always having been "rebellion against Sam and against . . . the worldly love which was inconsistent with love and enthusiasm. Not so had I worked for the Museum: not in that spirit had I endeavoured to help Sam by persuading Mother to alter her will."[54] Moreover, Sam had moved into Ned's world of art, and Ned was to retaliate by moving into Sam's world of business.

As Whitehill says, Ned blamed Sam for putting the museum's

money into building.[55] He decided in 1904 that henceforth Boston was no place for him. As Marshall said, "Under Sam's management the Boston Museum will flourish, perhaps as New York, with finances in magnificent order and all gentlemen and businessmen at the helm. . . . Good livers, over-dressed women, and fine society."[56] (Whitehill quotes this from Burdett and Goddard, and attributes it to Marshall; I think it may be Warren who wrote it—as is often the case, their text is unclear.) Ned had wanted art to be a refuge from all that.

Meanwhile he was busy at many other projects (this busyness is one of his striking characteristics). In 1900, for instance, he published by far his best piece of writing, a sophisticated fairy tale in the manner of Oscar Wilde entitled "The Prince Who Did Not Exist."

Warren's prince does not exist because he is a character in a story, but he loves a young lady reader who has principles. She can love only someone who does exist, who is real, so he is disconsolate; even his own beauty wearies him. He tries to escape from his story at its end, but it is so dull that he gives up, on page 167, weeping and leaving a damp spot on the page. Then he tries to escape at its beginning, but as he pushes back against the story line, all the letters hit him in the face; besides, at the very beginning he wasn't even born. However, when the young lady picks up the story again, she finds it more interesting because it is now all jumbled up by his efforts to escape: Characters answer questions before they are asked and fall in love after they are married. So she becomes quite absorbed in the story, *into* it, and so falls in love with the prince. (Unless someone else wrote or revised this antirealistic fantasy, Ned had literary gifts that his other writings sadly failed to show.)

He published "The Prince Who Did Not Exist" at the Merrymount Press, a privately owned press situated on Summer Street, opposite South Station, and founded in 1893 by Daniel Berkeley Updike. This press was also to publish the catalogue of Mrs. Warren's paintings, Cornelia's *A Memorial of My Mother,* and Fiske's *Enclaves of Economic Rent Yearbooks*. Updike was one of Ned's longtime aesthete friends; an Episcopalian bachelor from Rhode Island, born in the same year as Ned, he was an only child and devoted much of his adult life to his mother.

In his recent autobiography, *Self-Consciousness,* John Updike describes his older kinsman as "frail and shy, with protruding ears and a religious disposition."[57] He seems to have been the Warrens' friend, and especially Ned's, from early on. He worked twelve years for Houghton Mifflin, and then had been stirred to emulation by William Morris's work as a maker of books. He set up a press of his own, and for forty years produced a variety of books, circulars, pamphlets, and so on of high quality. For instance, he printed a number of Edith Wharton's books, by her special request to her publisher.

We don't know much about how he related to the rest of the Warren family, except that he bought some of Mrs. Warren's less expensive pictures at the auction. But Ned gave him his "Titian" Brusasorci (bought together with the Lippi), and in 1928 he and his foreman (later partner) John Bianchi were named as executors and trustees and residuary legatees in Ned's will.

The name of Updike's press is of course an allusion to Thomas Morton's hedonist and licentious establishment near Boston, attacked and destroyed by seventeenth-century puritans. Updike was not hedonist or licentious himself, any more than Ned Warren was, but he was an antipuritan aesthete, and the word "Merrymount" is an antipuritan slogan. One wonders if the Warren family could have patronized such a publisher if Mr. Warren had been still alive. Mr. Warren and Mr. Houghton were not natural Merrymounters. (Updike found Mr. Houghton, when he worked for him, "too much like the granite hills of his native Vermont.") In any case, the adoption of an aesthete press as publisher to the Warren family (except for Sam) is another small sign of Ned's sway within the family.

I was lucky enough to find a woman who had worked with Updike in his later years, and she told me anecdotes of him whose flavor suggests the bachelor milieux Warren frequented in Boston and Maine. For instance, Updike took an acid tone about his Beacon Hill acquaintance and told my informant he'd been thoroughly bored the night before, going out to perhaps the Somerset Club with X. "My people have known his people for three hundred years now; and for three hundred years his people have been boring my people."

But he was as often the victim as the victor in the game of social arrogance. He was a friend of several of the grande dames of Boston, and one day one of them, perhaps Mrs. Gardner, after an absence of a few months, greeted him with an enthusiastic invitation to lunch, because "we have so much to talk about." But when he arrived at her house he found that five or six other people had been invited. And telling this, perhaps fifty years later, his eyes misted over with the remembered pain. My informant "forgave him a lot for that."[58] Such were Warren's friends.

In 1903, Ned published a volume of verse, entitled *Itamos,* and sent a copy to Robert Bridges, with sadly comic results. Bridges was himself an aesthetic movement poet, but one whose verse made very discreet or obscurely bland statements. He wrote quite a flattering letter to Warren about his poems, approving of the latter's praise of carnal love. "As to your main subject or thesis," Bridges said, "I think that your creed really hits the essential motive which man will have to recognize when he has purged his religions."[59] But he had not grasped the kind of love object Warren meant.

It will be seen that, even in prose, Bridges too was addicted to vague and evasive statement, and without the excuse of having had the homosexual's social experience. The two poets were so transcendental and poetic they failed to communicate. When Bridges invited Warren to pay him a visit, what had been hidden in the latter's message gradually became apparent in conversation. Bridges then became embarrassed, and then harsh. He approved of carnality in certain cases, but "men differ so, and the average runs so low, that such a doctrine is not fitted for all. . . ." And finally, at the end of a letter dated July 10, 1904, "Your real meaning is therefore a great shock to me, and among all your enemies you will not find a more stubborn foe than me."[60]

Warren was still collecting, and not only antiquities. In 1900 he ordered from Auguste Rodin a version of his famous sculpture group now called *Le Baiser*. Rodin was of course a congenial spirit because of his eroticism, and a familiar one because of the Fothergill connection. The first version was called *La Foi,* and there was already a second version in existence, but Ned's, for which he asked certain changes (for instance, a complete male sex organ), is often considered the finest. It cost him £1,000 and arrived in Lewes in 1906. More than life-size, it was installed in the coach house until 1914, when Ned gave it to the Lewes Town Hall. In 1917 the Borough Council asked him to take it back because of the effect it might have on the public.

Rodin came and stayed at Lewes House in 1903 and wanted to exchange some of his own work for a Greek Aphrodite there. Warren bought altogether five of his sculptures. As we have seen, Rodin praised the Chios Head and defended Marshall's claims for it. In 1911 he wrote to Lewes House, saying that he shared their Greek religion, and proposed that Marshall should take him to Greece and be his guide there.[61] And though this was the most striking case of Warren's dealings with contemporary artists, it was not the only one. Through John Fothergill he was in touch with, for instance, William Rothenstein, and through him with James Tonks and Wilson Steer; and Roger Fry visited Lewes House and painted a watercolor of it, still preserved there.

On the whole, however, Warren was not very welcoming to contemporary art movements. On April 13, 1903, he sent Sam his judgment of a Degas painting; Sam had solicited his opinion on the museum's behalf. Ned found it "lacking in dignity or nobility of conception, ugly in composition, and not of a type of design which we should want to be followed by students who look to us for guidance, except in the mere technique of painting."[62] This we might call a very Bostonian conservatism, and it is probably representative of Lewes House. They were not modernists in art. Matt Prichard, one of the liveliest and most experimental minds there, drew the line at Picasso, although he admired Matisse.

We know less about Ned's taste in literature, but what little we know suggests a comparable conservatism. More than once he asked the Berensons to tell him of new poets, but adds, in a letter of 1917, that he wants one who does not write in the new style, which is too loose to interest him—"no texture."

Marshall's Marriage

Yet another painful factor in Ned's consciousness was Marshall's gradual separation from him. In their relationship Warren had always been the pursuer, Marshall the pursued, and in this decade the latter decided that he wanted to get married. He fixed his choice on someone (we don't know whom) in 1904–1905, but Warren ruined the project by a fit of jealousy. Then, in 1907, Marshall decided to marry Warren's cousin, Mary Bliss—described by Fothergill as a charming though sickly lady, much interested in the world of art and antiquities. The marriage was made possible by Warren's generosity, for he supplemented Marshall's income from the Metropolitan. (Between 1905 and 1908 he made three such marriage settlements on old friends. In 1904 he was said to have twenty dependents.)[63]

Mary Bliss had been left $5,000 in Mrs. Warren's will, as was Mrs. Warren's sister, Ellen Clarke Hammond, which suggests that the three women were collecting friends. Perhaps that $5,000 was her dowry, which would then be Mrs. Warren's last posthumous strike against Ned. After the marriage, Mary, with Marshall's help, began a collection of old lace. We know that Marshall got on well with Mrs. Warren, and he also seems to have been good friends with his Bliss brothers-in-law. They were all presumably easier to deal with than Ned Warren. The marriage was of course an event everyone interpreted as a defeat for Ned. Berenson heard the news from Erskine and Molly Childers when they visited him in the New Year of 1908, and wrote in exclamation to Mrs. Gardner "Poor Ned!"[64]

Marshall had recommended that Warren forget both his family and the firm: The various works of all of them together, he said, were not worth one of the books of classical archaeology he and Ned might write; books such as Furtwaengler's *Meisterwerke der griechischen Plastik* (1893). Out of the Warren family, only Ned's mother had ever helped him, Marshall said; so why not forget the family and the hundreds of people working day and night at the Cumberland Mills. He was not interested in Warren's idea of living at Westbrook: "It is your own business, I suppose, if you choose to spend your life at Cumberland Mills for six months of the year. I at least could not do so. The place is dreadful and the people worse."[65] He didn't believe in Warren's ability to deal with the businessmen at the mills, but, "You think your duty lies in Boston and I know you too well to try to stop you."[66] He also disapproved Warren's taking his lover, Harry Asa Thomas, with him to America in 1906.

When he heard the news of Sam's suicide, Marshall wrote Ned what sounds, in the excerpt we have, like a severe letter. He described him as being "mystical," apparently meaning that he was irrational; when left alone for a couple of months, Ned always got a scheme in his head that no argument could then drive out. "You made up your mind about Eros: you made up your mind about the Mill people. I could do nothing to get the things out of your head. You had identified your will with [the will of God]." This makes Ned "wonderfully strong" but "dreadfully uncanny." "You won't bend aside. Things must go down before you, you advance to your end in view, pitilessly, though no man is more pitiful, cruelly, though no man is more tender, recklessly, though no man is more patient."[67] "Uncanny" is Marshall's equivalent for the "crazy" that other people applied to Warren. And Sam was one of the things that went down before him.

For some time Warren had been anxious that he and Marshall

should get back to the writing of their discourse on the Greek idea. Collecting, he said, expressed his idea only by quotation and could not compare with direct exposition. His idea was his life. For Marshall, Warren told him in a letter of 1901, the person is everything, while Warren lived for an idea, not a friend.[68] These were the terms in which Marshall thought too; as early as September 1891, fearing death, he wrote that he himself "was a born lover, I think, and not quite right for a scholar: though I loved scholarship above all things, I always loved some man better."[69] Warren loved his idea best. Naturally enough, Marshall complained that he was only a symbol in one of his friend's schemes.[70] These terms do not always seem the best for comparing the two, but they do point to a striking difference between their respective commitments to their "idea."

Burdett and Goddard say that the year 1906 was the worst of all for the friendship. John Fothergill blamed Marshall for his heartlessness, but he also felt that Warren was in the wrong, was too intellectually and morally ambitious, too determined to spread his theory of "the Greek idea." He wrote him, "It is futile to sigh for the world of Pericles. . . . I believe that to a woman is given the means to satisfy men in the very highest sense. Your theory strikes me as essentially un-Hellenic and un-Christian as well."[71]

But occasionally Fothergill changed his mind and said that Warren was right; at certain illuminated moments of knowledge, he could see things the way Warren did. He spoke of Warren's solidity—his intellectual, moral, and spiritual capacity, something so impressive it "reconciles [Fothergill] to existence." And Burdett endorsed that judgment.[72]

Oxford

At Oxford there was another project: Warren had long wanted to promote the study of the classics in a "traditional"—that is, misogynistic—setting. He had known, in his first years at New College, Thomas Case, who became president of Corpus Christi in 1904—a man as recalcitrant as Warren himself about modern subjects and modern ways of teaching old subjects. Corpus Christi, moreover, already had a chair in classics and was traditionally strong in that subject. It therefore made sense to endow that college liberally enough to let it pursue a reactionary path, indifferent to modern theories.

One of the earliest letters by Warren in the Corpus Christi archive dates from September 1906.[73] In it he tells Case that he still has to extricate himself from the bonds of a Will and Deed of Trust, which will take him another year or two, before he has money at his disposal. His brother Fiske is helping him in breaking the trust. (Ned mentions this no doubt because Fiske and Gretchen had been living in Oxford since 1904 and were known to some of the dons at Corpus.) However, he continues, Fiske does not know what Ned wants the money for, and this is for the best as far as Fiske goes. In other words, Case should not broach the subject to the other pair. In fact, Ned's name should not be mentioned in the matter. (Ned always took pains to keep the people in his schemes from knowing about each other.)

In a letter of 1906 he assures Case that "The clause is in my will," although at other times he insists that he is speaking of intentions, not making promises. A letter of 1908 speaks of the sale of a Rubens, the price of which will allow him to endow the college, and another, of July 1909, promises two installments of £1,000 each for the Classical Fund. "The family knot," he adds, "was hard to untie, but is now certain to be untied." (This is another sign of his confidence that he had beaten Sam.)

The endowment finally came in two forms, or at least two stages: There was the Classical Fund, to help pay those who taught Latin and Greek at the college; and, when Ned died, there would be money to appoint a praelector in classics—a post never to be given to a woman, and if to a married man, then he must have rooms (not just classrooms or offices) in the college, or he must live in a house connected by a tunnel with the college so that he could reach the undergraduates all through the night. It was his particular desire, he said, that the Warren Praelector and those he taught should be in close contact at all hours. Special money was assigned for digging this tunnel. It was further specified that the praelector should teach only in the college, and only young men.

Around the end of this decade, Warren found another way to cast the spell of the Greek idea over Oxford undergraduates. He formed a significant friendship with John Davidson Beazley, who in some ways was to continue the work of Lewes House after Warren's death and to institutionalize some of the influence of Warren at Oxford. He became a world authority, indeed *the* world authority, on Greek vases. He distinguished the development of Attic vase painting over three hundred years, in terms of individual but related artists (masters and pupils, rivals and colleagues).

Beazley was well placed to appreciate Warren. He too had aspired to be a poet. He too, as a boy, displayed himself in a toga, and the display had the same sexual significance. He too played with the same defiance of authority and normality. But he was different in being strikingly handsome, academically brilliant, and able to make clear and ruthless decisions of self-discipline. At a certain moment he seems to have given up poetry and homosexuality, and most kinds of personal relationships; he devoted himself almost entirely to classical scholarship.

His scholarship was very pure, but still recognizably in alliance with the aestheticism of Lewes House. In an essay by John Boardman in Donna Kurtz's *Beazley and Oxford,* we can find a comparison and contrast, in terms of humanism, drawn between him and his predecessor as professor of classical archaeology, Percy Gardner, who held the post from 1887 to 1925. Beazley was more the scholar but narrower in his interests; fastidious is a word often used. Boardman speaks of the dramatic contrast between "Gardner—patriarchal, a figure of the 19th century, a pioneer and empire-builder [and] Beazley—the aesthete, poet . . . and with a total dedication mainly to one branch of classical archaeology. . . ."[74] Under him the cast collection ceased to grow; he didn't care about teaching.

In the same volume, Michael Vickers criticizes Beazley's approach, saying that Greek potters were really humble craftsmen, and that it was the influence of the modern arts-and-crafts movement that made us, or Beazley, see them as artists. Beazley wished this concept back upon the Greeks, according to Vickers. But for us this reaction against Beazley matters most as a sign of how long Warren's influence had lasted.

Though a brilliant student, Beazley's Fellowship at Christ Church College was not renewed in 1908 on the grounds of idleness and irresponsibility. He thought of himself as a poet in those days; later, after he had committed himself to scholarship and respectability, he would never mention his poetry. T. E. Lawrence wrote, "Beazley is a very wonderful fellow . . . who has written almost the best poems that ever came out of Oxford: but his shell was always hard, and with time he seems to curl himself tighter and tighter into it. If it hadn't been for that accursed Greek art, he'd have been a very fine poet."[75] He seems indeed to have abstracted himself from almost everything but his work, as a consequence of that initial act of self-discipline.

He found that lifework finally at Lewes House, working on Greek vases, and Warren gave liberally to Beazley's museum, happy to install there too the icons of virility. He was one of Warren's closest intellectual heirs, extending his influence at Oxford into the second half of this century. Born in 1885, he lived on until 1970.

These Oxford schemes, then, were on Ned's mind, as was his collecting, his ambitions at Westbrook, his relations with Marshall and Prichard, and above all his relations with Sam. It is difficult to disentangle these factors, but it seems clear that they worked together to exasperate the always irritated feeling between the two brothers. He wrote his attorney, who had reproached him with extravagance: "I do not like to miss ripe fruit when it is ready to fall into my hands; and I feel it hard to do the obvious thing [retrench?] while Sam has money to spend on his machines."[76]

By this time Ned had quite reoriented his loyalties within the family. His primary loyalty went to his father (and against his mother). "I wasn't good to him [my father] while he was alive but he was big enough to pardon me, and I have done amends since his death by the honour in which I hold him."[77] This is the feeling we find in "Alcmaeon," together with the more luridly colored matricide. He blamed his upbringing for his character, as we have seen.

In a letter to Berenson dated May 18, 1903, he ascribed the distrust in which he was held by Bostonians to several causes—none of them touching on his sexuality. First came his behavior during the long years when he was "recovering from my melancholia." Then his lack of any real friend at the M.F.A., with the partial exception of Robinson. Then the defection of Prichard and Fisher to Sam's side, and Cornelia's believing their version of things. Above all, he acknowledged, his work was all done in revulsion against his antecedents and training. He was not a dutiful son to his mother; he rebelled against the tradition maintained by her and handed down to his sister—the court of female arbitration. This feminism is entrenched in middle-class life. It is the old battle, he declared, between those natural enemies, the bourgeois and the artist.[78]

When he spoke of Bostonians this way, we may be sure that he thought of Sam and Mabel and their friends. But did he, one wonders, also mean Cornelia's friends of Denison House, and Henry's friends, and Fiske's? And what did those quite various groups think of Ned Warren, whose doings must have held a certain interest for them?

Fiske

Fiske, as we have seen, was on Ned's side in the quarrel, emotionally and as one of the heirs. While legally he was on Sam's side, as both a trustee and a partner, he had in fact been squeezed out of both functions by Sam and spent his time on other matters. His allowing Ned to present him as an ally seems to show that he resented this. But he also seems to have been quite passive in the suit; an ineffective ally for Ned and susceptible to pressure from Cornelia, who was mostly on Sam's side. Of course his first trip to the Philippines covered a good deal of 1901 and 1902. Then he was based in Oxford in 1904 and 1905, and from there went back to the Philippines; and the same thing again in 1907; so he was absent from Boston most of the time.

He was leading an exciting life, in a style quite unlike the other Warrens'—reported in newspapers, and sometimes hitting the headlines. On October 18, 1901, the *Boston Evening Transcript* carried the cry FISKE WARREN A SUSPECT and told of treasonable and inflammatory proclamations found in his baggage on the boat to Manila. Fellow passengers said that he and Sixto Lopez had shaken hands in mutual congratulation when they heard of President McKinley's assassination. He was the first man to have to take the oath of allegiance when he arrived in the Philippines (otherwise he would not have been allowed to land). This contretemps had been in a sense foreseen by the officers of the Anti-Imperialist League, and at their suggestion Fiske had resigned from his position on the executive committee before setting out, in order to avoid compromising the league.

He gave his Harvard classmates his own account of all this in the Class Report for 1907; since 1900 he had been involved in the Philippine question, through Sixto Lopez and his Australian secretary, Thomas Patterson. The oath of allegiance exacted from him, illegally, in 1901 showed that the government was lying when it said that the Filipinos welcomed the American presence. In 1905 he had been able to win acquittal for the editors of *Renacimiento*, who had been prosecuted for exposing the concentration camps in which rebels and their families were kept. He cited his articles of 1907 and 1908 in the *Springfield Republican* on Philippine topics.

Fiske was certainly the most eccentric of the Warrens, but it was a recognizable, and in some ways comfortable, Yankee style of eccentricity. It is notable that he was the one who kept up with his

Harvard classmates; Sam seems never to have sent in a reply to the report, which is perhaps a sign of the strain of disorder in him. Fiske was in some sense the stereotypical Yankee, full of odd quirks of prudence and principle, who asked to be treated as a "character." For instance, in November 1906 he refused to subscribe to the museum on the grounds that institutions should get money from the state or else from those who make use of them.

On the boat from Hong Kong with Fiske in 1902 was a woman named Olive Cole Smith, who long after wrote a description of him in a letter to his daughter. She was a Midwesterner and evidently found Fiske a typical New Englander—challengingly standoffish. When she reproached his absence of mind, "with such a memory you'll never be President of the United States," he replied, "Who wants to be? I don't like the kind of men they select to be Presidents." "What! Not even Lincoln?" "No. He was a vulgar, crude man." Mrs. Smith was shocked by his elitism, and (at that time) by his anti-imperialism.[79]

Gretchen Warren, as we know, had her portrait painted by John Singer Sargent at Fenway Court in 1903, a picture often regarded as one of his best. She studied philosophy at Oxford until 1907, and at the end of her stay took examinations administered by F. C. S. Schiller of Corpus and J. A. Smith of Balliol and was given a certificate that she deserved a double First. On her return to America she was offered both a lectureship at Wellesley and a deanship at Radcliffe. On William James's recommendation, an essay of hers on the philosophy of science was published in the *Monist* in 1910.

The style of her philosophy, at least in its much later expression, is suggested by this excerpt from her essay "Art, Education, and Nature": "Man is more than physical. If the artist, the poet, the scientist draws upon the tremendous panorama of past and present life spread before him, still more must the whole man seize upon all that he sees and feels of beauty and intelligent order, eager for it as material for the shaping of his mind and will."[80] She sees everything from the angle of the creative mind, like a latter-day Transcendentalist.

Fiske was also much engaged at the end of this decade by the Single Tax movement, which derived from Henry George's philosophy as expressed primarily in his *Progress and Poverty* (1879). (Fiske read the book in 1909 and was an immediate convert.) Henry George (1839–97) began his writing career as a muckraking journalist in San Francisco, hostile to the rich, but in *Progress and Poverty* he presented Labor and Capital as partners in affliction, their joint enemy being the landlord: "The Boston collar-manufacturer who pays his girls 2 cents an hour may commiserate their condition, but he, as they, is governed by the law of competition, and cannot pay more and carry on his business."[81]

Georgism could thus be seen, and was in fact welcomed, as being a less threatening alternative to Marxism: a more welcome alternative because it was not Socialist, did not declare a class war, and had in fact its elements of idealism and spiritualism.

It seems to have been this side of George's thinking that attracted Fiske, though he makes a great show of facts and reason in his own writings in that vein. (In his *Enclaves of Single Tax* yearbook for 1922, Fiske speaks of his socialism as being of a scientific, not a utopian and propagandistic kind.) Moreover, by choosing to espouse the Single Tax movement, as opposed to other parts of Georgism, and by interpreting it in exclusively economic as opposed to political terms, he arrived at a form of radicalism that was as unthreatening to the capitalist class as possible. Personally, Fiske was quite abrasive, and yet winsome, and his varieties of ideology were combined according to the same receipt.

C. A. Barker, in his *Henry George,* says that when George's idea seized a political mind it became a part of progressivism; when it seized a mind of legalist bent (like Fiske Warren's) it became the Single Tax movement. Barker sees George as offering America a Jeffersonian ideology, adapted to an industrialized economy. It is also worth noting that the time of *Progress and Poverty*'s publication was the time of Tolstoy's conversion to the simple life—two of the starting points for the New Age.

At the end of *Progress and Poverty,* George writes, in quite a religious style: "Behind the problems of social life lies the problem of individual life. . . . Out of the inquiry has come to me something I did not think to find, and a faith that was dead revives. The yearning for a further life is natural and deep. It grows with intellectual growth, and perhaps none really feel it more than those who have begun to see how great is the universe." This sounds like Vida Dutton Scudder's Franciscan socialism. "When we see that economic law and moral law are essentially one, and that the truth which the intellect grasps by toilsome effort is but that which the moral sense reaches by quick intuition, a flood of light breaks in upon individual life."[82] One can see why Fiske Warren would find this attractive, but also why Karl Marx would describe George's book as the capitalists' last stand.

Another of George's lieutenants was Father James Huntington, the founder of the Order of the Holy Cross, the first Protestant monastic order in America. Several of the women of Denison House became Companions of the Holy Cross, and Vida Dutton Scudder wrote Huntington's biography. Cornelia Warren must have heard a lot about George's theories from them as well as from Fiske, which shows again the parallelism between her interests and her brother's.

Fiske has been described, in articles devoted to him, as a leading spokesman for Georgism, but none of the books on the latter topic mention Fiske Warren. Among the many concerns that come under the heading of Georgism, his primary interest (he has an article on this topic in the *Single Tax Yearbook* of 1917) was the single tax enclaves; various attempts to run a small community by collecting from all who live there the "economic rent" as George defines that, and paying local taxes out of that fund. Fiske himself started up several such enclaves: the first, Tahanto, begun on his farm at Harvard, in 1909; another up at Westbrook; and a third, in 1916, in Andorra. In 1911 he set up a Raiffeisen system of cooperative credit in a previously existing colony, Arden, in Delaware. He had studied this system in 1905 in Ireland, where Horace Plunkett had introduced it. This was the first application of the system in the United States.

The *Boston Sunday Globe* carried an article on Fiske on December 29, 1907, with pictures of Lopez, Fiske, Gretchen, and their home. He was presented as a society man converted to politics and as a thorn in the side of Secretary Taft. When in Manila, he had been ostracized by official society as a renegade. At a banquet there, apparently, a Reverend Dr. Rossiter offered to have the war veterans duck "a certain little anti-imperialist." The *Globe,* in quite a friendly and admiring style, described him as an enthusiast and idealist like Wendell Phillips and William Lloyd Garrison.

Cornelia

Cornelia Warren was engaged primarily in work centering around Denison House. In 1902 a book entitled *Literary Boston of Today,* by Helen M. Winslow, refers to her *Miss Wilton* as "a successful novel" and reports that the author intends to write again as soon as she has leisure, but all her time and energy go now to settlement work.

She was also involved in forms of profit-sharing among her employees at Cedar Hill and drew up similar plans for the workers at the mills. She consulted Brandeis about these schemes in 1900. In

the same year he was advising her about the purchase of Old Colony Church in order to convert it into a gymnasium for the benefit
of Denison House people. (She bought the building for $1,100 and
rented it to the city for a nominal sum for five years. Vida Scudder
was one of those involved.) Cornelia invited Italians out to Cedar
Hill, for instance on Decoration Day. (Presumably they were shown
her Italian painting, the Filippino Lippi tondo.) The Denison House
women had considerable success with the Italians there, and Alice
Freeman Palmer was leader of a group devoted to welcoming Italians to America.

There is, however, less to report about both her work and that of
the house in this decade. Following a pattern familiar to feminists,
the public record was inscribed by men, and the work of male
institutions either did, or seemed to, eclipse that of Denison House.
It was, for instance, Robert Woods of South End House who wrote
the books on settlement work in Boston. Denison House did not
have a Jane Addams—its nearest approach was Vida Scudder. And
the settlement movement as a whole began to lose its impetus as
professional social workers began to be trained and as political
theory began to favor radical militancy.

In 1918, Mabel Warren wrote to her daughter Sylvia that Cornelia Warren had given her mother's Lowestoft china and Italian
vases to Denison House, and now "the old cats" are going to sell
them. One would not expect Mabel to show much sympathy for
settlement workers at any time, but perhaps twenty years earlier she
might not have been quite so reckless in her scorn. At least the
phrase shows the gulf between the two branches of the family.[83]

Superficially, the settlement house movement had been successful. There were apparently more than four hundred of them by
1914. In that year a questionnaire was circulated among workers to
which 145 replied; seventy of them had been in residence between
one and five years. Of these, sixty-nine declared themselves in
sympathy with labor organizations; ten specified the A. F. of L., and
eight the more radical I.W.W.; several stressed their belief in
women's unions. Forty said they were Socialists, and 101 declared
for women's suffrage. But in Caroline Gordon's "Conclusion" to the
report on the Boston house, there was a heavy stress on the way
official agencies were taking over its functions, and its current need
therefore to justify itself qualitatively, not quantitatively, in terms
of "spirit."[84] To sound that innocuous note was, implicitly, to sound
the movement's death knell. The volunteer was being replaced by

the trained specialist, the amateur by the professional. Vida Scudder moved from Denison House back to Wellesley in 1912. In 1917 she wrote that settlements were now entirely accredited, thoroughly established, and so "they present no challenge to the chivalry of youth."[85] At least in the reading and writing community, Cornelia's line of work, like Fiske's, did not prove as fruitful as Ned's. The aesthetic movement had absorbed or diverted idealistic energies.

Looking back in 1914, moreover, Denison House saw itself as having moved away from direct education toward public hygiene and the development of the artistic impulse by *racial* crafts.[86] Denison House's constituency came to be largely Syrian and then Chinese—Tyler Street runs parallel with, and one block over from, Harrison Avenue, now counted as part of Boston's Chinatown; and so the issues of immigration and cultural pluralism were much discussed there.

Robert Woods urged his staff to "Appreciate the distinctive genius of each type and to sympathize with its traditions."[87] In 1902 he called assimilation a two-edged sword and stressed the value of the immigrant edge—the value of preserving the culture of the immigrant home.[88] This had its effect on Zionism, and therefore on the development of Louis Brandeis. Woods was an ally of Brandeis; he had worked with him against the Boston Elevated Railroad proposal and for savings-bank insurance. These groups were all allied. In 1905, Joseph Eastman left South End House to become secretary to Brandeis's Public Franchise League and work against the Elevated Railroad.

A major theorist in the matter of cultural pluralism was Horace M. Kallen, a rabbi's son who went to Harvard, studied with William James, and then became a Zionist. He and Henry Hurwitz organized the Harvard Menorah Society, with President Eliot's support. He got to know Brandeis in 1905, and together they spread the idea of Jewish progressivism and idealism. "The Jew is essentially a Democrat," said Brandeis. The first issue of the *Menorah Journal* in 1915 had both an article by Brandeis and a flattering biographical note.

Brandeis

That, however, lay in the future. Brandeis did not speak about Judaism before 1905, and only joined the Zionists sometime in 1912–1913. Meanwhile he moved further left politically. In 1890 he had donated his services in a fight against lobbying by the liquor and railway interests, and in 1897 began the five-year struggle against the Boston Elevated Railway Company. In 1908 he led the less successful Anti-Merger League against the formation of the New Haven, Boston, and Maine Railroad. In the same year he read H. G. Wells's *New Worlds for Old* and began to take an interest in contemporary attempts at socialism. A little later he made alliance with Senator La Follette. All of which built up opposition to him in Boston's legal circles and elsewhere. For instance, the American Jewish Committee was hostile to Brandeis because it included investment bankers, and because of the role he played in, among other things, the Ballinger-Pinchot case about mining interests' exploitation of Alaska, where one of his adversaries was Daniel Guggenheim. The Morgan-Guggenheim group had been assigned five thousand acres of coal-bearing land, and that was connected to a scandal in the Department of the Interior, of which the secretary was Richard Achilles Ballinger. That case both made Brandeis a national figure and took his energies away from the Warren suit.

He was becoming a prominent leader, and J. P. Morgan was one of his great enemies. Morgan was also, for instance, behind the New Haven merger, where Brandeis suffered his greatest defeat. "Mr. Morgan," he said, "may be regarded as the father of monopoly for this country. . . . We have no place in the American democracy for the money king, not even for the merchant prince. We are confronted in the 20th century, as we were in the 19th century, with an irreconcilable conflict. Our democracy cannot endure half free and half slave. The essence of the trust is a combination of the capitalist, by the capitalist, for the capitalist.[89] [And] private monopoly in business and industry is an exact analogy of political despotism."[90]

These were the matters that were preoccupying him in 1910, at the time of the Warren suit. Because he was in Washington, busy with the Ballinger-Pinchot case, he did not come back to Boston to defend Sam; instead he asked his associate, Edward McClennen, to conduct the case. He did not take it seriously because he could not take Ned seriously, it was said. And then we must take into account the division in politics between him and Sam.

After 1905, according to Gal, Sam refused to follow Brandeis's lead in politics. His links were by then with State Street, and Allan Forbes, a State Street financier, replaced Brandeis as his closest friend.[91] "Warren evidently did not accept Brandeis's invitation in November 1905 to attend a meeting on the 'subject of insurance of working men' despite his earlier interest in the conditions of labor. He is not mentioned in the literature or surviving papers concerning the savings-bank insurance movement. Nor is Warren mentioned in the voluminous papers connected with the fight against the New Haven merger. Warren's evasiveness in these matters undoubtedly caused his friendship with Brandeis to degenerate."[92]

Ned and his attorneys seem to have aimed their complaints at Brandeis from early on, before the suit was even filed. It is a standard maneuver to excuse the object of one's indictment—and claim charitable feelings for oneself—by pointing to a sinister figure in the shadows behind him. Brandeis's absence from the courtroom became evidence against him.

Brandeis told his friend Norman Hapgood in 1913 that he had just begun to get into the Warren suit when the call came from *Colliers* magazine to take part in the Ballinger case, and that he had been reluctant to delegate the Warren suit to his associates because of his personal feeling for Sam.[93] Probably he detected some anti-Semitic feeling in Youngman's indictment, although the explicit charge (or a main one) was simply that Brandeis had acted for both sides of the dispute, the heirs and the partners, even though they were at odds with each other.

In Sam's will, which was drawn up in 1906, before feelings reached their bitterest peak, the eleventh and last article says that the testator is not unmindful that his executors and trustees (who again included Brandeis) may have to act in situations when the interest of one of them conflicts with that of a beneficiary. The will authorizes such a trustee to act in that situation and directs that he shall not be impeached unless positive evidence of ill-doing is provided. It seems clear enough what threat that article was intended to ward off. Sam was, in advance, protecting Brandeis against charges relating to Sam's estate, like those already being raised about the family trust.

The Suit

The decade's most important events, for our story, had to do with the suit over the Mills Trust. In 1906, Ned's attorney, Youngman, produced a seventy-page report arguing that the trust had worked to the advantage of the partners in S.D. Warren and Company but at the expense of the heirs. This report was the result of three years of investigation of the firm by accountants, and its cost was divided equally between Ned and Fiske. Both brothers were rebelling against Sam.

Fiske seems to have needed Ned's taking the initiative before he could himself protest against Sam. If he did feel such a passivity or inferiority, that explains his so often yielding to or favoring Ned in, among other things, financial matters. Another reason might be a guilt that, as long as he was a minor partner in the firm, Fiske shared in Sam's suspect prosperity. According to Ned's attorneys, Sam was making nearly $100,000 a year, and Fiske $30,000 to $40,000— before his share was so radically diminished, that is.

Another factor in the situation was Ned and Fiske's desire to intervene in the company's running of the mills. Ned had proposed to install himself, as a six-month-a-year resident, at Longley House, across the road from the mills. This was where members of the family stayed on visits to Westbrook and where the managers met. Ned saw himself living there, unobtrusively listening to the managers' conferences and making occasional proposals: to win the workers' trust with a swimming bath (in the Byzantine style) or a series of lectures on Shelley; and to suggest to the management the purchase of, for instance, property with water rights, such as the Saccarappa Falls, when such became available.

He had also some straight businessman criticism to offer on the nepotism at the mills. In a letter to Cornelia in 1908, Ned said, about the running of the mills, "I demur to hereditary succession and traditional management at the mills." This objection was a matter of business policy, he said, as much as the things he had criticized, and they had finally conceded he *should* criticize, in the company offices on Devonshire Street. He wanted to send an investigator to Westbrook, the way he had sent Youngman to the latter place.

On June 10, 1909, he sent Cornelia a long account from Longley House of a conversation he had had with a disaffected workman who had much to complain of in the administration of the mills. Ned gives an admirably objective-sounding account of what this "A.B." had told him. And on February 15, 1910, he explains his desire to live in or near Westbrook. Sam had once said the Warrens *should* spend their summers on the Presumpscott, whence their fortune had come, but he now objected to Ned's living there. (During the hearings he had repeated that objection.) So the latter had leased Fewacres, a mile or so away, as the next best thing. "Often when I rode on the downs with Johnnie and heard only of collecting, my thoughts were of the mill people," but the collecting was a big job, and he had waited till that came to its natural end before beginning something new. He would never have interfered "after my experience of Sam's Museum work, the principle was fixed in my brain that a man must not exceed his own province."[94]

We gather from Burdett and Goddard that Ned had face-to-face arguments with both Sam and Brandeis during the suit.[95] But since it seems that Brandeis was not often present in Boston (at least once the suit was filed) perhaps written arguments coming from him are meant.

For the time being Ned saw himself as a social reformer. "Poor mill-hands!" he exclaimed, "I am longing to go to the rescue, but I can't go faster . . . my business is for the moment to be content with their discontent."[96] He composed a satirical sonnet about the hardheaded or hard-nosed company and its plans for the workers:

> But paper made of pulp, and pulp of men
> Appears the end of its accomplishment . . .
> . . . for, hard of head,
> Their owner thinketh not, or, thinking, could
> Only produce more paper out of wood,
> And is alike to them, alive or dead.[97]

Perhaps he saw himself at that moment as like the Shelley of the revolutionary sonnets.

Finally, on December 13, he wrote to Sam that he had filed suit but hoped to withdraw it and be friends again. He then presumably went to Fewacres for Christmas.

Ned had devoted a lot of energy to furnishing Fewacres and remained very fond of it. Some of his mother's furniture from Mount Vernon Street was there, as was a Chinese vase, a fourth-century B.C. statuette of Artemis, and an architectural capital. It is still a striking house. He wrote one of his better poems about the place, which began:

> The scent of wooden fires is all
> about the house. By rushing breeze
> shaken, the burdens of the trees
> fall.[98]

Living there, he was not far from a cousin, or second cousin, of whom he was fond: Lois Warren Shaw, the daughter of John E.

Warren. His correspondence with her shows his ability to relax and play even in the grim circumstances then surrounding him.

The first letter that survives, dated September 22, 1908, begins, "I took your illness lightly, as I think that woes should be taken when lightness will cure them: heaviness won't. But of course a serious ailment should be taken seriously, and I should be as serious as is possible (to me) if I understood the ailment. . . . My nostrums are faith, hope, and charity, by none of which do we gain anything except everything." He believed that nothing makes a soul suffer as much as wanting too much, though he admitted the virtue of large desires. However, once the desire has been achieved, the soul either resumes unhappy striving or "it stands behind chairs and serves other people. This last stage, which includes happiness after a fashion, is called blessedness. . . ." (This we might take as a rationalization of his own behavior with Marshall and others.) Ned preached neither detachment nor attachment. "We need the fireplace, but freshness is without the window." He ended by saying, "Don't you think that I ought to don a cassock and bands?"[99]

They corresponded mostly about furniture and family gossip, but it seems clear that there was a substantial affection between them, and one letter, undated but obviously written soon after Sam's suicide, tells us more about Ned's feelings than any other document. In it he said it had taken him years to find out the truth about the trust and the company, and what he had discovered was what he had long suspected from his knowledge of Sam, though not what he had expected from Mort. "You probably think," he said, assuming her agreement with his account of things, "that men of business are not always all that they think themselves and that they are furious when caught up by" a nonbusinessman like Ned, who "has obviously no business to meddle with them. Further you think that . . . it is always an advantage not to have had a sound commercial education."

His feelings about the family were very sore, and the most striking parts of the letter are his self-defense against Cornelia and his reproach to Fiske, already quoted. He says nothing directly about Sam, but observes that Bambo (Sam's eldest son, who took his place) "believes, I suppose, that a Prince Imperial should succeed an Emperor." The stress he laid on the word "emperor" sounds satirical and bitter. He wrote from England and claimed that everyone there is on his side in this particular matter, as well as in the whole structure of their thinking.

He declared, to another correspondent, that Sam was not really keen on the business, any more than he was on collecting; Ned claimed to have Fiske's support in this diagnosis. What was Sam keen on? In museum matters, Ned said, all Sam cared about was conservative financial policy, family dignity, and their mother's memory.[100] This last seems to be a reference to giving the Lippi to the M.F.A. in her name.

If there was to be no revision of the trust, with a trustee board of all four siblings, Ned wrote, he was resolved to sell out (and Fiske would probably do the same) to someone like J. P. Morgan.[101] According to his investigation of the trust, he was getting only 40 percent of his due. Youngman claimed that $1.5 million (counting interest, $2 million) had been appropriated by the partners at the expense of the heirs since 1888. Ned's share of that would be about $600,000.

That was the situation in September 1909 when Ned sailed from England, on the mission that, five months later, ended with Sam's death. At least those were the facts and figures of the situation as Ned described it to people at a certain distance. We do not know what he felt. We do not know what he said to, say, Marshall about it, much less what he said to Sam. Nor do we know what Sam felt about Ned by any direct expression of those feelings.

All we know for certain is that Sam went out to Needham Junction by train on February 18, walked to Karlstein, and after an afternoon of log-splitting, turned his gun against himself. He was suffering various defeats in his business life; he may well have felt abandoned by Louis Brandeis; and he does not seem to have found consolation in his domestic life. He left no note to his family and made no attempt to disguise his suicide as a shooting accident. His son had to discover the body and conceal the disgrace.

Karlstein seems to have been something of a Bayard house. Mabel Warren's father and at least one sister were often there, yet we do not hear of Sam's siblings visiting. Mr. Bayard lived there for a while, actually died there, and outside the front door stood a brass cannon presented to him by the people of England after his time in London. The elaborate stables and the weekend polo and riding parties also had a rather Southern style. A man as tense as Sam Warren may have felt, on occasion, as lonely among the Bayards, and even the Bayard-Warrens, as he did among his own siblings. But we can only guess. There are just the few letters cited.

Yet even if we did know what the two brothers said to and about each other, we should not necessarily believe that that was what they felt. What they wrote falls far short of hatred, and the same may have been true of their conversations: There are many reasons why destructive emotions are not expressed, at least not directly. But if we look at the jagged pattern of each man's behavior, the fissures in his personality, and the impact third parties felt from them during these months and more, there can surely be no doubt that there was fierce psychic tension between the two—a psychic field not wholly dependent on the individuals—or that the bullet fired in Karlstein was exploded and directed by that tension as well as by the gun's mechanism.

7

Posthumous

*The Captain first touched his cap, and then proffered a
broad and muscular hand, clean and well-shaped, but
bearing evident signs of having done rough work. In that
frank grasp, though it was gentle enough, Oliver's
unprepared fingers felt a bit thin and hesitant. But how
could a sea-captain look so very fresh and youthful and
sportsmanlike? And when he said* How do you do?
*how could his voice and air be so singularly engaging
and unembarrassed? Ah, he was English.*

—George Santayana,
The Last Puritan

We have now passed the climax of our story, but we need fear
no sense of anticlimax as we follow out the rest of the Warrens'
lives. In its mutilated form, the family continued various forms of
energetic work.

There is a rough pattern of ten- or eleven-year intervals between
their deaths: Mr. Warren died in 1888, Henry in 1899, Sam in 1910,
Cornelia in 1921, Ned in 1928, and Fiske in 1938. But at least in
the case of the last two there was no relaxation of drive, no deflec-
tion of purpose, in the years after 1910.

Immediate Reactions
First of all of course there was the reaction to Sam Warren's death.
Considerable shock was felt in Boston, and the circumstances of

Sam's death had to be adequately explained, someone had to be blamed. There were three individuals or groups who were said to be responsible for it: his enemies at the M.F.A., Brandeis, and Ned.

On February 23, Mrs. Gardner reported Sam's death to Berenson (and presumably to Prichard at about the same time) as an appalling loss. "He was the only one who cared and worked for the Art Museum. The consequence is that the staff are heart-broken, and the trustees etc. know and realize *not*. He has not been well, but his death from apoplexy was very sudden."[1] (Mrs. Gardner, it would seem, did not read the *Evening American*.)

She and Prichard directed their first anger against the people at the museum. Prichard saw Warren's death as a sequel to the drama that had involved the two men equally, ending with their joint resignations from the museum in 1906. We have noted, moreover, that the reporter from the *Evening American* also asked immediately how much money Sam had left to the museum—and that Brandeis replied that he didn't suppose he had left any. Prichard, who was in Paris, heard rumors of anger in Boston because Sam had *not* made a sizable bequest. (Indeed, Sam's family seems to have closed its purse strings as far as the museum was concerned: Mabel Warren, after Sam's death, sent it $10 when solicited for a contribution.) These details show us that there was, and was known to be, bitter feelings between the Sam Warren party and the museum; bitter enough to be invoked at the time of his death.

To understand this feeling we must retrace the events that began with Prichard's appointment in 1902. He, Sam Warren, and Mrs. Gardner had quickly formed a high-spirited and mocking alliance against the duller and more conventional trustees. In 1904, when Warren, Robinson, and the architects hired by the museum sailed to Europe to look at models for the new building, Prichard became temporary director. And the 1904 *Communication to the Trustees* was, as we have seen, dominated by Prichard's aesthetic movement ideas.

Things were moving fast in the direction the "conspirators" wanted. But by that same speed they were inviting an indignant reaction. Prichard wrote to Mrs. Gardner on January 3 about how great his temporary responsibilities were: "It is not the loss of Robinson that counts so much as that of Warren, who did an immense amount of work for us."[2] His tone about Robinson is often gaily disparaging, but more significant is the assertion about Warren, who had, in the museum, as in the trust and the business and the family, the habit of taking over from other people.

In August 1905, Robinson resigned. On August 12 he wrote a letter of explanation to every member of the board of trustees, which was printed in the *Boston Transcript* on August 22, saying he was not in sympathy with the policy of the museum, especially in matters affecting the position (the powers) of the director. The board referred the matter to a committee, consisting of Charles Eliot Norton, Charles William Eliot, John Chipman Gray, Charles Sprague Sargent, and William Endicott—the senators of Boston culture. They interviewed nearly everyone at the museum and reported that the director had indeed not been allowed enough independence and authority, and that imprecise definitions of power had created strained relations and confusion.[3] They proposed changes to the bylaws and hoped that Robinson would withdraw his resignation. However, he persisted, and on December 9 they accepted it.

On December 19 the *Boston Herald* gave a headline to its story about the quarrel in the art world, reporting demands that Warren and Prichard resign, and that "the social clique of which Mrs. Gardner is the recognized head shall cease to dominate in the direction of the affairs of the museum." Later came a cartoon of the committee in session, with Prichard and Mrs. Gardner just offstage. The photograph of Warren showed him in a polo cap, his mark of caste.

He was not officially reproved by name, but on January 12 Prichard was demoted to the position of bursar (a more or less nominal post). Meanwhile, on December 18, Robinson had been appointed assistant director at the Metropolitan. Mrs. Gardner's friend Morris Carter says that in Boston this appointment was felt to vindicate Robinson and his supporters, and "great was the indignation against the foreigner [Prichard] which had resulted in this loss to Boston. This indignation was also directed in less degree to Mr. Warren, who would gladly have resigned at once, but . . ." he wanted to see the plans for the new building put into effect.[4] In February 1906 the *Bulletin* announced that new bylaws would relieve the trustees of the detailed supervision of administrative matters. In July, Prichard resigned, and Warren announced that he would not run for reelection as president. (According to a manuscript in the Gardner Museum Archives, they both announced their resignations on July 19, 1906.) Warren paid glowing tribute to Prichard in his last President's Report and stayed on the Building Committee until 1909, but he was inactive, according to Whitehill. Warren was in semi-retirement, as it were. Whitehill also points out that the new building, which Warren had done so much for, opened only a few months before his death.

We know something about the feelings of the trustees in the case of William Sturgis Bigelow (student of Buddhism and collector of Japanese art). He was a friend of Ned's and an enemy of Prichard's, one of those against whom Prichard and Mrs. Gardner conspired. He attended the trustees' meeting of January 26, 1906, and voted against Sam Warren's reelection as president, and was so angry because Prichard was only demoted, not fired, that he resigned and decided to cut the museum out of his will.

He had intended to give the museum, and in 1911 did in fact give, 26,000 items of Chinese and Japanese art. His anger was in part the thought that after his death Prichard "might have played Hell's bells with my thirty years accumulations, on some crazy theory or other." He wanted to expose Prichard as a homosexual; he had heard of the poem by Lord Alfred Douglas dedicated to Prichard, and, writing to Henry Cabot Lodge, wondered if Henry James or someone in the American embassy in London could tell them of scandals touching Prichard. "If we could show that Matthew S. Prichard (or Pritchard) left his country for reasons connected with the late Oscar Wilde, we should have quite a handle to work with, and might even reach Mrs. Jack. . . ."[5]

These events were of course observed by Ned Warren, and we can guess at his feelings. Any defeat for Sam was bound to be something of a triumph or consolation for Ned—and vice versa. In 1902, with Sam happily allied to Prichard and Mrs. Gardner, Ned felt defeated. On March 15 of that year he wrote to Berenson about his idea of selling all his Boston capital and keeping only annuities and antiquities thereafter. On May 22 he told Berenson his museum work had all been blasted, and the M.F.A. had not stood by him. On September 19 he suggested that he and Berenson might join forces "in New York," presumably working for the Metropolitan.[6]

This mood deepened in 1903 during the fiasco of the Lippi. Ned felt especially close to Berenson at that time, seeing their fates as sadly parallel. On January 20, 1905, he wrote to Mary Berenson that he liked her husband the better that he was bitter: "One should feel strongly about the few real things in life." He and Berenson, he said in a letter dated April 15, 1906, had never claimed to be indifferent to injustice. On April 23, 1905, he told her that he is writing the whole history of his relations with the M.F.A., and letting Sam, Prichard, and Robinson know. They will then have the chance to write their defenses.

But then came Robinson's resignation from the M.F.A. and the time of Sam's troubles there. On April 5, 1906, Ned told Berenson he had sent to Boston an essay that was an attack on the management of the museum, and Sam, his friend Denman Ross, and the whole committee, though unnamed, would know who was meant by its various indictments. The article, which appeared as a very long letter in the *Transcript* on May 8, 1906, seems to be all that came of the larger project.

In it Ned described his buying for the museum under its first two presidents as a kind of golden age. He did not name Sam, or describe *his* presidency, but implies that the new building was a mistake, and also cites instances of bad buying. The museum paid $90,000 and $50,000 for two Velázquez, which could have been got for $35,000 and $16,000. It thus threw away $140,000, and thereby lost the chance for classical antiquities at bargain prices. He also complained of the committee's parsimony with him in 1902, and its imposition everywhere of "an unsympathetic and amateur control" on its agents. He ended with a stern reference to the difficulties the museum committee has complained of facing: "Is it intended that we are to stand by the management which creates the difficulties?"

He told Berenson that the row at the M.F.A. put Sam in a very bad light, "a light fatal to such a figure." That last phrase—the imagery is one of which Ned was fond—came to have a sinister ring.

Perhaps the most surprising twist to this story was that, on January 5, 1907, Sam and Ned sailed together and alone from Boston to Naples. As Ned wrote to Mary Berenson, "You will open your eyes." He added, "It means, however, only that we have so much to fight about that we can afford to leave out what is personal. Hence majestic attempts at intimacy"—which neither succeed nor fail, he says.[7] Ned saw "how different are our ground ideas," but the reader is bound to see more than that. By January 1907 the relations between the two brothers were so bad on so many fronts that to choose to be alone together for several days was quite extraordinary. It was Sam who took the initiative: He bought the tickets; Ned seems to have succumbed in amazement. Sam's were the majestic attempts at intimacy. We can only understand them as a last-ditch attempt to dissolve Ned's bitter hostility, which was driving them both, or him, toward disaster. Of course it failed: Ned saw no disaster ahead for him; for him the hostility between them was a field of freedom.

He seems rarely to have felt embarrassed or divided in these situations, and to have shrewdly chosen the moves that would be to his ultimate advantage. Earlier, for instance, during the battle of the casts, when Sam asked what his position was (saying that he thought he knew), Ned refused to commit himself.[8] Since he was certainly on the side of originals versus casts, of art versus education, this must surely mean that he wanted to keep free from any entangling alliance with Sam and Prichard—in order to keep open the option of alliance with Robinson. It is also notable that after Sam's departure from the presidency, Ned resumed his relationship with the museum. He was very good friends with Arthur Fairbanks, the new director. In 1908, for instance, Ned sent the museum as a gift his collection of obscene art, known at the museum as the Warren Gift Collection. A nude that Robinson had rejected in 1903 was accepted (as a gift from Fiske) in 1908. At the same time, 1907–1908, the museum agreed to buy Ned's collection of 119 Greek coins for $6,400, and later, in the 1920s, they bought his collection of engraved gems. In the years after 1906 there were always gifts from Ned Warren: in 1908, fifty-one "miscellaneous objects" (presumably the erotic art) attributed, with three vases and a statuette, to him and Fiske; in 1913, ninety-two classical objects— but Sam's name is missing. It is to Ned, not to Sam, that catalogues are dedicated.

To return to Robinson's resignation, however, it is clear that Sam Warren was in some sense reproved by the investigating committee and squeezed out by his enemies on the board of trustees. And these men were the proper Bostonians whose approval and comradeship he had committed himself to win—whom he had in some sense preferred to Ned, and even to Brandeis. In 1906 the twenty-nine trustees included two Longfellows, two Lowells, two Coolidges, a Cabot, a Higginson, and of course Charles William Eliot and Charles Eliot Norton. This was the roll call of "Boston," and their votes were cast against Sam Warren.

It was the first in a series of defeats he suffered, which climaxed in 1910. In the museum case, paradoxically, he was punished for being carried away by Prichard's ideas—for being a member of the aesthetic movement, as that was acted out in the museum. He said so, in almost so many words. In the Annual Report for 1906 he explained that he had resigned "for personal reasons" and added: "With ever deepening interest and conviction, I have taken part in an important movement initiated within the museum, directed . . . to quicken the sense of beauty and promote a sound standard of taste among the people. The outcome of this movement, when understood, will be accepted." It was a claim that his archenemy, Ned, might have made for himself.

This explains both the fierce loyalty of Prichard and Mrs. Gardner, with their anger at the trustees, at the time of Sam's death; and the close alliance between Prichard and Mabel Warren in the years after. These people formed a party, almost a sect, and Sam had been a martyr to their cause—in some sense, a lost cause.

From the start Prichard took a very high line about the matter. He wrote to Mrs. Gardner on March 3, 1910, "You will be awaiting a letter from me after a long silence and to hear an echo from Europe of the message of Sam Warren's death." Fisher, he reported, is stabbed to the heart about it, and so are others, but for Prichard the matter is cosmic, not personal. "Sam Warren had got beyond the individual to such a point that the workaday intelligence had long lost sight of him. . . . If you turn to the teaching of Buddha you will find an extraordinary correspondence between the conditions of the Path and the practise of Sam Warren. No one was more detached from the pettinesses of life than he and no one free as he was freed from the fetters of lust, ill-will, and delusion. I cannot help feeling that he was aware of his end. . . . It was entirely to him that I was dedicating my little efforts. . . . It needs the childlike acceptance of a man like Sam Warren, one who indeed fulfilled the conditions demanded by the Master, to be attuned to the subtle harmonies of life." His was a life like a great symphony.[9]

This extravagant language bears witness partly to the effect that Kakuzo Okakura's Buddhism had had on Prichard and Mrs. Gardner since his appointment as the M.F.A.'s curator of Oriental art at the turn of the century. Born in 1862, Okakura, at the age of twenty-four, had been sent abroad by the Japanese government to study European art, but he had become an aesthetic nationalist and won many European and American converts to Japanese art and spirituality. We read of Berenson, for instance, entertaining Okakura, Prichard, Fisher, and five others at dinner.

This is an example of the Boston influence of that religion, which affected so many people in this story and whose texts were supplied by Henry Warren. And though later there was a post- or anti-Buddhist reaction, often using a Christian ideology, that testified in its own way to the same phenomenon. There are obvious connections between Prichard's ideas in the second half of his career, when he listened to Bergson's lectures, and the thinking of T. E. Hulme and T. S. Eliot (who cites Henry Warren in *The Waste Land* and is supposed to have written one of Prichard's obituaries). Prichard, who certainly knew Eliot, came to believe, for instance, that the only pure art was that which expressed the religion of the community, so that Byzantine art was in some sense the purest of all. (Another Byzantinist, Royall Tyler, was a friend of Sam's whom Prichard knew in Boston and again in Paris before the war.) To arrive at this preference for the formal and hieratic, having started from Bergsonian premises—a paradox of taste to be found in both Eliot and Yeats—was the mark of a small but distinguished branch of the aesthetic movement after the war.

On April 10 and 11, Prichard wrote again about Warren: "An embodiment of life, he drew what was positive from all and left them the negative in its packing untouched." The museum is the result of the unconscious cooperation of a number of forces marshaled by him. He was ousted because he was alone and unsupported, and was "killed by none of these, but at the end of another story and stabbed in the heart." This seems to be a reference to Ned, and in an undated letter to Mrs. Gardner, Prichard wrote: "Will you let me know something? Tell me if Sam Warren's brother continues to beat the air in the halls of justice. . . . Is it not the greatest tragedy that you have known in life?"[10] This seems to be as near as Prichard can let himself come to naming Ned and discussing the part he had played.

He was more open about the museum people. On April 24, 1910, he wrote Mrs. Gardner, having read in the April *Bulletin* of the museum the trustees' dry and meager "tribute" to Sam: "I have read the Bulletin note on dear Sam Warren, and have found a use for the Trustees. They can all go to hell—and sit as a committee to assist Rhadamanthus and company in judging the souls of the righteous! Their very hearts must be made of compressed broadcloth." And on September 18, 1913, when Okakura died: "Two mouthpieces of life, Okakura and Sam Warren, are gone. I have never arrived at understanding why Life robbed us of one and now the other is gone too."[11]

He and Fisher remained friends of Mabel Warren and her children, to whom Fisher continued to act as tutor. At Prichard's intervention, Matisse made three drawings of Mabel in Paris in the fall of 1913. She seems to have felt herself impoverished, after her husband's death (in a letter of December 1913 to her daughter Sylvia she says her income that year was $10,000 less than in 1913), but her situation was not what most of us would call poverty. In a letter of 1920 she reports that her son Bayard has just told her that the company made $330,000 that September. She seems to have separated herself and her children from the other branches of the Warren family, taking a very sharp tone about Cornelia, for instance, who "writes a letter just like Ned or Grandma." (And "it is a sad story that includes Fiske—or Ned"; in a letter of 1914, apropos of something Fiske had done.) She also deplored the way Cornelia smelled, but one gathers from her letters that anyone was liable to give offense to Mabel. (She often complained of men who failed to rise from their chairs when she approached.)[12]

Denman Ross, among Sam's allies there, gave the museum a fifteenth-century Spanish panel in Sam's memory, and Ned gave a Greek head, but this too was a cause of scandal. He had long been trying to sell this head to this and other museums, according to Mrs. Gardner, and so had it in some sense left on his hands. She knew of another and much better head that he might have offered but didn't—the Chios Head (both are now displayed in the museum).

Mrs. Gardner herself, writing to Berenson, clearly blamed Ned. On March 4 she wrote, "Sam Warren's death is unrealizable as yet. It is a terrible loss. His brother Ned's law proceedings killed him. Ned is crazy. That is his only excuse."[13] On March 19, Berenson replied that he was truly sorry and regretted immensely that Ned should seem connected, saying that poor dear Ned had a heart of gold. "He may be a trifle mad, I grant, but I do think him incapable of conscious wrong-doing or deliberate mischief."[14]

From Westbrook we might cite the opinion of John E. Warren, written in his Memoranda, preserved in the Warren Memorial Library there. He was in fact away on a cruise when Sam died. His comment is naturally very discreet; he says that Sam had been "very severely taxed for some weeks" by his contest with E. P. Warren, which had put him under severe strain. Whether this was the cause of his death is a question. But "I feel a sense of personal loss greater than anyone else connected with business in 43 years . . . in spite of his seeming severity and autocratic ways he was a man I was always glad to work for and confer with."

According to Norman Hapgood (writing to Woodrow Wilson in 1913), Louis Brandeis wanted to continue the suit after Sam's death and to defend Sam's record against Ned, but the family did not want to expose Ned's character. As for Brandeis's guilt by involvement, Richard W. Hale of the Boston Bar said that Sam's family and friends thought his death was hastened by the ingratitude of Brandeis's desertion of him at a critical moment.[15] Sam, the soul of honor, had stood accused of being a rascal, for doing things that Brandeis had planned. Also Brandeis was blamed for the original trust and for bad professional ethics in acting for two groups with mutually opposed interests, the heirs and the trustees.[16]

He was being ostracized in Boston in a number of ways. In the same year, 1910, just a few days after Sam's death, the Dedham Polo Club burned down. Instead of rebuilding, most members wanted to merge with the Norfolk Country Club in Westwood. (All but Brandeis were already members of the Brookline Country Club, the first in the country.) Brandeis opposed the move, and when it nevertheless happened, he resigned; the new club's atmosphere was more socially exclusive.[17] Also in 1910 there was a racism scandal over realtors in Roxbury and Dorchester refusing to sell or rent to Jews. The atmosphere of Boston was becoming decidedly anti-Semitic. As late as 1909, Brandeis had been undecided on the issue of restricted immigration; Sam Warren asked for his thoughts on the subject that year. But in 1912 he spoke out against restrictions.

Brandeis had begun to invest his hopes in Washington and federal politics, first by attaching himself to Senator La Follette and, later, after the latter fell sick in 1912, to Woodrow Wilson.

Clearly, then, by 1910, Brandeis was much disliked by some Boston leaders, including other Boston lawyers who did not want to see him represent Boston on the Supreme Court. Asa P. French spoke of an aristocracy at the Boston Bar: high-minded, distinguished men, "But they cannot, I think, consider with equanimity the selection of anybody for a position on the great court of the country from that community who is not a typical, hereditary Bostonian."[18] This was said to the Senate subcommittee appointed to consider Brandeis's nomination to the Supreme Court.

Woodrow Wilson had come to rely on Brandeis's advice, especially on economic matters, and wanted to make him attorney general, and then secretary of commerce, in 1913, but Henry Lee Higginson—one of the president's biggest backers since his early days at Princeton—prevented that. (Norman Hapgood was given the job of investigating the complaints of Massachusetts and other big businessmen.) According to Lief, "The forces arrayed against Brandeis were the New Haven, the United, Kidder-Peabody, Lee-Higginson, Fitzgerald, and many other Wall Street interests."[19] He was held, in rumor, to have cost New England stockholders in the New Haven Railroad millions of dollars.[20]

When he was nominated for the Supreme Court, to replace Justice Joseph R. Lamar, the Warren case was one of the blackest pages in the dossier compiled by newspaperman Clarence W. Barron. This was brought to Washington in February 1916 together with a petition against Brandeis, signed by fifty-four leading Bostonians, including Lawrence Minot, A. L. Lowell, and C. F. Adams. He was accused of deciding legal and constitutional issues on "sociological" grounds and of being "unreliable"; above all, he "lacked the judicial temperament." The hearings lasted four months.

Brandeis said that he had had little to do with the Boston Bar since 1900, and nothing since 1910, the year of the Warren suit. Other lawyers said that he had been ostracized from 1892 on.[21] The hearings began in Washington on February 15, 1916. The *Warren v. Warren* case was reviewed at great length; the senators often protested at the detail, saying they were not an appeals court. Hollis Bailey, one of Ned's attorneys, first presented the case against Brandeis, or against the trust he had set up; charges for repairs, which were the partners' responsibility, had been called "additions and improvements," and so paid for by the trustees (and ultimately the heirs). Later, Youngman gave evidence, saying that Sam had been troubled about the trust and had consulted Brandeis about it, but Brandeis had put Warren's brains and conscience to sleep with legal chloroform.[22] Moorfield Storey, Fiske's attorney, said that Brandeis's acting for both sides in the trust had been bad practice; Storey bore a grudge against Brandeis for helping destroy the New England railroad, but he also said that what Brandeis did was commonly done in Boston.

Curiously enough, both sides repeated that family relations among the Warrens were excellent until the suit was filed. This is curious on the part of those attacking Brandeis, because so much depended on whether another attorney or an "independent mind" should have been involved in the trust. His defenders said there was no need for one because these people were all men of one family, and they all wanted each other's good. But it would have been to the advantage of Bailey and Youngman to establish that Ned and Sam were nearly always at odds, so that Ned needed someone to watch what Sam's friend was doing. Presumably they could not say this because Ned was a true Warren at least in his horror of exposing the family to public scandal.

According to Norman Hapgood, Brandeis wanted to pursue the case after Sam's death, but the family would not allow it. They wanted to forget it as quickly as possible. "The suit was something you abstained from talking about if it could possibly be avoided," McClennen told the Senate subcommittee. "Mrs. Warren was a sensitive, high-natured woman . . . [the daughter of a Southern senator] . . . and was—I do not know that I can characterize the situation in which she was left by the death of her husband."[23] Brandeis said that nothing could excuse Ned "except the theory that he was insane."[24]

The Warren family in some sense rallied around Brandeis. For instance, Cornelia and Mabel both wrote to McClennen in 1910 to say they were entirely satisfied with his conduct of the case.[25] And on February 16, 1916, Cornelia wrote to Brandeis of her indignation at reading in the evening paper accusations against him apropos the Warren case. She hoped that the committee considering his appointment knew that Ned was the only one to conduct that bill in equity. (Fiske had hired an attorney to investigate the trust, but he did not, apparently, sue.) Brandeis replied asking her and "members of Fiske's family" to get in touch with the committee; to say that Brandeis had *not* been acting for both sides in disputes over the trust, but for neither side, neither the heirs nor the partners; and to say that Mrs. Warren and Henry had also approved the way the trust had been set up. But in August 1916, Brandeis resigned from his post as Sam's trustee, presumably as a result of the events of that year. The connection between him and the Warrens was finally broken.

Barron's *Boston News Bureau* had an editorial entitled "An Unfit Appointment" as soon as Brandeis's nomination was announced; the editors called it "an insult to New England and the business interests of the country."[26] (This newspaper was the property of Clarence W. Barron, longtime editor of the *Wall Street Journal* and, appropriately, one of Brandeis's bitterest enemies.) Moorfield Storey told the Senate subcommittee that Brandeis's reputation was that he was ruthless, unscrupulous, and not to be trusted; he lacked the confidence of a representative class of men in the community.[27] Francis Peabody, a lawyer friend of Sam's at the polo club, said Brandeis had a reputation for being untrustworthy, not always truthful, and "sailing under false colours."[28] Sherman L. Whipple exonerated Brandeis of all moral charges, but said he would not have been so misjudged "if Mr. Brandeis had been a different sort of man, not so aloof, not so isolated, with more of the comradery of the bar . . . [if he had said to other lawyers] 'Boys, what do you think about it?' " But he was aloof, "intensely centered in carrying out his own ideas and his own ideals . . . does not . . . consult with anybody or take them into his confidence. . . ." He rested "in the security of the purity of his own mind."[29]

Though there is no written record of Brandeis's feelings, which must have been complex, it seems that he cherished the memory of his early friendship with Sam Warren until his death in 1941. His biographer, Alpheus T. Mason, tells us that when he talked with Brandeis in his last years in the study of his house at Chatham on Cape Cod, there were a few photographs thumbtacked to the wall, and one of them, the oldest, was of Sam Warren, seen at the helm of an old sloop.[30]

Brandeis and Berenson lived on long after Sam and Ned. They died full of years and honors while the Warrens slipped into echo-less obscurity. Even for those who know nothing about Louis Brandeis, his name is evocative—of the university in Waltham. (The Warrens began in that town, but their name is not attached to any such college.) The name Berenson evokes his museum-villa, I Tatti. The one is a public, to some degree an ethnic, institution. The other connotes a private, cosmopolitan, aesthetic prestige. Many books have been written about each of them, but probably the readers of the one set are nonreaders of the other. The Berenson biographies are the more elegantly written; those on Brandeis are the more closely linked to the substance of American law and politics. Women have played a larger role in preserving the Berenson legend; the Brandeis story, so lacking in erotic interest, has mostly been told by men. It would be hard to say which one's image has been more influential, but each one's fate makes a striking contrast with that of the Warren to whom he was indebted, and alongside whom he began adult life.

It was of course Ned whom the widow and her children blamed for Sam's death. They asked him not to attend the funeral and severed all relations with him—and indeed with Fiske. As usual we do not know what Fiske felt, but Cornelia was certainly angry and cut Ned out of her will. Mabel seems to have blamed both of her husband's brothers equally: "It's a sad story that has Fiske in it—or Ned."

Fiske is said to have assumed, even after the suicide, that the trust issue might be resolved by adopting Ned as a trustee—to replace Sam, perhaps? This is probably best understood as an example of Fiske's refusal to acknowledge certain kinds of reality, to know what other people were thinking. This is the form of low-key bravura that characterized much of his behavior, and Ned's, and perhaps helps explain the sympathy between them. Ned observed in his autobiography, with apparent complacency, that he was generally known, or supposed, to be unaware of what other people were thinking.

Ned and Oxford

What Ned was thinking, after Sam's suicide, we do not know. He evidently did not leave the country immediately, but he fairly soon wrote to Lois Shaw from Lewes House, expressing very sore feelings about how family members had treated him. He thought of changing his citizenship but found that it might complicate his legal and financial situation. He had withdrawn his suit, and after protracted negotiations sold his share of the trust to Fiske and Cornelia; the arrangement being reached on Thanksgiving Eve, 1910. He is said— according to Burdett and Goddard—to have regretted but not repented his brother's death, and there is no record of emotional disturbance. (The biographers say he spent some time "recounting his faults, as he frequently did when alone.")[31]

The financial accommodation was reached on McClennen's initiative, according to the latter.[32] Ned was given $1,770,000, which Youngman claimed included $250,000 of reparations, acknowledging the justice of his case. The million and a half was guaranteed by a mortgage on the mills property. The book value of his share of the trust was something over $1,161,000, but he also had $250,000 from his mother's estate. The *Boston News Bureau* told the world about the settlement and described Brandeis as having been the power behind the Warren throne, the man who had made the "cheating plot" that the suit unmasked.[33]

There was no pause in Ned's busyness; he was soon at work on an essay on Swinburne, which Robbie Ross promised to place for him. His recommendation won for William J. Young a post at the Boston Museum of Fine Art, where Mr. Young remained forty-seven years, until he resigned, as director of its research laboratory. (In a letter of July 24, 1989, Mr. Young remembers Ned always carrying amber worry beads wrapped around his left hand.) And Ned continued his patronage of American museums. During the 1920s he bought largely for and also gave quite a few things to the Rhode Island School of Design, where Mrs. Gustav Radeke was building up a collection. In 1925, for instance, the school bought twenty-five Greek vases through him, and he "sometimes 'tossed in' a few gifts of his own."[34] In 1926, when the new Radeke building was opened, a bronze Aphrodite was acquired with Warren's help. (Mrs. Radeke belonged to the Metcalf family, who were to the Rhode Island School of Design Museum what the Warrens wanted to be to the M.F.A.) According to H. W. Parsons, who also bought for them, Warren was responsible for the two or three good pieces of Renaissance sculpture there.[35] It is also interesting to note that, besides the classical art we expect from him, we find two pieces of English furniture of the last quarter of the eighteenth century among his donations there.

He also continued his complex negotations with Corpus Christi College, Oxford. He was able to announce to President Case in December 1910 that he had sold his property, but that he would only receive the payment gradually over twenty years; while for 1910 and 1911 all his income must go to pay lawyers' fees, etc. By 1916, he figured, the college should get £8,000 for its Classical Fund.[36]

In 1911 some quarrel developed between Case and Warren, after which the former apologized and suggested the scheme of establishing a praelectorship, which had been proposed long ago by the founder of the college. Warren agreed to this and found £2,000 to get Corpus out of some immediate financial difficulties.[37] The two were after all allies in the cause of classical studies. The postwar debates at Oxford, which led to the university's abandoning compulsory Greek, drove Case in particular to despair.

In November 1913 a committee at the college reported on a Draft Deed for a Classical Fund, which had misogynist provisions: No woman was to teach, and though women students might attend lectures by a lecturer paid out of the fund, no woman might come to a tutorial. In 1926, Ned added a scheme for buying a piece of land for a bathing place for Corpus undergraduates. P. S. Allen, the president who succeeded Case, always referred to this piece of land as "Warren's Piece." (Providing young men with such bathing places is a motif that runs through several of Ned's benefactions; it is obvious enough what voyeuristic associations swimming holes had for him, and we should not forget—though there seems no need to dwell on it—the related pleasures of those Greek sculptures and vases.)

During the war Warren (like Santayana) spent a lot of time in

Oxford, and indeed in Corpus, which made him an Honorary Fellow in 1915. This was a triumph for Warren—and for Case, who wired him the news as soon as the vote was cast. Apparently there was some opposition among the Fellows to giving him the honor. We have to guess at its grounds, but in 1913 he had brought out a second volume of verse, *The Wild Rose.* The preface explained that a wild rose (a canker, or cancer) is the symbol of profane love, as the cultivated rose is of Christian love. It must have been an open secret, by that time even to Bridges, what kind of profane love was being recommended.

There were few undergraduates then in residence, because the physically able were conscripted for war service, but Warren was lucky enough to find at least one, E. H. Gropius, who was susceptible of the same enthusiasm for classical studies as himself. This man, who went up in 1915, changed his name to Goddard after the war, when he began a very successful career as a secondary school teacher, and co-wrote Warren's biography. As his name suggests, he was of German parentage, and it is tempting to associate that heritage with his susceptibility to "ideas": His published works include, besides the biography of Warren, an essay in the Spenglerian philosophy of history and some translations of Rudolf Steiner. It is one of the defining marks of Ned's friends that intellectually several of them learned from that German galaxy of historical speculators, so many of whom were sexologists, from Bachofen and Nietzsche on. (There is, in Marshall's papers, ample evidence of Nietzschean studies—for instance, lengthy notes on Halévy's life of Nietzsche—and Matt Prichard, who went on from Nietzsche to Bergson, was certainly a vitalist.) It comes as a surprise to realize this only because they didn't write out such ideas—except for Ned in his *Defence of Uranian Love.*

In a 1916 letter from Warren at Oxford to Marshall in Italy, we glimpse what both the dons and the undergraduates meant to him. Warren says he feels a worm in his relation to the dons: "not myself precisely, a worm, but what they know of me worm-like. So it all rests on amiable manners, if I have any . . ." or on their kindness, which is great. "You may count even Bridges, not as a friend, but he could have prevented my election. I suspect that he achieved a victory of conscience." As for the students, he'd seen in the Oxford theater a play he disliked, but in the audience undergraduates who "confirmed Henry James's dictum that the English are the handsomest men in the world. Our best [Americans] are all right, but the nation runs to hoy-polloyishness. . . . It did me good to hear the young men laugh when they were supposed to weep, and mimic the loving passages as they went out."[38] By sympathy and tendency he is at his subversive work still; it is no wonder he feels like a worm when with the dons.

John Fothergill says that Ned was scared of the Corpus Fellows; who do sound, in some anedotes, like the dons in Evelyn Waugh's satire *Decline and Fall* in their internecine plottings.[39] Fothergill reports dreaming of Corpus Christi, as if it haunted his imagination— perhaps because of Warren's stories.[40] It was a small college, concentrating heavily in classical studies; in 1926 the governing body consisted of four classics Fellows, plus a president and chaplain, also classical scholars, plus one mathematician, one historian, and an ex–army officer bursar. In any case, Ned seems to have been uncomfortable there.

A picture of Ned at Corpus is sketched in Santayana's autobiography, *My Host the World.* The two men were much in Oxford during the war years. Santayana tells us he too was courted by Corpus: Robert Bridges tried to get him to become a Fellow there in 1919, and F. C. S. Schiller always invited him to dinner whenever Santayana was in Oxford in the 1920s. So did Ned, but *he* always saw Santayana in his rooms, "where we might be tête à tête, and freely discuss Boston and other delicate subjects."[41] The two men had indeed a lot in common, with their shared grudge against Boston as an organizing center.

At that time Santayana was, he says, at home in that Oxford atmosphere created by moderately comic anecdotes and sly hints at one another's heresies. (The word "heresy," like the word "delicate," probably hints at sexual matters, among others.) The college apparently commissioned Ned to sound the other man out again about becoming a Fellow. Santayana didn't want to be so tied down with so little financial recompense, but still less did he like the alternative of earning extra money by teaching the undergraduates. Education was not one of his enthusiasms.

Santayana says he might have accepted such an offer from another college but not from Corpus, where he would have been sponsored by Schiller and Ned: "They were both individuals that a novelist might like to study, interesting cases; but to be sandwiched between them as though I were such another tramp (as externally indeed I was) would have been a perpetual mortification. Warren was unfortunate, yet I objected to him less than to Schiller, because I pitied him, and our connection with Boston was a true link."[42] One can guess that these conversations, and Santayana's study of Ned, were part of the process by which he evolved his novel *The Last Puritan*.

Through J. D. Beazley, Warren was perpetuating his presence at Oxford in another way. In 1918, *Attic Red-Figured Vases in American Museums* appeared, dedicated to Warren and Marshall, "in gratitude for constant kindness and recognition of their unwearied labour. . . ."

Bowdoin and Beazley

Bowdoin College, in Brunswick, Maine, was in a sense the local college for Westbrook and S.D. Warren and Company. After the college built its Walker Art Gallery in 1894, the first major donor was George Warren Hammond, Ned's cousin and Aunty's husband. Ned, who introduced himself at the college as Hammond's nephew, gave altogether about six hundred objects, making a much more impressive donation than his uncle.

His serious giving seems to have begun in 1916, to judge by Warren's letter of December 19, 1915, in which he says that a friend of his is planning to bequeath Bowdoin an archaeological library as a way to repay him for favors received. This makes Warren think of being more systematic in his donations and creating "a good little illustrative collection of antiquities." He suggests that the college might fund a scholarship in classics and archaeology (feeling the two subjects should always be paired). "My notion is to provide exceptional opportunities for the exceptional among Bowdoin men."[43] Then, as usual, he asks his correspondent "not to talk about this."

The connection with the college gradually became important to him. Warren was given an honorary degree, and his last visit to the college was on November 21, 1928, only a month before his death. The collection's strongest feature was the painted pottery; the second best the gems, coins, and figurines; and last the sculpture.[44] Kevin Herbert quotes J. D. Beazley on Warren's philosophy of collection: "A coin, a gem, a vase, a statuette, would speak of Greece in the heart of Maine; and sooner or later there would be a student whose spirit would recognize them. There was no hurry; an acorn in the forest."[45]

This presents what one might call the positive side of Warren's motivation. He himself declared the negative side more important—

he cherished his gifts' power to disturb the decorum of idealism and refinement. So it is worth complementing Beazley's phrases with something more sardonic from Warren himself—also apropos Bowdoin: "I'm afraid I'm not much for the evangelization of American youth by art. Art is inevitably for the few, and a museum is a lighthouse to rescue them from unhappiness. It is a traitor to the modern cause, lodged amid utilities for the succor of renegades." This comes from a letter written in 1916.[46]

Beazley, however, wrote eulogies at the time of Warren's death for the *Times* and the *Oxford Magazine,* which make one think he understood Warren better than most of his friends—or perhaps he just knew better how to write about him. It is he, for instance, who mentions that Warren spoke of Westbrook, as well as of Harvard and Mount Vernon Street, "with the loving precision of a Bewick vignette." (In most memoirs Warren is depicted mentioning America only satirically, and never mentioning Westbrook.) Lewes House Beazley calls an image of its mentor, with its severe front on the street and its back a silent lawn, offering calm and work and friendship.[47]

Perhaps the most interesting point for our story is that in the history of connoisseurship Beazley's achievement was to assign the growing mass of Greek vases in museums to individual artists (masters and pupils, colleagues, and rivals). This whole enterprise, enormously prestigious in its day, is now under attack, but what matters to us is the parallel between this and Berenson's work on Italian paintings. Both men may be said to have developed Giovanni Morelli's system of identifying artists by means of their treatment of details. They erected a realm of knowledge (apparent knowledge) where none was before. They were leading connoisseurs of their generation. And like Berenson's, Beazley's career owed as much to Warren in practical ways as it did to Morelli in theoretical ways. Beazley was significantly helped by Warren and Marshall early on. They got his first book published in America in 1918. And in 1920 he published *The Lewes House Collection of Ancient Gems.*

Forgeries and Fakes

The recent reaction against Beazley's work bases itself on skepticism about the importance of the auteurs of these vases. But there have been other recent forms of reaction against connoisseurship, two of which have brought Ned Warren's name to attention again: skepticism about the authenticity of works procured by him and

Marshall for museums, and excitement at the game of "unmasking the forger." This last phrase is the title of a recent book by David Sox that pays special attention to Warren and Lewes House. Sox says, for instance, "There is no doubt that for a long time there has been an attempt to keep controls on the E. P. Warren/John Marshall/Harold Parsons stories. . . . The Warren-Marshall relationship had an extraordinary impact on the future collections of several museums."[48]

Marshall, when he died in February 1928, was investigating stories of forgery with what must have been a sinking heart. He was also worried about the Etruscan warriors he had bought for the Metropolitan. If they were seen to be fakes, they immediately became totally shameful, and especially the shame of John Marshall. Parsons discusses the case in an *ArtNews* article, published much later, entitled "The Art of False Etruscan Art." He says that no one should ever have been deceived, because the bodies are far too massive for the legs they stand on. The figures could never have been designed to stand.

In another scandal in which Marshall was involved, a brother connoisseur was losing face. Marshall tried to persuade Wilhelm Bode of the Berlin Museum that the sixty-centimeter painted wax Flora, bought by the latter for 160,000 deutsche marks in 1909, believing it to be the work of da Vinci, was in fact the work of an Englishman in 1846. These anxieties and conflicts are said to have brought on Marshall's death (some of Warren's letters confirm this). According to Fothergill, Marshall made two trips to Berlin to argue with Bode.

It has been said that Bode's death the following year marked the end of a period of connoisseurship, the period of the great collectors of classical antiquities. (Warren and Marshall died in 1928, Bode and Studniczka in 1929.)

One of the principal figures in Sox's book, therefore, as also in Thomas Hoving's *King of the Confessors,* is Warren's protégé Parsons, in his role of forgery detective and accuser of museums. He is important to us also as a main continuer of Warren's work of supplying American museums—moving westward, the Rhode Island School of Design, the Worcester Art Museum, the Cleveland Art Museum, and the museums in Kansas City, Missouri, and in Omaha, Nebraska. Soon after 1930 (soon after Warren's death), to judge by his correspondence with Berenson, Parsons began to devote most of his energy to the detection of forgeries. He felt that the great collecting days were over. In 1949 he wrote Berenson that classical antiquities ended with his old masters, Warren and Marshall: "There are no more to be had."[49]

The search for truth, in Hoving's story, is paradoxically embodied in Parsons, who yet appears, in Hoving's account as in other people's, as implicitly dishonest. Yet Hoving remains full of ambivalent enthusiasm about Parsons—about his dishonesty, among other things. His too-elegant suit, for instance: *"That* I'd never seen before! The man's *accent!* I'd never heard anything like that either, an effervescent combination of Boston and Oxford, cadenced in a never-ending chain of skillful pleasantries."[50] This cloven, ambiguous, and suspect character of both the connoisseur and his accuser is crucial to our understanding of Warren and all his friends.

Lewes House

Besides the collecting and the writing, Warren engaged in 1911 on a new and unpredictable enterprise by adopting a four-year-old child. Despite the 1980s sound of this—gay parents adopting—it was not a totally new idea with him. He referred to another child as "my boy" in a letter of 1909 to Lois Shaw; that child's name was Dennis and perhaps he died very young—Warren uses the phrase "if he lives." He refers to the second boy as Travis (presumably that was already his name) and engaged a governess to look after him for a few years. The child grew up at Lewes House and Fewacres, calling Ned Papa. In his will Warren alludes to a deed drawn up on October 31, 1911, between himself, the boy's mother, and some public official (perhaps someone representing a Church of England adoption agency). The deed was simply a guarantee that Warren would look after the boy financially, but it seems clear that it was part of the adoption process.

Exactly when the child was born we don't know, but he was still a minor in 1928 when the will was drawn up; by origin, Ned said, he was "of good birth." Among the memoirists only Fothergill refers to him, and then only as "the child." In fact he was a love child born out of wedlock in Paris to the daughter of a Cornish vicar, and the father was apparently a local squire.[51]

Warren told Lois Shaw in September 1911: "I think that I have found a boy to adopt, but shall not know till my return to England. He is of good birth and healthy. I am a little afraid of him, because he seems likely to be of some account and therefore troublesome."

(A little later, however, he decided that Travis had no soul—"that immortal disturber of human peace.") He wanted to have him at home, but "the gentlewoman who had charged [sic] of Dennis at Lewes now lives near London, and he would have to be in her charge till he is seven . . . if it is to be this boy, this handful, he must have a man about, to take after. I won't do: I know that. Harry [Thomas] would. He admires Harry, but Harry hates his tantrums. Harry, you see, is not keen on children. Neither am I."[52]

In 1917, however, there were four children at Lewes House, according to Warren's letter to Berenson of June 23: Travis, and Harry's son and daughter, and Nan Thomas's brother, Fred.

Travis Warren was sent to Winchester, one of the great public schools. Doing badly there—he was apparently rather backward—he was sent to Tonbridge, the school E. M. Forster had attended. Athletics were said to be his strong point.

From his brothers and sisters Ned was not long estranged—at least not long from Cornelia and never from Fiske. (Mabel was unforgiving and perhaps resented the other Warrens' willingness to get back on terms with him.) Though Cornelia did not reinstate him in her will in the position he had held, she left him $10,000 and her share of the Filippino. She was corresponding with him soon after 1910; perhaps there was no time at which they were completely out of touch.

Cornelia

As mentioned, Cornelia also kept in touch with Louis Brandeis and the quite different activities he represented. On August 29, 1911, she wrote to Brandeis inquiring his judgment on a proposal to establish by law a minimum wage in Massachusetts, which was, she said, "subversive of the ideas on which I was brought up."[53] This was an idea sponsored in this country by Florence Kelley, long associated with Jane Addams's settlement house in Chicago. Kelley was a close friend of Josephine Goldmark, Brandeis's sister-in-law and a leading figure in the National Consumers League, which Cornelia supported. Brandeis replied that he kept an open mind on the subject himself but hoped that she would cooperate with the state's investigation of the proposal. She also kept in touch with Denison House; Helena Dudley lived at Cedar Hill until Cornelia died in 1921.

Cornelia's will provided that three trustees should be appointed to dispose of the real estate, but to provide out of it a playground, houses for a gardener and estate supervisor, and the mansion to be a rest home for women. The trustees decided to give seventy-five acres, including the mansion, to the Girl Scout movement; other parts of the estate went to make a park, to the Harvard School of Landscape Architecture, and to the Massachusetts Agricultural College.

Cornelia's obituaries treat her entirely as a public figure and seem to express no intimate understanding or appreciation. The only one that shows some insight was written by Katherine Lee Bates and appeared in the June 8 *Boston Evening Transcript*. It quoted a line from *Miss Wilton* in which it is said of a character that she "disguised herself under a veil of kindness." That is the feeling other accounts give, by omission.

The obituary also said, more platitudinously, "The law of her life was Christian service. The achievement of her life was Christian character." The religious adjective there seems to be used rather cosmetically. But there is something that sounds true in the assertion that she liked plain ways, plain speech, and plain life; and that she was so convinced that discussion was sometimes vain and cooperation sometimes difficult.

Cornelia's brothers seem to have been struck by what Miss Bates had to say. Fiske wrote to thank her for the obituary, saying that his sister's work at Wellesley—presumably including Denison House—had been the best part of her life. And Ned wrote that "A tree looks well in a light that suits it. My sister looks well in a Christian light. I, according to you, in some other."[54] The other light is probably pagan.

In Cornelia's name Ned gave an Etruscan "Bust of a Woman in High Relief" to the Boston Museum. *The Lady Athaia* belongs to the second half of the second century A.D. and is said (in Vermeule's book on stone sculptures) to present a thoroughly Eastern face, foreshadowing Greco-Buddhist sculpture. It suggests a Buddhist withdrawal and impersonality. The head is elaborately dressed and jeweled but has indeed a veiled look that corresponds suggestively with the phrases in Miss Bates's obituary.

Fiske

Fiske promised to make good to Ned the amount the latter had lost when Cornelia cut him out of her will. But the negotiations over just how much that was were complex and were still not completed when Ned died in 1928.

Fiske and Gretchen lived on—he until 1938, she until 1959. She published a good deal of poetry, succeeded Amy Lowell as president of the New England Poetry Society, and ran a salon that T. S. Eliot as a Harvard student is said to have attended. (It is believed in the Warren family that Gretchen Warren was the original of the lady in his "Portrait of a Lady.") She is often cited in Cleveland Amory's *Proper Bostonians* (1947), where she is presented as "A woman of rare charm, she dedicates herself conscientiously to her salons and her writing . . . seldom leaves her antique-studded Beacon Hill home at all—never, if she can help it, for purely social engagements."[55] Guests, according to Amory, distributed themselves around a large dining room, among fragile seashells and almost equally fragile chairs, sipped tea or sherry, and discussed poetry and philosophy.

Every year from 1918 to 1933, Fiske issued an *Enclaves of Economic Rent Yearbook.* They were privately printed by the Merrymount Press and officially edited by Charles White Huntington, who had been the official author of his genealogy back in 1894. They gave the year's news of these mild social experiments. In form they varied slightly, but for several years they began with an anecdote from Aristotle's *The Constitution of Athens,* in Greek. (Greek epigraphs were used by Fiske, Ned, and Sam.) The introduction to the tenth yearbook said that humanity was in prison but the door was unlocked, and that openable door was the economic enclave. "This way has been followed by a few persons, and the thirteen resulting areas in which land is free [the enclaves] shine like minute white stars against the darker background." This idealism was linked to pragmatism in a familiar American way. The 1925 issue contained an essay by Henry Ford.

The rhetoric remained semi-religious; indeed it became more so as time went on. A poem by Gretchen is quoted:

> *When wars are done . . . a second Calvary shall rise . . .*
> *A Hill immense, resplendent, high . . . [Where we shall see]*
> *. . . burn with phoenix fire*
> *The flame of purged desire.*

Fiske said the enclaves exemplified the law of Moses as well as that of Henry George, and that the movement meant the brotherhood of man and the fatherhood of God. He used the language of the

Lord's Prayer sometimes about the enclaves. He traveled as much as he had in his youth but now went to international single tax conferences, going third class or steerage. He was a pilgrim and a polemicist, visiting holy places and congregations of the faithful, raising the question of enclaves everywhere.

He claimed that infantile paralysis and infant mortality were strikingly low in enclaves of economic rent. In 1920 he and his cousin Phillips Mason became the trustees of the Georgian Trust, founded to promote Henry George enclaves. Seen from a common-sense point of view, they look like summer retreats for liberal-minded academics and artists. The 1921 yearbook mentions, as living at Tahanto, Wallace W. Atwood, the president of Clark University; Roland B. Dixon, the Peabody Museum curator of ethnology; the chairman of the Philosophy Department at Bowdoin, and so on.

The same yearbook says that the enclaves are very like English garden cities. Certainly both ideas had a strong flavor of William Morris about them. For instance, the residents of Arden, one of the earliest enclaves, were known as the Ardenfolk; they had gilds and practiced handicrafts. Fairhope offered Organic Education; its 1913 constitution began, "Believing that the economic conditions under which we now live are unnatural and unjust . . . at war with the nobler impulses of humanity. . . ." Free Acres had an open-air theater, an archery gild, and tournaments in Robin Hood costume. Pageants were a characteristic art form of the American enclaves. But perhaps the most famous was the very small Sant Jordi in Andorra, founded in 1916; the *New York Times* published an article on it, and it was the proposed place of exile for Erskine Childers. The remoteness and the smallness of Sant Jordi (only seven acres) was a sign of the ineffectuality of the movement.

Imaginatively, however, or perhaps fancifully, the idea was striking. Each successive yearbook always listed some new enclave or enclaves, either set up by Fiske or endowed by him, or simply discovered. One in the first category was Shakerton, close to Harvard, where he bought the land that the last Shakers finally abandoned in 1921, thus making an appropriate link between his kind of social-spiritual experiment and those of the past. (A recurrent theme in his claims for enclaves was that they would make war impossible.) One of those in the last category, and it is described in the last yearbook (1933), was the German commune near Berlin called Eden. The people of Eden practiced nudity in the summers (so did Fiske), suckled their children, and worked cooperatively. It had been founded in 1893 and was one of a network of communes founded at that time. One of the headquarters of that network was at Ascona (it is described in *Mountain of Truth*).

The great historical manifestation of that impulse is the Gandhi movement in India, and it is appropriate that Fiske should have been in contact with a Gandhian in his last years. Fiske's cousin Herbert Mason bought an estate on the eastern shore of Maryland in the 1930s and on it lived a man named Frank Boland who had been to India and lived with Gandhi. He conducted religious, or spiritual, services to a mixed-race congregation, and Fiske often visited.

As he grew older Fiske became more eccentric and was the subject of many anecdotes. His daughter Rachel told of meeting him at a garden party, making conversation, and then being appalled to hear him say, "You remind me of my daughter Rachel." According to another story, when he and a friend took a horse and trap from Portland to Westbrook, he tied a ribbon to the wheel of the trap and sat obsessively watching and counting its revolutions all the way there.[56]

Most striking of all, perhaps, was when his cousin Phillips Mason met him in Boston and they took the train west together—one to Weston, the other going on to Harvard. Fiske insisted on saying good-bye and discharging all the duties of politeness as soon as they were aboard. By doing this he could then begin talking (monologuing) on single tax matters, with no need to break off as the train approached Weston and his cousin got off. Perhaps he went on talking, all alone, as the train carried him on. But the characteristic thing is his "rational" organization of the occasion.[57]

When Fiske died the *Boston Globe* obituary compared his politics with those of his brother-in-law, Erskine Childers. The latter said that the highest patriotism was to prevent your country from domineering over a smaller one, and that was the inspiration of Fiske's work for the Philippines. The article compared Fiske's enclaves with Brook Farm and Robert Owen's nineteenth-century community, called Harmony. He was the subject of an article in the *National Cyclopaedia of American Biography* and another in *Who's Who in America* for 1936–37. The *Boston Herald,* on July 24, 1929, gave a portrait of him in a series entitled "People You Ought to Know."

Fiske left an estate of a little more than a million dollars, and his will was short but typically testy and puzzling. Article 1 declared that doctors could conduct an autopsy on his body if they wished.

Article 3 said that all the property was to go to whoever it would have gone to if he had died intestate. And Article 6, "Unless it appears that my wife was living thirty days after my death it shall be as if she had predeceased me."

There is one reference to Gretchen staying at Fewacres in a letter of 1923 written by Charles Murray West to Lois Shaw: "We have Mrs. Fiske here for a few days, she is very amusing, and some of her theories are interesting, she eats nothing and is very strong, and to my horror she suggested that I should not eat meat at all, or possibly a little once a day."[58] That suggests both what Mrs. Fiske Warren had in common with Fiske and the tone Ned took about them both. He lumped Gretchen in with the other women of his family, and indeed American women in general. He told Lois Shaw in 1925 that "Mamma, Cornelia, Mabel, and Gretchen, with greater opportunity, don't seem to me to have attained what you have attained . . . ," which is defined, by negation, as a wise humility. So many American women are not bad, but "too confident in their powers, so that they disregard and override that of which they cannot judge. I've told you that in my opinion American men become so little what a man should be that American women may naturally be relatively worthy of the confidence which they place in themselves."[59]

One wonders what model of womanly behavior Warren would approve—what his "English" as opposed to his "American" woman was like. The best clue comes in a letter to Berenson of May 18, 1903, that cites Isabel Burton, the infinitely patient and adoring wife of the traveler and adventurer Richard Burton. Warren had been reading about both Burtons, for in another letter of that year he reminds Berenson how Burton used to say that a man must choose between honors and honor.[60]

No one could be much less like Burton in his line of achievement than Warren. It's obvious, and uninteresting, that Ned liked to contemplate the Burtons' relationship, because there was a man who seemed never to have suffered humiliation at the hands of women. What's striking is that he did make himself as much like Burton as he could—saw his collecting in terms of adventure—and tried to make his young men (like Fothergill) resemble Burton.

Ned's Work

Fiske is mentioned in a 1914 letter to Lois Shaw from Lewes House: "Fiske was delighted to find me amid babies and women." Ned reflected that it was only natural that Fiske "understood the life with babies and with women, but had never understood the collecting enterprise, nor now my pen-work, and that, if the second is as good as the first, those friends are right who reckon my well-doing according as I accomplish it, and regard the babies and women as its enemies." But on the other hand, Ned presents himself as pleased with his own late success in domesticity: "Also as my theory was that a man after an education was not of necessity a dolt in 'business,' so I believed a solitary not inhuman."[61]

His secretary in these last years was Charles Murray West, remembered by Mortimer Warren as "straight out of P. G. Wodehouse." This was of course the 1920s, the age of Bertie Wooster. Apparently the household at Fewacres was run along the lines of an English country house, complete with butler and afternoon tea. And West, who seemed to the Americans who remember him a "lightweight," drove around Maine at high speeds in an enormous Pierce-Arrow.[62] Ned shared with Lois Shaw various unsuccessful schemes for promoting "Murray's" intellectual development.

Meanwhile, in the last decade of his life, Warren did a lot of writing or publishing. In 1918 he produced the pamphlet called "Classical and American Education," a contribution to the debate at Oxford over the continuance of compulsory Greek. He was no pamphleteer; it is hard to grasp his innuendoes or—in even a simple sense—to read his tone, and harder yet to find a consecutive argument in what he writes.

Warren is most striking in his sharp remarks about Harvard and his fond memories of the relief he found at Oxford on his first arrival there. Should Oxford now be "reformed"? In place of the aristocrats he had found there they would put "the average man"? From that time on Harvard students would have no reason "to travel to England to behold him and admire." They could find the average man at the quick-lunch bar near the underground trolley junction in Harvard Square.[63]

Finally, in 1928, the year of his death, the long promised discourse on pederasty, *A Defence of Uranian Love*—in three volumes—began to appear. (The word "Uranian" was first used by Karl Heinrich Ulrichs, but to describe adult homosexual love. Warren used it for men's love of boys also, indeed primarily.) It presents itself as a scholarly work, with copious notes, citing sources in six languages.

The Greek idea of virtue, seen at its best in the age of Pindar, was characterized by *grandeur* or *nobility*. This was a masculine idea linked to the cult of aristocracy and to the subordination of women. The modern idea of virtue is radically different, with *sublimity* replacing grandeur (Lionel Johnson said that Francis Thompson was never noble, only sublime) and with links to democracy, Christianity, and the exaltation of women. Hence modern shibboleths like "the greatest happiness of the greatest number" were heartily to be distrusted.

The supreme historical event in the sequence that brought about this change was the French Revolution, and the supreme contemporary and local manifestation of this idea is Boston, Massachusetts. It is important for us to give full weight to the historical dimension of Warren's idea. Whatever one's judgment of its plausibility, it was a reinterpretation of world history, and so an idea in the largest sense. It was just this that alienated Marshall and his other English friends; of course, they entertained the proposition as a *jeu d'esprit*, but they could not take it seriously, and it is just this that makes him more interesting than they.

In its day, Warren said, the Greek idea of virtue had been inseparable from the practice of "Uranian" love, most typically a boy's tutoring in virility and sensuality. The essential argument is that the love of boys, as well as the love of women, includes spiritual as well as carnal elements. Moreover, only the boy who embodies the promise of manhood will attract a lover, so such relationships are in themselves a cult of virility.

In modern times, however, classical scholars have averted their eyes from homosexuality, while practicing homosexuals "were astonished that a personal inclination should be expected to bear a philosophy. . . ."[64] This last can be taken to refer to his friends at Lewes House who so uniformly and glumly discouraged him. He himself kept the faith. In one of his last letters to Beazley, Warren said he had achieved three things in his life: the Boston Collection, the *Wild Rose*, and the *Defence*. One would wish to excise *The Wild Rose* from that list and substitute the life at Lewes House, including the relationship with Marshall, but one is glad to see him make such a claim.

Volume I of the *Defence* is autobiographical. In a family home like Warren's own a youth is shocked to read in the Book of Psalms that the Lord "rejoiceth not in the strength of a horse, neither delighteth he in any man's legs," and is inconsolable when told that the Venus de Milo will not be found in heaven.[65] (At its best, this first volume can remind a reader dimly of the first part of *Lolita,* but of course with the difference that Humbert Humbert was heterosexual; it is Humbert's sadder and dimmer pederast friend, Gaston Godin, whom Ned most reminds us of.)

There is a chapter on strength, describing how the youth exults in the masculinity he enthrones; and then one on gentleness, which is an equally valuable quality, for this is essentially a moral enterprise: "There is no education like that which a lover [an older man] can give." The latter's love life will be a rather heroic succession of attachments to boys and young men, in which he will give constantly, without any equal return.

He will save the youth from subjection to women—something easier to do in "countries blessed with a deep culture and dignified institutions," such as church and crown, and secluded and segregated universities. In new countries (the references to old and new translate to England and America) "men are claimed mostly by personal interests, and woman becomes the only partisan of the ideal." Women then invent "refinement" (a *bête noire* for Warren), something that it is the merit of Greek art to lack. Women are also to be associated with "passion" and "unrequited passion." In Greek romantic literature, the opposite of the case in modern literature, it is only women who suffer unrequited love, never men.[66]

According to this philosophy, "To magnify an Eros characteristic of the masculine is now to turn the world upside down."[67] Such an Eros would be by "Christian" standards amoral, for a man is or should be "his own centre and the reason of his doings,"[68] morally indifferent to the object of his love, and needing no justification from outside. In certain ways the modern world *is* morally superior to the Greek one: in honesty and in charity; but on the whole the balance inclines the other way.

Volume II, on Greek thought, has twenty-five chapters stressing that thought's casual and materialist and masculine orientation. Male beauty is more firmly bounded than female; the lax and undulating means a want of restraint and so *impotentia*. While a woman gives herself to whatever or whomever she believes in, a man must give everything else, but never himself. Men must remain substantial. Even in their tragedies the Greeks were less concerned with sin and hubris than with the greatness of the men who fell and died. Not that the tragedies are the best of Greek culture; Warren warns us against the canker of doubt even in Aeschylus. As we already know, Plato's androgynous idealism is even further from what Warren admires. Severity and heroism, and the distrust of pity and self-sacrifice, are what we have to learn from the Greeks. We cannot wince away from the world's inherent cruelty.

The chapter entitled "The Severity of Apollo" begins, "There is unhappiness, injustice, pain in the world." This cannot be excised. "There is something cruel in that shutting of the door whenever we come in for the night. . . ."[69] Marriage and family themselves are unjust exclusions; so is art—can any ode or painting *deserve* our full attention? We do not and cannot live by what we conventionally call an ethical code. We live by a canonization of the noble.[70]

Volume III concentrates on the enlargement of the idea of love that Christianity brought with it. This was a kind of moral progress, but such enlargement was not simply a good thing. It is of course Roman Catholic, not Protestant, Christianity to which Warren concedes this much, and even the best of Christianity is criticized as an escape from the truth into the sublime. The Christian hero is victim, not victor; so Homer would have seen no heroism in St. John of the Cross. (Warren is not so interested in what St. John would have seen in Homer.)

The book ends with an appeal to remember the "poor boy [Orestes], just over the threshold of boyhood, knocking at his mother's door and bringing death to her. With the first day of manhood the whole weight of manhood has fallen upon him. He must vindicate for himself that possession and bear that rule which he has never had."[71] He has only one boy friend, Pylades, to help him as he dares the Furies. But years later his body will be found and laid to rest in the Forum in Rome, as guardian of Roman government.

Many of the ideas of this discourse are familiar to readers of Nietzsche, or indeed of D. H. Lawrence and E. M. Forster. They were in fairly wide circulation in the aesthetic movement of England in the 1880s and 1890s, which was when the discourse was first conceived. Naturally, such ideas remained in circulation after that to some degree, even after newer ones replaced them in fashion. For instance, Warren read (with enthusiasm) Emile Faguet's *Culte de l'Incompétence,* which echoed Nietzsche, though Faguet "just missed understanding Nietzsche's greatness."[72] This was a widely read manifesto for the aristocracy, or at least against the democracy, of 1913. A parallel book of the same year was D. H. Lawrence's *Twilight in Italy,* another attack on Enlightenment commonplaces. Warren says that the nineteenth century had been dominated by a passion for the commonplace, but "According to Dionysius, there is a God in a deep but dazzling darkness. . . ."[73]

The project was laid aside during the years of collecting, though Warren kept referring to it. It was revived when Marshall spoke of leaving him and was clearly not going to write it, though much of the writing seems to have been done later, in 1913. There seems to have been a general nervousness among all of Warren's English friends about both his speculative boldness and the social penalties such a self-declaration would bring. The biography says that one of Ned's friends (perhaps Burdett himself) warned him against publishing it, comparing it with *Dorian Gray* to its disadvantage. The latter was humorous, fantastic, and vulgar; three traits that won the book some popularity, and somewhat offset the hostility it aroused, while the *Defence* would simply make life uncomfortable for the author's friends. One sees the point: *A Defence of Uranian Love* does not make an impressive argument. But it was Warren's obstinacy that wins him to some degree the status of an intellectual.

In 1923, Warren also began to write his autobiography, which makes up the bulk of Burdett and Goddard's volume. In the form it has now, the writing is unimpressive, but who knows what cuts or editing they have given it. He himself thought it was important; writing it, he told Lois Shaw, gave him "inexpressible pleasure. It is like unpacking boxes of treasures bought on a journey. What I have thought and felt during a longish life comes out and seems to me worth the trouble which I had about it. The record of the trouble is, indeed, not pleasant to write out. . . . But at times it has seemed so impossible of accomplishment that I rejoice to find it gliding from my pen."[74]

Ned's Last Years

During his years in residence at Oxford during World War I, Warren seems to have played the part of a Socratic tutor to the undergraduates, to at least his own satisfaction. He was obviously an important teacher to E. H. Gropius/Goddard. After 1918, however, he got less response from the ex-servicemen who filled the colleges. Fortunately, after Mary Marshall's death in the early 1920s, Warren was again able to busy himself taking care of Johnny. Between 1907 and 1924, though the latter had visited Lewes House, sometimes with but more often without Mary, the two men had been more or less estranged. Now Warren was again active in supervising Marshall's diet, holidays, medicines, lodgings, and he persuaded him to resign from the Metropolitan, though in fact the letter of resignation

was never posted. Warren promised Marshall £2,600 a year and
guaranteed that in his will. Marshall died first, however, early in
1928, and bequeathed Warren his American estate after the deaths
of his sisters Priscilla and Ellen. (Ned in his will looked after not
only these sisters but Johnny's two brothers.) According to Fothergill, Marshall became diabetic, but the causes of his death included
also the nervous trouble caused by the rumors of art forgeries.

In a letter to Lois Warren dated September 27, 1926, Warren
refers to Marshall's health being affected by unpleasant news (later
proved to be mistaken) and a worry that he took too seriously, both
pertaining to his "business." These had thrown him wholly out of
health and left behind palpitations. They were, Warren said, "big
worries," and he didn't think Marshall would ever cure his heart
trouble unless he gave up "business." (Warren always put quotation
marks around the word.) It seems certain that this agitation derived
from the question of art forgeries.

The friends were together the last two and a half months of
Marshall's life. Burdett and Goddard imply that Warren was at
Marshall's deathbed, where the latter several times repeated
"Good-bye, Puppy." We cannot doubt that Warren was deeply
affected; theirs was certainly a love story. But he reported himself
as being as busy as ever immediately after and undistracted from
prosecuting his various schemes: "You needn't sympathize or suppose me knocked out. It is my nature to go on and not to brood over
sad facts."[75]

Fothergill quotes a few rather nice lines Warren wrote about
Marshall; or perhaps about himself:

> *And happier thus the shrouded soul,*
> *at stretch and watch for none,*
> *dies when his task of life is done,*
> *lives in a dream that few divine,*
> *eats of his figs and drinks his wine,*
> *rolls up his heaven like a scroll,*
> *and hides his sunlight from the sun.*[76]

These lines might do for an epitaph for either of them. The
shrouded soul applies especially well to people who, like the two
of them, had to conceal so much. But in a different sense, the phrase
seems to fit Sam and Cornelia Warren too.

Ned Warren died on December 28, 1928, in a London nursing

home after an abdominal operation presumably for one of those intestinal complaints that had plagued him for so long. He was given a *Times* obituary on the thirty-first, which was supplemented by a letter to that newspaper on January 15, 1929, from his old friend A. G. B. West, rector of St. Dunstan's-in-the-East. West said there were scores of men, his friends or their sons, now in learned professions or positions of trust because of the start Warren gave them. (In many ways the most interesting side of Ned's activities was his getting young men *out* of the learned professions.)

The two Oxford obituaries I have found are much more to the point. One was by Goddard in *The Pelican,* a Corpus publication. He praised Warren as being a far better Grecian, truer to the message of Greece, than for instance Walter Pater. (Goddard means, presumably, that Pater betrayed the Greek idea by sublimating its sexual component, or by praising Athens and forgetting Thebes.) He and Marshall were passionately and aesthetically attached to the Greek idea and distressed that so few scholars had any aesthetic spirit.[77] Warren himself would have been the perfect candidate for the praelectorship he endowed, able as he was to inspire a passion for the beauty of the great athletic age of Pindar before the philosophers had weakened that idea.

Goddard himself was apparently a remarkable teacher, and I met one of his pupils who had, at Bradford Grammar School, received Warren's passion for Greece through that intermediary and, in 1926, while still a schoolboy had gone to Rome at Easter, where he met Warren. Apparently, when Goddard married, Warren had given him a sum of money to make a trip to Rome with his wife, but she was not interested and so the money was used by Goddard to bring two schoolboys with him instead. It must have seemed appropriate to Warren that the passion for classics should run in the masculine line. Goddard was perhaps Warren's one true intellectual heir. So when he talks, in the biography and elsewhere, of the frustration of the Corpus Christi praelectorship scheme, one hears a note of regret in his voice, which suggests that he had hoped to fill that post himself. He had certainly shared Warren's dream of installing a Socratic tradition at Oxford. If the college, he says, now has to wait fifteen years for enough interest to accrue before they can appoint such a praelector, they will never find the Socrates he wanted, but at best a philologian (i.e., it will be too late for Goddard).

The second Oxford obituary was J. D. Beazley's in the *Oxford*

Magazine on January 24, 1929. Beazley clearly understood Warren, as a collector but also as a man; it was to him that Warren wrote, in one of his last letters, about his three great achievements. He said Warren was remarkable because he was neither an opportunist nor a dreamer; he had studied himself as a young man and had chosen for himself a purpose, involving high and difficult tasks. (Perhaps Warren's life is as much characterized by a restless multifariousness of purpose, and Beazley's phrase applies better to himself, but that self-identification with the older man is itself a tribute.) He loved that earlier Greece—athletic, aristocratic, and heroic—which became articulate in Pindar, Aeschylus, Critius, and Myron. He had a deep understanding of the Greek mind as well as a subtle sense of the language.

Beazley ended by citing a passage he had often discussed with Warren about a great oak tree, taken from Pindar's magnificent fourth Pythian Ode. In his chapter entitled "Warren as Collector," Beazley strikes off another such image, speaking of the happiness Warren said he felt standing in the Salone del Toro in Naples; a sense of ease, gaiety, and well-being, as if he were in the middle of a more radiant world.[78] It is what D. H. Lawrence felt standing in the Etruscan tombs.

Warren's final literary work was his will, a forty-four-page document signed November 23, 1928. It was not probated in England until July 1931, and what with the stock market crash having occurred during the long period of probation, an estate that might have been worth $2 million was worth only $1.2 million, and several of its benefactions could not be carried out immediately.

There are eighteen articles. The first eleven list various payments, lump sums and annuities, to be paid as soon as possible. Harry Asa Thomas got Warren's English real estate and $10,000; Fiske got the family portraits. Goddard, Burdett, and C. R. S. Harris of All Souls College, Oxford, were made literary executors, with the implicit charge to write a biography. The Boston Museum was given the chance to buy the collection of intaglios and cameos for $87,500. Charles Murray West was to get Fewacres and money to buy more land to go with it.

Then, in Article 12, a trust was set up with many provisions (subparagraph cc alone covers the elaborate arrangements at Corpus). The adopted son, Travis, was given $3,000 a year from his guardians (Thomas and Burdett) up to the age of twenty-eight. Between that age and thirty-two his trustees (heretofore his guardians) were to give him a sum of not more than $20,000, and $200 a month, and in the same period they could invest up to $30,000 on his behalf in a business that interested him—if he had shown any business competence. And when the trust ended (it ran for twenty-one years) he was to get $3,000 a year. All this seems to express distrust of at least the young man's practical abilities; he was described by some who met him as "light-weight." That distrust was perhaps justified by subsequent events: Travis was reduced to poverty by the end of his life.

Various members of the West family inherit large sums, almost as large as Thomas's. If Corpus failed to keep to the terms of the trust the money left it was to be reassigned, one-third to the Boston Museum and two-thirds to Bowdoin. And finally, Warren's ashes were to be taken to Italy, to rest beside Marshall's in the Acatholic Cemetery in Bagni di Lucca. Frank Gearing, Warren's Lewes House secretary, took them. (Warren was cremated at Golders Green, and according to Fothergill's memory, there were few or no people in the chapel besides himself and Thomas, though outside were several of the servants from Lewes House.)

Warren's carefully appointed houses were soon dismantled. Neither Thomas nor Murray West preserved what he left them. Fothergill mentions attending the auction at Lewes House and seeing the Tudor table sold for £2,100. In America, Warren's "Choice Collection of English Furniture," plus bronzes, statuary, brocades, velvets—altogether about 250 items—were sold at the Anderson Galleries in New York in November 1930. And Fewacres itself was sold a few years later.

Ned's Heritage

More interesting to the historian than the fate of Ned Warren's money and real estate is the fate of his idea, his presence, his achieved self. The most obvious place to look for this is the museums, especially their departments of classical antiquities; a book is needed to show completely the pattern of his donations and his sendings, his relations with American curators and Greek and Italian dealers. But it all adds up to an idea much narrower than the one his whole life gives us, and this larger, looser idea is what is most interesting to follow in its posthumous career.

Warren was never portrayed or studied by a major novelist, but what we might call his ghost came within Evelyn Waugh's purview while the latter was a schoolboy at Lancing. Waugh practiced script and lettering there, and a man named Francis Crease, who attended chapel at the college and "took an interest in the better looking boys," as Waugh says in his autobiography, admired Waugh's work knowledgeably and asked to meet him. Despite some custodial scruples, because Crease displayed many of the behavioral traits associated with homosexuality, he was allowed to give Waugh private instruction once a week in his own house. Waugh says, "I think he had been some kind of companion-secretary-almoner to a rich American, who held an honorary fellowship at Corpus and in his company met most of the university and collected some fine china and silver."[79] The reader can guess who this rich American was. And in fact the second codicil to Warren's will left £200 a year to a Francis Crease. (It is tempting to think that Crease's tales, heard from Warren, of life at Corpus may have been material for *Decline and Fall*.)

Waugh describes Crease in terms that would apply to some degree to Warren himself: He was plump, pink and white with a nunlike complexion, wore rural-aesthetic dress of soft tweeds, capes, and silk shirts. He was partly an invalid, and his gait was delicate, almost mincing. He spoke in soft tones that rose to shrillness when he was excited. Despite the masters' suspicions, he seemed to be "entirely without sexual interests"; yet he was once arrested on suspicion of being a priest who was wanted by the police for unnatural vice. He drew black and white decorations in the Beardsley or Walter Crane style.

His worst trait, says Waugh, was secretiveness: He was "a neuter, evasive, hypochondriacal recluse" of whom Waugh nevertheless was, and remained, fond, admiring, respectful. Part of the writer's interest in Crease derived from the contrast he made with the other man who at that time made a claim on Waugh's imaginative loyalties. This other man, J. F. Roxburgh, won the competition in the short run. He was a strong, virile presence, a brilliant teacher, who went on to become a powerful figure in the world of English pedagogy. He had the will and skill to succeed, while Crease was a failure, and Lancing worshipped success, Waugh says. Yet Roxburgh *was* a homosexual.

Waugh is interested in that paradox but also—implicitly—in the values Crease embodied, values Waugh prefers, as he writes the autobiography. Indeed Waugh's novels too celebrate the probity as well as the pathos of failure. That was half the attraction Catholi-

cism had for him. Crease and Warren jointly remained a figure in
all his imaginative work.

Crease was not exactly like Warren, obviously. But there is a
likeness between them that also extends to include Marshall, and
Robbie Ross and others of their friends, and Maurice Magnus and
Forster and Gide, and so on. Moreover, there are other links between Warren and Waugh. Waugh's father must have known Warren at Oxford; they were at the same college in the same years and
knew the same people. Arthur Waugh wrote about Lionel Johnson
in his memoirs.

Indeed, he does so also in an essay in *Tradition and Change.* But what
is most interesting in that volume is its dedication to Waugh's
sixteen-year-old son Evelyn, who is presented as a modernist: "You
are born into an era of many changes; and, if I know you at all, you
will be swayed and troubled by many of them." For instance, Evelyn has already frescoed his old nursery with "strange Cubist pictures." (Mr. Waugh presents literary history as leaping from the
high Victorians, with whom he identifies himself, to the moderns.)
As for Evelyn, "I wish you nothing better than to change gently."
Thus Waugh was cast, in early adolescence, in a drama of decadence
and aestheticism, with figures like Johnson, Crease, and Warren as
co-players. (Crease became to some degree a friend of the Waugh
family and obviously fitted into Mr. Waugh's categories.) Evelyn's
first book was on Dante Gabriel Rossetti, one of the aesthetes'
precursors.[80]   `

As everyone knows, the crucial imaginative experience for
Waugh and his friends (including Harold Acton, John Betjeman,
and others who came to be the collective voice of a generation) was
Oxford in the 1920s, where young men defied the middle-class
reality principle. The supreme fantasy expression of that experience
is *Brideshead Revisited,* and the factual basis for the fantasy has been
fully explored in recent scholarship. It was, in many ways, the same
Oxford as Ned Warren had known forty years before; behind the
excitements of dandyism, aestheticism, aristocracy, and Catholicism stood the threat and promise of homosexuality.

Waugh and his friends never mention Warren, so far as I know,
but in indirect and shadowy fashion—through other people—he
was shaping that experience for them, pulling the strings of their
puppet theater. For instance, John Fothergill cut an important figure
in that Oxford. His Spread Eagle Inn at Thame was much frequented by Waugh's group. Waugh gave him a copy of his first

novel, *Decline and Fall,* inscribed to "John Fothergill, Oxford's only civilizing influence." Fothergill kept the copy in the lavatory of the inn, chained against the risk of theft.[81]

In one of his evocations of Oxford, Waugh writes, "In those days of broad trousers and high-necked jumpers and cars parked nightly outside the Spread Eagle at Thame, there had been few subdivisions; a certain spiritual extravagance in the quest for pleasure had been the sole common bond between friends, who in subsequent years had drifted far apart . . ." and he goes on to describe them.[82] One of those he was thinking of was certainly Harold Acton, also a friend of Fothergill, who mentions him in his memoirs. The latter praised Acton's novel, *Humdrum,* which "might have been written by the young Wilde."[83] Thus there *were* a few subdivisions or categories, and one was of Waugh, Acton, and their friends—those influenced, however remotely, by Warren and Lewes House.

As Fothergill writes his reminiscences of those days he keeps citing and evoking Warren. He says he is badly in debt but hopes to recover because "E. P. Warren's legacy ought to be released very soon."[84] (He had been left £20,000 in the will, but like other legatees had to wait while the capital accrued enough interest to pay off all the benefactions.) *Confessions of an Innkeeper* is dedicated to Harry Asa Thomas, among others, and in it he says that his last batch of bills at Thame were cleared by Warren and Thomas.[85]

My Three Inns ends with Fothergill recommending to the reader Harold Acton's autobiography, *Memoirs of an Aesthete,* published just before his own book. In the *Memoirs,* Acton names another Warren friend, J. D. Beazley, as the only Oxford don he and his friends could take seriously. They appreciated Beazley in much the way Christopher Isherwood and his friends appreciated E. M. Forster; Beazley and Forster were hidden away in their respective universities, intensely quiet and discreet personalities, but they held within them an explosive charge for these young dissidents.

Fothergill puts Acton and Waugh together several times in his memoirs—speaking of their joint influence on Oxford—and indeed Waugh dedicated *Decline and Fall* to Acton. Fothergill's last book has a long penultimate section reminiscing about Warren. And at the Spread Eagle, as well as the undergraduates brought by Waugh and Acton, he entertained Beazley—and no doubt Warren himself. It was an extension of Lewes House.

In his *Memoirs,* Acton speaks of Fothergill's affability and erudition, but his real enthusiasm is reserved for Beazley. On his first visit to Oxford the young Acton saw "Nearby, sipping champagne from a tankard in a pregnant silence as on some lonely Grecian isle, was the pale and pensive Professor Beazley, the fount of all our knowledge of Greek vases."[86] He and Mrs. Beazley shared the Judge's Lodgings at Oxford with a Miss Price, a friend of Warren and Berenson, "a practical aesthete of the 1880s."[87] In their house Acton found the harmony he could not find elsewhere in Oxford—an Aegean calm. He traveled with this household to Spain.

Thus Fothergill and Beazley were two major conduits through which Warren's ideas and interests touched Waugh's generation, though their temperaments and presences were quite different from each other and from him. One would not speak of Fothergill, like Crease, as a ghost of Warren, but one might call the Spread Eagle a house haunted by him. (For instance, the plum puddings at the Spread Eagle were always made according to Warren's "extravagant American receipt,"[88] and Fothergill's memoirs are full of tales about Warren, Marshall, and Lewes House.) What we see here and in those named before (and we might add Santayana, and others) is a family or brotherhood or order (a defrocked order) of aesthete heretics at their secret work of subversion of "the normal" and "the moral." Their social setting is nowadays the academy, broadly interpreted; that is where the aesthetic movement has lodged itself in our society.

On the whole we probably look on those people as figures of comedy. They represent to most of us options of freedom, alternative lives, escapes from the norms, kinds of relaxation and occasions for laughter. That is what "civilizing" signals, as Waugh applies it to Fothergill, or "Aegean calm," as Acton applies that to Beazley. But the story of the Warren brothers, of the manifold conflicts in the Warren family—our story when set in the actual districts of Boston, and not in the ideal groves of academe—should remind us that such eccentricity is more than comic, that a figure like Ned Warren has its tragic and its threatening dimensions.

ENDNOTES

KEY

Alcmaeon	E. P. Warren's *Alcmaeon, Hypermestra, Caeneos*
Burdett and Goddard	Osbert Burdett and E. H. Goddard's *Edward Perry Warren*
D. H. Papers	Denison House Papers at the Schlesinger Library
Hadley	Rollin van Ness Hadley's *The Letters of Bernard Berenson and Isabella Stewart Gardner*
I Tatti Papers	Berenson Archives at the Berenson Library at I Tatti
Memorial	Cornelia Warren's *A Memorial of My Mother*
M.H.A. Papers	Warren-Clarke Family Papers at the Massachusetts Historical Association
Miss Wilton	Cornelia Warren's *Miss Wilton*
S. D. Warren	*S. D. Warren: a Tribute from the People of Cumberland Mills*
Senate Hearings	*U.S. Senate Committee Hearings on the Nomination of Louis D. Brandeis to be Justice of the Supreme Court*
Whitehill	Walter Muir Whitehill's *The Museum of Fine Arts, Boston*

Introduction

1. M.H.A. Papers.
2. *Senate Hearings*, p. 860.
3. The Marshall-Warren Papers in the Ashmolean Museum.
4. Ibid.
5. *Senate Hearings*, p. 895.
6. Ibid., p. 897.
7. Ibid., p. 896.
8. Ibid., p. 898.
9. Ibid., pp. 897–98.
10. Ibid., pp. 898–99.
11. Letter in the possession of Mrs. Rhoda Shaw Clark.

Chapter 1

1. *S. D. Warren*, p. 59.
2. Letter in the Houghton Library, Harvard University.
3. *Memorial*, p. 51.
4. *Miss Wilton*, p. 323.
5. Ibid., p. 184.
6. Ibid., p. 185.

7. Ibid., p. 169.
8. Ibid., p. 246.
9. Ibid., p. 318.
10. *Memorial*, p. 157.
11. *History of the S.D. Warren Company*, p. 32.
12. Mason family papers, in the possession of Herbert Mason.
13. *Highlights of Westbrook History*.
14. *National Register of Historic Places: Description; Cumberland Mills District*.
15. *S. D. Warren*, p. 94.
16. Ibid., p. 109.
17. Ibid., p. 107.
18. Ibid., p. 10.
19. Ibid., p. 58.
20. *History of the S.D. Warren Company*, p. 33.
21. Ellen Ballou, *The Building of the House*, p. 47.
22. One of Fiske Warren's Familiar Letters; a term he seems to have used to mean "familial"; at the Warren Memorial Library.
23. Charles C. Calhoun, "Bowdoin and the Ancient World," in *Bowdoin*, vol. 61, no. 1, September 1987.
24. *Memorial*, p. 78.
25. Ibid., p. 77.
26. Burdett and Goddard, p. 1.
27. Ibid., p. 2.
28. *Memorial*, p. 151.
29. Ibid., p. 101.
30. Ibid., pp. 102–103.
31. Ibid., p. 127.

Chapter 2

1. *Memorial*, p. 138.
2. Ibid., p. 139.
3. Burdett and Goddard, p. 5.
4. Erica Hirshler, "The Great Collectors," in *Pilgrims and Pioneers*, eds. Alice Faxon and Sylvia Moore (New York: Midmarch Arts Press, 1987), p. 27.
5. Burdett and Goddard, p. 64.
6. Ibid.
7. Ibid., p. 67.
8. Ibid., p. 9.
9. Ibid., p. 14.
10. Ibid., p. 9.
11. Ibid., p. 11.
12. Ibid., p. 13.
13. *Memorial*, p. 121.
14. I Tatti Papers, letter of March 1902.
15. *Memorial*, p. 117.

16. Burdett and Goddard, p. 23.
17. *Memorial,* p. 143.
18. H. C. Warren, *Visuddhimagga,* Foreword.
19. Interview with Fiske Warren in the *Boston Herald,* July 24, 1929.
20. *Memorial,* pp. 148–49.
21. Ibid., p. 134.
22. Burdett and Goddard, p. 38.
23. Ibid., p. 2.
24. Ibid.
25. Whitehill, p. 142.
26. Santayana, *People and Places,* p. 140.
27. Ibid., pp. 87–88.
28. Ibid., p. 53.
29. Ibid., p. 180.
30. Ballowe, *George Santayana's America,* p. 20.
31. Santayana, *People and Places,* p. 208.
32. Ballowe, *George Santayana's America,* p. 10.
33. Santayana, *People and Places,* p. 165.
34. Ibid., p. 209.
35. *Memorial,* p. 151.

Chapter 3

1. M.H.A. Papers, letter of March 9, 1894.
2. Burdett and Goddard, p. 4.
3. Ibid., p. 5.
4. M.H.A. Papers, Mrs. Warren's letter of March 1894.
5. Ibid., letter of April 15, 1894.
6. *Descriptive Catalog of Paintings Collected by the Late Mrs. S. D. Warren,* p. viii.
7. Hirshler, "The Great Collectors," p. 28.
8. Taylor, *Babel's Tower,* p. 20.
9. Ibid., p. 31.
10. Burdett and Goddard, p. 6.
11. E. P. Warren, *A Defence of Uranian Love,* I, p. 42.
12. *Alcmaeon,* pp. 16–17.
13. Ibid., p. 17.
14. Ibid., p. 21.
15. Ibid., p. 18.
16. Burdett and Goddard, p. 21.
17. Ibid., p. 16.
18. Ibid., p. 19.
19. E. P. Warren, *A Defence of Uranian Love,* I, p. 42.
20. Letter in the Nutter, McLennen and Fish Archive.
21. Alfred Lief, *Brandeis,* New York, 1936, p. 28.
22. Ibid.
23. Ibid., p. 344.

24. Mason, *Brandeis,* p. 238.
25. Gal, *Brandeis of Boston,* p. ix.
26. Lief, *Brandeis,* p. 32.
27. Ibid., p. 28.
28. Ibid., p. 31.
29. Mason, *Brandeis,* p. 389.
30. Ibid., p. 59.
31. Brandeis, *The Letters of Louis D. Brandeis,* p. 38.
32. Gal, *Brandeis of Boston,* p. 6.
33. Mason, *Brandeis,* p. 61.
34. Strum, *Louis Dembitz Brandeis,* p. 62.
35. Ibid., p. 63.
36. Letter in the Nutter, McLennen and Fish Archive.
37. Mason, *Brandeis,* p. 3.
38. Ibid., p. 47.
39. Anecdote from Herbert Mason.
40. Burdett and Goddard, p. 56.
41. Palmer, *The Autobiography of a Philosopher,* pp. 125–26.
42. Ibid., p. 14.
43. Palmer, *The Life of Alice Freeman Palmer,* pp. 147–48.
44. Ibid., p. 111.
45. *Memorial,* p. 152.
46. Ibid., p. 153.
47. Burdett and Goddard, p. 32.
48. Ibid., pp. 34–35.
49. Ibid., p. 36.
50. Ibid., pp. 42–43.
51. Ibid., p. 45.
52. Ibid.
53. Wilde, *Collected Works,* III, p. 99.
54. Ibid., pp. 99–100.
55. Ibid., p. 102.
56. Burdett and Goddard, p. 46.
57. Ibid.
58. Ibid., p. 48.
59. Ibid., p. 6.
60. Hadley, p. 14.
61. Sprigge, *Berenson,* pp. 102–103.
62. Simpson, *Artful Partners,* p. 47.
63. Ballowe, *George Santayana's America,* p. 39.
64. Ibid.
65. Ibid., p. 40.

Chapter 4

1. *Journal of the American Oriental Society* 16, no. 66 (1896).
2. Morison, *Three Centuries of Harvard,* p. 381.

3. Harvard University Archives.
4. Introduction to the Harvard Oriental Series.
5. H. C. Warren, *Visuddhimagga.*
6. Harvard University Archives.
7. E. P. Warren's memoir of his brother, in H. C. Warren, *Visuddhimagga.*
8. H. C. Warren, *Buddhism in Translations.*
9. Warren family papers, in the possession of Mrs. Margaret Warren.
10. *S. D. Warren,* p. 35.
11. Ibid., p. 55.
12. Paper, *Brandeis,* p. 219.
13. Lawrence M. Friedman, "The Dynastic Trust," *Yale Law Journal* 73 (1964): 547–92, esp. 547.
14. *Senate Hearings,* pp. 486–87.
15. Quoted in Chester, *Inheritance, Wealth, and Society,* p. 132.
16. Burdett and Goddard, p. 63.
17. E. P. Warren, *Classical and American Education,* p. 17.
18. Ibid., p. 18.
19. Burdett and Goddard, p. 51.
20. Ibid., p. 58.
21. E. P. Warren, *A Defence of Uranian Love,* I, p. 6.
22. Ibid., p. 7.
23. Ibid., p. 8.
24. Ibid., p. 13.
25. Ibid., p. 14.
26. *Alcmaeon,* p. 27.
27. Ibid., p. 37.
28. Ibid., p. 38.
29. Burdett and Goddard, p. 54.
30. Ibid., p. 116.
31. Ibid., p. 255.
32. Simpson, *Artful Partners,* p. 57.
33. Walter Pater, *Marius the Epicurean,* London, 1918, pp. 149, 157.
34. Santayana, *People and Places,* p. 210.
35. E. P. Warren, *A Defence of Uranian Love,* II, p. 25.
36. Burdett and Goddard, pp. 328–29.
37. E. P. Warren, *A Defence of Uranian Love,* II, p. 7.
38. Fisher, *An Unfinished Autobiography,* p. 140.
39. Santayana, *The Middle Span,* p. 8.
40. Ibid., p. 17.
41. Santayana, *Character and Opinion in the United States,* p. 170.
42. Santayana, *The Middle Span,* p. 44.
43. McCormick, *George Santayana,* p. 83.
44. Ibid., p. 56.
45. Santayana, *People and Places,* p. 188.
46. Ibid., p. 190.
47. Santayana, *The Middle Span,* p. 58.
48. Burdett and Goddard, p. 62.
49. Ibid., p. 63.

50. Ibid., p. 111.
51. Ibid., p. 66.
52. Ibid., p. 100.
53. Ibid., p. 400.
54. Ibid., p. 104.
55. Ibid., p. 113.
56. Ibid., p. 106.
57. Ibid., p. 107.
58. Ibid., p. 126.
59. Ibid., p. 127.
60. E. P. Warren, *A Tale of Pausanian Love,* p. 13.
61. Ibid., p. 24.
62. Ibid., p. 36.
63. Ibid., p. 75.
64. Ibid., p. 83.
65. R. M. Ogilvie, *Latin and Greek,* London, 1964, p. 55.
66. Ibid., p. 136.
67. Ibid., p. 137.
68. Ibid., p. 141.
69. Ibid., p. 147.
70. Ibid., p. 143.
71. Gal, *Brandeis of Boston,* pp. 20–21.
72. *Senate Hearings,* p. 1290.
73. Gal, *Brandeis of Boston,* p. 36.
74. Ibid., p. 29.
75. Ibid., p. 30.
76. Ibid., pp. 36, 230.
77. Brandeis, *The Letters of Louis D. Brandeis,* p. 73.
78. Ibid., p. 76.
79. Edel, *The Life of Henry James,* I, p. 649.
80. Leon Edel, *The Letters of Henry James,* I, London, 1978, p. 408.
81. Thoron, *The Letters of Mrs. Henry Adams,* p. 416.
82. *Senate Hearings,* p. 840.
83. Paper, *Brandeis,* p. 35.
84. Ernst and Schwartz, *Privacy: the Right to Be Let Alone,* pp. 45–46.
85. James H. Barron, "Warren and Brandeis, *The Right to Privacy,* 4 Harvard Law Review 193 (1890): Demystifying a Landmark Citation," XIII 4 *Suffolk University Law Review* (Summer 1979): 875–922.
86. Paper, *Brandeis,* p. 36.
87. Barron, "Warren and Brandeis," pp. 888, 905.
88. Ibid., p. 907.
89. See Forbes, *Sport in Norfolk County,* chapter on polo by W. Cameron Forbes.
90. Arthur T. Cabot, in a memorial eulogy of 1910, in the Warren family papers in Mrs. Margaret Warren's possession.
91. Ibid., p. 13.
92. Ibid.
93. Burdett and Goddard, p. 145.

94. Ibid., p. 146.
95. Patricia Palmieri, *Adamless Eden: A Social Portrait of an Academic Community at Wellesley College 1875–1920* (unpublished manuscript).
96. Palmer and Palmer, *An Academic Courtship,* p. xv.
97. Palmer, *The Life of Alice Freeman Palmer,* p. 138.
98. Palmer and Palmer, *Academic Courtship,* p. 101.
99. Woods, *The City Wilderness,* p. 34.
100. Scudder, *Socialism and Character,* pp. 5–6.

Chapter 5

1. Letter of March 14, 1967, in the Bowdoin College Archives.
2. Burdett and Goddard, p. 134.
3. Ibid., p. 147.
4. Fothergill, *An Innkeeper's Diary,* p. 260.
5. *Poèmes* (Paris: Editions du Mercure de France, 1896), p. 182: cited in Akiko Murakata, *Selected Letters of D. William Sturgis Bigelow* (Ph.D. Dissertation at George Washington University, 1971), p. 275.
6. Ibid., p. 273.
7. Osbert Burdett, *The Beardsley Period,* London, 1925, p. 169.
8. Ibid.
9. Fothergill, *My Three Inns,* p. 232.
10. Rothenstein, *Men and Memories,* p. 343.
11. Fothergill, *My Three Inns,* p. 233.
12. Ibid.; p. 232.
13. Ibid., p. 3.
14. Lawrence, *Aaron's Rod,* p. 208.
15. Ibid., pp. 213–14.
16. Lawrence, *Phoenix II,* p. 303.
17. Ibid., p. 304.
18. Ibid., p. 306.
19. Ibid., p. 307.
20. Ibid., pp. 311–12.
21. Ibid., p. 305.
22. Ibid., pp. 323–24.
23. Fothergill, *An Innkeeper's Diary,* p. 171.
24. Fothergill, *Confessions of an Innkeper,* p. 182.
25. Ibid.
26. Ibid., p. 87.
27. Letter at Bowdoin College.
28. Fothergill, *My Three Inns,* p. 239.
29. Osbert Burdett, *Memory and Imagination,* London, 1935, p. 175.
30. Ibid., p. 176.
31. Biographical manuscript on Prichard in the Gardner Museum Archive.
32. Ibid.
33. Burdett, *Memory and Imagination,* p. 171.

34. Burdett, *The Art of Living,* p. 131.
35. Furbank, *E. M. Forster,* I, p. 66.
36. Ibid., p. 67.
37. Forster, *Two Cheers for Democracy,* p. 233.
38. Berenson, *A Sketch for a Self-Portrait,* p. 51.
39. *Senate Hearings,* p. 872.
40. Samuels, *The Making of a Connoisseur,* pp. 245–46.
41. M.H.A. Papers.
42. Letter of March 15, 1915, at the Cleveland Museum of Art.
43. Letter of April 21, 1915, at the Cleveland Museum of Art.
44. Burdett and Goddard, p. 176.
45. Fothergill, *Confessions of an Innkeeper,* pp. 195–96.
46. Fothergill, *My Three Inns,* p. 237.
47. Burdett and Goddard, p. 400.
48. Letter in the Museum of Fine Arts Archive.
49. Burdett and Goddard, p. 344.
50. Letters in the M.H.A. Papers.
51. Ibid.
52. Ibid., letter of September 3, 1892.
53. Ibid., letter of June 1, 1894.
54. Ibid.
55. Ibid., letter of January 9, 1896.
56. Ibid., letter of December 10, 1896.
57. Fothergill, *My Three Inns,* p. 235.
58. Letters in the M.H.A. Papers.
59. Burdett and Goddard, p. 191.
60. Ibid.
61. Ibid., p. 208.
62. Ibid., pp. 86–87.
63. Hadley, p. 100.
64. Letter of December 10, 1896, among the M.H.A. Papers.
65. Letters at I Tatti.
66. Whitehill, p. 215.
67. Ibid., p. 148.
68. Ibid., pp. 146–47.
69. Herbert, *Ancient Art in Bowdoin College,* p.2.
70. Whitehill, p. 147.
71. Burdett and Goddard, p. 154.
72. *Miss Wilton,* p. 120.
73. Ibid., p. 123.
74. Ibid., p. 130.
75. Ibid., p. 131.
76. Ibid., p. 227.
77. Ibid., p. 256.
78. Ibid., p. 576.
79. Ibid., p. 273.
80. Ibid., p. 417.
81. Letter of March 4, 1892, among the M.H.A. Papers.

82. G. H. and A. F. Palmer, *The Teacher,* Cambridge, Mass., 1908, pp. 3, 4, 8, 9.
83. Article on Boston in the 1911 edition of the *Encyclopaedia Britannica.*
84. Davis, *Spearheads of Reform,* p. 26.
85. D. H. Papers.
86. Davis, *Spearheads of Reform,* p. 42.
87. Scudder, *On Journey,* p. 147.
88. Gal, *Brandeis of Boston,* p. 10.
89. Ibid., p. 53.
90. Mason, *Brandeis,* p. 389.
91. Ibid., p. 4.
92. Ibid., p. 95.
93. Gal, *Brandeis, Progressivism, Zionism,* p. 143.
94. *Senate Hearings,* p. 284.
95. Ibid., p. 867.
96. Ibid., p. 472.
97. Ibid., p. 881.
98. M.H.A. Papers.
99. *The Nation* 68, 1750; January 12, 1899, p. 24.
100. *Memorial.*
101. Letter of August 1896, among the M.H.A. Papers.
102. Letter of July 15, 1897, among the M.H.A. Papers.
103. Letter of August 6, 1898, among the M.H.A. Papers.
104. Harvard Oriental Series Descriptive List, p. 388.
105. Ibid., p. 389.
106. Harvard Oriental Series, General Introduction, p. xxiv.
107. M.H.A. Papers.
108. Boyle, *The Riddle of Erskine Childers,* pp. 121–22.
109. Ibid.
110. Fisher, *An Unfinished Autobiography,* p. 153.
111. *Senate Hearings,* p. 860.
112. Letter of March 1894, among the M.H.A. Papers.
113. Burdett and Goddard, p. 153.
114. Tompkins, *Anti-Imperialism in the United States,* p. 123.
115. Ibid., p. 90.
116. Ibid., p. 3.
117. Schirmer, *Republic or Empire?,* pp. 242–43.
118. Ibid., pp. 247–48.

Chapter 6

1. Wells, *The Future in America,* p. 225.
2. Ibid., pp. 233–34.
3. Ibid., p. 235.
4. James, *The American Scene,* p. 232.
5. Ibid., p. 248.
6. Burdett and Goddard, p. 225.

7. Letter in the M.H.A. Papers.
8. Letters in the Archive of the Paintings Department of the Museum of Fine Arts, Boston.
9. M.H.A. Papers.
10. Ibid.
11. Ibid.
12. Gardner Museum Archives.
13. M.H.A. Papers.
14. Neilson, *Filippino Lippi,* p. 121.
15. Ibid., p. 122.
16. Letter of July 22, 1902, in the Museum of Fine Arts Archive.
17. Letters in the Archive of the Paintings Department of the Museum of Fine Arts, Boston.
18. Ibid.
19. Letters at I Tatti.
20. Conversation with Susan Sinclair.
21. Museum of Fine Arts Archive.
22. Whitehill, p. 221.
23. Ibid., p. 227.
24. Burdett and Goddard, p. 219.
25. Museum of Fine Arts Archive.
26. Whitehill, p. 167.
27. Ibid., p. 183.
28. Ibid., p. 188.
29. Ibid., p. 189.
30. Ibid., p. 200.
31. Ibid., p. 201.
32. Ibid., p. 202.
33. *Museum of Fine Arts Bulletin* 4, p. 47.
34. Whitehill, p. 209.
35. Ibid., pp. 212–13.
36. Ibid., p. 214.
37. Ibid., p. 175.
38. Repository, University Museum Archives, University of Pennsylvania, Curatorial Records—Mediterranean Section, Box 1 (Sam Yorke Stevenson)—Correspondence.
39. Burdett and Goddard, p. 73.
40. Whitehill, p. 157.
41. Burdett and Goddard, pp. 338–40.
42. Museum of Fine Arts Archive.
43. Burdett and Goddard, p. 340.
44. Ibid (taken from *Boston Evening Transcript*), p. 341.
45. *Mitteilungen,* p. 74. ("There is in this head the vigour, the health, even an astonishing health, and a prodigious force . . . the essential features [of antiquity] are force and health. . . . No vagueness. . . . Thanks to it I have understood Praxiteles, I who thought that the Parthenon was the summit of art.")
46. Ibid., p. 77.

47. Ibid., p. 87.
48. *Monthly Review,* London, February 1902, pp. 78, 80.
49. Ibid., p. 97.
50. Ibid., p. 99.
51. Ibid., p. 100.
52. Ibid., p. 101.
53. Burdett and Goddard, pp. 222–23.
54. Ibid., pp. 145–46.
55. Whitehill, p. 162.
56. Burdett and Goddard, p. 227.
57. Updike, *Self-Consciousness,* p. 191.
58. Conversation with Sylvia Berkman.
59. Burdett and Goddard, p. 283.
60. Ibid., p. 290.
61. Ibid., p. 262.
62. Museum of Fine Arts Archive.
63. Burdett and Goddard, p. 236.
64. Hadley, p. 417.
65. Burdett and Goddard, p. 226.
66. Ibid.
67. Ibid., pp. 395–96.
68. Ibid., p. 394.
69. Ibid., p. 135.
70. Ibid., p. 226.
71. Ibid., pp. 234–35.
72. Ibid.
73. All the letters to Corpus Christi College are in that college's archive.
74. Kurtz, *Beazley and Oxford,* p. 51.
75. Sherwood, *No Golden Journey,* p. 59.
76. Burdett and Goddard, p. 75.
77. Ibid., p. 76.
78. Letter at I Tatti.
79. Warren family papers, in the possession of Mrs. Margaret Warren.
80. Gretchen Warren, *Art, Nature, Education,* p. 19.
81. George, *Progress and Poverty,* pp. 253–54.
82. Barker, *Henry George,* p. 304.
83. Warren family papers, in the possession of Mrs Margaret Warren.
84. D. H. Papers.
85. Davis, *Spearheads of Reform,* p. 231.
86. 1914 Questionnaire Report in the D. H. Papers.
87. Gal, *Brandeis of Boston,* p. 147.
88. Ibid., p. 148.
89. Lief, *Brandeis,* p. 205.
90. Ibid., p. 266.
91. Gal, *Brandeis of Boston,* p. 121.
92. Ibid., p. 123.
93. Mason, *Brandeis,* p. 240.
94. M.H.A. Papers.

95. Burdett and Goddard, p. 240.
96. Ibid., p. 246.
97. Ibid., p. 230.
98. Fothergill, *My Three Inns,* p. 234.
99. Letter in the possession of Mrs. Rhoda Shaw Clark.
100. Burdett and Goddard, p. 221.
101. Ibid.

Chapter 7

1. Hadley, p. 467.
2. Whitehill, p. 182.
3. Ibid., p. 206.
4. Ibid., p. 209.
5. Murakata, *Selected Letters of D. William Sturgis Bigelow,* p. 275.
6. These, and the next letters to Berenson to be cited, are at I Tatti.
7. Letter of January 29, 1907.
8. Letters of December 30, 1904, and January 7, 1905, in the Museum of Fine Arts Archive.
9. Gardner Museum Archive.
10. Ibid.
11. Ibid.
12. Warren family papers, in the possession of Mrs. Margaret Warren.
13. Hadley, p. 468.
14. Ibid.
15. Mason, *Brandeis,* p. 239.
16. Ibid.
17. Gal, *Brandeis of Boston,* p. 173.
18. Mason, *Brandeis,* p. 241.
19. Lief, *Brandeis,* p. 260.
20. Ibid.
21. Gal, *Brandeis of Boston,* p. 41.
22. Paper, *Brandeis,* p. 218.
23. *Senate Hearings,* p. 867.
24. Mason, *Brandeis,* p. 389.
25. Ibid., p. 240.
26. Ibid., p. 471.
27. *Senate Hearings,* p. 271.
28. Ibid., p. 750.
29. Lief, *Brandeis,* p. 361.
30. Mason, *Brandeis,* p. 582.
31. Burdett and Goddard, p. 248.
32. *Senate Hearings,* p. 867.
33. Lief, *Brandeis,* p. 179.
34. Rhode Island School of Design Museum Handbook, p. 30.
35. I Tatti.
36. Corpus Christi College Archive.

37. Burdett and Goddard, p. 369.
38. Letter in the possession of Dr. Carlos Picon.
39. Fothergill, *My Three Inns*, pp. 238–39.
40. Fothergill, *Confessions of an Innkeeper*, p. 58.
41. Santayana, *My Host the World*, p. 97.
42. Ibid.
43. Bowdoin College Museum of Art Archive.
44. See Herbert, *Ancient Art in Bowdoin College*.
45. Ibid., pp. 8–9.
46. Ibid., p. 7.
47. *Oxford Magazine*, January 24, 1929, pp. 303–304.
48. Sox, *Unmasking the Forger*, pp. xi, 21.
49. I Tatti.
50. Hoving, *King of the Confessors*, p. 92.
51. Letter from Perry Warren, March 1989.
52. Letter in the possession of Mrs. Rhoda Shaw Clark.
53. Brandeis, *The Letters of Louis D. Brandeis*, II, p. 482.
54. Burdett and Goddard, p. 396.
55. Amory, *The Proper Bostonians*, p. 125.
56. Anecdote from Herbert Mason.
57. Anecdote from Adelbert Mason.
58. Letter in the possession of Mrs. Rhoda Shaw Clark.
59. Ibid.
60. I Tatti.
61. Letter in the possession of Mrs. Rhoda Shaw Clark.
62. Letter from Mortimer Warren.
63. E. P. Warren, *Classical and American Education*, p. 23.
64. Burdett and Goddard, p. 302.
65. Ibid., p. 132.
66. E. P. Warren, *A Defence of Uranian Love*, I, p. 38.
67. Burdett and Goddard, p. 307.
68. Ibid., p. 306.
69. E. P. Warren, *A Defence of Uranian Love*, II, p. 55.
70. Ibid., p. 64.
71. Ibid., III, p. 80.
72. Burdett and Goddard, p. 250.
73. Ibid.
74. Letter of August 24, 1923, in the possession of Mrs. Rhoda Shaw Clark.
75. Burdett and Goddard, p. 399.
76. Fothergill, *My Three Inns*, p. 239.
77. *Pelican Record* XIX.
78. Burdett and Goddard, p. 334.
79. Waugh, *A Little Learning*, p. 148.
80. Waugh, *Tradition and Change*, pp. vii–viii.
81. Fothergill, *An Innkeeper's Diary*, p. 203.
82. Waugh, *Scoop and Put Out More Flags*, p. 224.
83. Fothergill, *An Innkeeper's Diary*, p. 224.

84. Fothergill, *My Three Inns,* p. 81.
85. Fothergill, *Confessions of an Innkeeper,* p. 190.
86. Harold Acton, *Memoirs of an Aesthete,* London, 1948, p. 114.
87. Ibid., p. 141.
88. Fothergill, *An Innkeeper's Diary,* p. 14.

BIBLIOGRAPHY

Amory, Cleveland. *The Proper Bostonians.* New York, 1947.

Ballou, Ellen. *The Building of the House.* Cambridge, Mass., 1970.

Ballowe, James. *George Santayana's America.* Urbana, Ill., 1967.

Barker, C. A. *Henry George.* New York, 1955.

Berenson, Bernard. *A Sketch for a Self-Portrait.* London, 1949.

Boyle, Andrew. *The Riddle of Erskine Childers.* London, 1977.

Brandeis, Louis Dembitz. *The Letters of Louis D. Brandeis,* ed. M. I. Urofsky and D. W. Levy. Albany, N.Y., 1971.

Chester, Ronald. *Inheritance, Wealth, and Society.* Bloomington, Ind., 1982.

Comstock, M. C., and C. C. Vermeule. *Greek, Etruscan, and Roman Bronzes in the Museum of Fine Arts, Boston.* New York, 1971.

Davis, Allen F. *Spearheads of Reform.* New York, 1967.

Descriptive Catalog of Paintings Collected by the Late Mrs. S. D. Warren. Boston, 1903.

Edel, Leon. *The Life of Henry James.* London, 1977.

Ernst, Morris L., and Alan Schwartz. *Privacy: the Right to Be Let Alone.* New York, 1962.

Fisher, H. A. L. *An Unfinished Autobiography.* London, 1940.

Forbes, Allan. *Sport in Norfolk County.* Boston, 1938.

Forster, E. M. *Two Cheers for Democracy.* New York, 1951.

Fothergill, John. *Confessions of an Innkeeper.* London, 1938.

———. *An Innkeeper's Diary.* London, 1931.

———. *My Three Inns.* London, 1949.

Furbank, Philip. *E. M. Forster.* New York, 1977.

Gal, Allon. *Brandeis of Boston.* Cambridge, Mass., 1980.

———. *Brandeis, Progressivism, and Zionism.* Ph.D. dissertation, Brandeis University, 1976.

George, Henry. *Progress and Poverty.* New York, 1982.

Grundy, G. B. *Fifty-Five Years at Oxford.* London, 1945.

Hadley, R. V. N., ed. *The Letters of Bernard Berenson and Isabella Stewart Gardner.* Boston, 1987.

Hapgood, Norman. *The Changing Years.* New York, 1930.

Herbert, Kevin. *Ancient Art in Bowdoin College.* Cambridge, Mass., 1964.

Highlights of Westbrook History. Westbrook Women's Club, 1952.

History of the S.D. Warren Company, 1854–1954, anon., Westbrook, 1954.

Hoving, Thomas. *King of the Confessors.* London, 1981.

Howells, W. D. *The Rise of Silas Lapham.* New York, 1984.

James, Henry. *The American Scene.* Bloomington, Ind., 1968.

———. *The Letters of Henry James,* ed. Leon Edel. Cambridge, Mass., 1974.

Kurtz, Donna. *Beazley and Oxford.* Oxford, 1985.

Lawrence, D. H. *Aaron's Rod.* New York, 1961.

———. *Phoenix II.* New York, 1968.

Mason, Alpheus T. *Brandeis.* New York, 1946.

McCormick, John. *George Santayana.* New York, 1987.

Morison, S. E. *Three Centuries of Harvard.* Cambridge, Mass., 1936.

Neilson, Katharine B. *Filippino Lippi.* Westport, Conn., 1938.

Palmer, Alice Freeman, and George Herbert Palmer. *An Academic Courtship.* Cambridge, Mass., 1940.

Palmer, G. H. *The Autobiography of a Philosopher.* New York, 1930.

———. *The Life of Alice Freeman Palmer.* Boston, 1910.

Paper, Lewis J. *Brandeis.* Englewood Cliffs, N.J., 1983.

Reitlinger, Gerald. *The Economics of Taste.* London, 1961, 1963.

Rothenstein, William. *Men and Memories.* London, 1931.

Samuels, Ernest. *The Making of a Connoisseur.* Cambridge, Mass., 1979.

Santayana, George. *Character and Opinion in the United States.* New York, 1920.

———. *The Middle Span.* New York, 1945.

———. *My Host the World.* New York, 1953.

———. *People and Places.* New York, 1944.

Schirmer, Daniel. *Republic or Empire?* Morristown, N.J., 1972.

Schueller, Sepp. *Forgeries, Dealers, Experts.* London, 1960.

Scudder, Vida D. *A Listener in Babel.* Boston, 1903.

———. *On Journey.* New York, 1937.

———. *Socialism and Character.* Boston, 1912.

S. D. Warren: a Tribute from the People of Cumberland Mills. Cambridge, Mass., 1888.

Secrest, Meryle. *Being B. B.* London, 1980.

Sherwood, John. *No Golden Journey.* London, 1973.

Simpson, Colin. *Artful Partners.* New York, 1987.

Sox, David. *Unmasking the Forger.* London, 1987.

Sprigge, Sylvia. *Berenson.* Cambridge, Mass., 1960.

Strum, Philippa. *Louis Dembitz Brandeis.* Cambridge, Mass., 1982.

Taylor, Francis H. *Babel's Tower.* New York, 1945.

Thoron, Ward, ed. *The Letters of Mrs. Henry Adams.* Boston, 1936.

Tompkins, E. B. *Anti-Imperialism in the United States.* Philadelphia, 1970.

United States Senate Committee Hearings on the Nomination of Louis D. Brandeis to be Justice of the Supreme Court. Washington, D.C., 1916.

Updike, John. *Self-Consciousness.* New York, 1989.

Vermeule, C. C., and M. C. Comstock. *Sculpture in Stone.* Boston, 1976.

Warren, C. *A Memorial of My Mother.* Boston, 1908.

———. *Miss Wilton.* Cambridge, Mass., 1892.

Warren, E. P. *Alcmaeon, Hypermestra, Caeneos.* Oxford, 1919.

———. *Classical and American Education.* Oxford, 1918.

———. *The Prince Who Did Not Exist.* Forest Park, Ill., 1958.

———. [pseudo. Arthur Lyon Raile]. *A Defence of Uranian Love.* London, 1928.

————. *A Tale of Pausanian Love.* London, 1927.

————. *The Wild Rose.* London, 1909, 1913, 1928.

Warren, Gretchen. *Art, Nature, Education.* Oxford, 1943.

Warren, H. C. *Buddhism in Translations.* Cambridge, Mass., 1896.

————. *Visuddhimagga of Buddhaghosacarya.* Cambridge, Mass., 1950.

Waugh, Arthur. *Tradition and Change.* London, 1918.

Waugh, Evelyn. *A Little Learning.* London, 1964.

————. *Scoop and Put Out More Flags.* New York, 1961.

Wells, H. G. *The Future in America.* New York, 1906.

Wilde, Oscar. *Collected Works.* New York, 1923.

Whitehill, W. M. *The Museum of Fine Arts, Boston.* Cambridge, Mass., 1970.

Woods, Robert A. *The City Wilderness.* Boston, 1970.

INDEX